D0879272

BARRON'S BUSINESS LIBRARY

Purchasing

Michael Harding and Mary Lu Harding

BARRON'S

General editor for BARRON'S BUSINESS LIBRARY is George T. Friedlob, professor in the School of Accountancy at Clemson University.

All inquiries should be addressed to:
Barron's Educational Series, Inc.
250 Wireless Boulevard
Hauppauge, New York 11788

Library of Congress Catalog Card No. 91-9151

International Standard Book No. 0-8120-4552-1

Library of Congress Cataloging-in-Publication Data
Harding, Michael.
    Purchasing / by Michael Harding, Mary Lu Harding.
        p.   cm.—(Barron's business library)
    ISBN 0-8120-4552-1
    1. Industrial procurement.   I. Harding, Mary Lu.   II. Title.
    III. Series.
HD39.5.H37   1991
658.7'2—dc20   91-9151
                                                                         CIP

PRINTED IN ITALY

1234 9929 987654321

Contents

Introduction

Purchased materials is the largest element of the cost to manufacture goods in most industries. Even in service industries, the percentage of cost that purchased materials represents is steadily increasing. The growing financial impact and importance that purchasing has within any business enterprise is the focus of this book.

The historical roots of prevailing attitudes toward purchasing as a profession will be examined in this book, as will the impact that purchasing has and should have on the profitability of a business.

HISTORICAL PERSPECTIVE

The function of purchasing existed before the beginning of recorded history. The activities of buying and selling were commonly conducted between individuals, often in the form of bartering. Large-scale coordinated procurement started when it became necessary to equip the armies of princes or kingdoms with weapons and provisions.

When the Industrial Revolution began at the turn of the nineteenth century, the purchasing of goods was in the hands of business owners and entrepreneurs. Materials represented only 10 to 20 percent of the cost to manufacture. This was a relatively small percentage, and owners exercised their personal judgment in the spending of funds. In fact, negotiating for the supply of materials added to the owner's prestige. There was a certain pride in making purchasing "deals" that involved a high level of business acumen.

As businesses grew, entrepreneurial decisions had to be delegated to specialized functions. However, the function of purchasing was one of the last to be relinquished by business owners, because their own money and prestige was at stake. Even when a purchasing function was established within a business, it was often limited to the processing of paperwork, while contract decisions were retained in the hands of owners or upper managers. It was only at the beginning of the twentieth century that purchasing began to be recognized as a legitimate profession.

In the last fifty years there has been a significant change in the percentage of purchased materials in manufacturing. Automation and technology have reduced the value added to products by direct labor and increased the cost impact of purchased materials. However, management's views and expectations of purchasing are changing much more slowly.

CURRENT ATTITUDES

Anyone can buy. Spending money is something with which every person can identify, and most people enjoy doing. In fact, the commonness of the activity helps to support a belief that no special skills are required for purchasing.

Purchasing, like many manufacturing-related disciplines, is undervalued in the business world. Purchasing is part of manufacturing, which is viewed as the "dirty" part of making money. The professions that manipulate money rather than create it are more highly prized. Engineering and business schools continue to attract people who wish to succeed financially. Yet manufacturing (and especially purchasing) is where the money is really made.

Purchasing personnel have been valued for their steadiness and loyalty. Applicants for buyer positions who come from the production function bring a knowledge of products and processes. Those who come from other companies bring the purchasing skills and practices of their former companies. However, often there is insufficient training or direction for purchasing personnel and departments. This book presents the skills and structure a purchasing organization needs to be effective.

A NEW DIRECTION

As a national average, 60 percent of the cost to manufacture is attributable to purchased materials. In the electronics industries, the percentage exceeds 90 percent. If the purchasing function controls over 60 percent of the costs in a product, then resources and talent must be focused on this function if the business is to stay healthy. An investment made in the hiring, training, and development of purchasing personnel that allows them to function with greater effectiveness has the potential for significant payback.

THE OBJECTIVE

This book has been written to address many of the areas of knowledge you will need to perform the purchasing function well. It may be used as a training tool in both new and existing corporate purchasing departments.

Organization and Administration

INTRODUCTION AND MAIN POINTS

The purchasing function is organized to support the work that is done within it. By examining what that structure looks like, we can draw conclusions about the nature of purchasing tasks. This chapter will examine the organization of the purchasing function (and the organization of the company within which it resides) and the administrative tasks that are a part of it.

After studying the material in this chapter, you will be able to:

▬ Determine which tasks of purchasing are value-added work and which are not.

▬ Organize the purchasing function to do the work that is of value.

▬ Determine the appropriate tasks of purchasing administration.

THE CORPORATE ORGANIZATION

The first step in analyzing the role of purchasing within a corporation is to examine the corporate reporting structure. Where is the top level of purchasing within the corporation? How high in the organization is it? To whom does it report? How strong is the functional leader? This information reveals the perception of the purchasing function held by other employees and departments: the higher in the organization purchasing is, the more it is perceived as a business contributor. Conversely, the lower in the organization purchasing is, the more it is perceived as an administrative function only.

Communication channels also reveal the relationship of purchasing to the larger corporate organization. To whom do the members of the purchasing department communicate on a regular basis? Normally there are strong ties to the finance, quality, and materials-management functions. Is there also a strong link to the technical-design community? Is there significant input to the sales plan and the production plan?

ORGANIZATION OF THE PURCHASING FUNCTION

The organization of the purchasing function itself should follow from a definition of the work to be done and which work is adding value to the corporation.

Value-added work is work that creates a business difference. Non–value-added work is work that serves an administrative function but does not affect the results of the business. For example, negotiation of a business arrangement with a supplier is value-added work. Expediting a shortage, while necessary in the short term, is not an activity that adds value to the business. In general, establishment of relationships, agreements, and contracts with the supplier base constitute the value-added work of purchasing. Establishment and maintenance of purchase orders and the clerical administration that accompanies those tasks are not adding value to the business. A major premise of this book is that it is in purchasing's interest to maximize the resources devoted to value-added work and to minimize the administrative tasks that add no value. Yet when asked why they spend so little time on the value-added tasks, buyers commonly respond that they are so buried in daily paperwork and fire-fighting that they have no time to do the things they really want to do. This is a self-fulfilling prophecy. If no time is spent on business arrangements that can simplify the paperwork, the result is that buyers must devote more attention to that paperwork. (Reduction of paperwork is discussed in more detail in Chapters 6 and 16.)

Job descriptions and departmental organization are tools that can help shift the balance of work toward the value-added variety. Job descriptions for the positions of buyer and any higher positions should emphasize establishment of business arrangements with suppliers as a primary task and requisitioner satisfaction as a primary measurement. Emphasis on placing purchase orders and on expediting delivery should be minimized. Those functions may still be performed, but if they are not stressed as primary functions, they will command less time and attention.

Proper organization of the purchasing function also assists the shift toward value-added work. In general, the flatter the organizational hierarchy and the more comprehensive the responsibility of buyers, the greater the ease with which the work shifts toward value-added tasks.

Division of labor within the purchasing function is also important. Buyers must have control of their items long enough to do the work of creating sound business arrangements. This is not the case in many companies. For example, requisitions may go to the buyers who are least busy, thus making it difficult for them to organize a group of items.

A better arrangement is division of work among buyers based on commodity. If a buyer is responsible for a commodity in its entirety, all requisitions for that commodity will come to him or her. The buyer will be able to develop a unified vision that encompasses requisitioners' needs, the demand for the commodity, the suppliers, and the kind of arrangements that best satisfy requisitioners while lowering costs and administration for purchasing. A commodity should remain with the same buyer long enough for the buyer to learn the market and negotiate appropriate arrangements for supply (for at least two years.)

Many companies have combined the jobs of buyers and inventory planners into a single function called "buyer-planner." Buyer-planners have greater visibility of demand patterns and more control over order patterns and inventory levels. Combining two jobs into one means that more work must be done per item. Buyer-planners normally manage fewer items per person than do buyers. Buyer-planners receive an MRP report or a demand signal from the user community, plan and maintain an appropriate inventory level, manage the supplier base, and structure the resupply mechanism with suppliers to ensure a smooth flow of incoming materials. They may also place purchase orders, if that is the resupply mechanism of choice.

Some companies focus more on inventory levels and less on the purchasing portion of the buyer-planner function. Thus, the quality of goods purchased, prices paid, and formation of supplier partnerships can become subservient to the value and amount of inventory carried. When this happens, inventory levels—not the effectiveness of the entire supply system—may become the primary measure of the contribution of the buyer-planners.

Broadening the scope of buyers makes the buyers significantly more valuable to the company and is much more rewarding for the individual. Any change that broadens the buyer's job scope and/or flattens the organizational hierarchy should be implemented if possible.

Another purchasing function that deserves close scrutiny is expediting. In some organizations, there is a separate function called "expediting." In others, expediting is performed by buyers. To choose which alternative is appropriate for your organization, you should consider several factors. The first is whether the work itself is value-added or not. Expediting a delivery that is late and causes delays in your company's manufacturing process may be viewed as a necessary part of the purchasing process. However, the reason that expediting is needed at all is that an event that was scheduled to happen did not. If commitments that were made were kept, expediting would not be necessary. A shift of emphasis away from paperwork and toward establishment of a better buyer-supplier relationship may ultimately make expediting unnecessary.

A second factor to consider is that once a task is created, it tends to perpetuate itself. If a separate position called "expediter" is created, there may be a tendency to create work for it simply because it exists. Both nature and business abhor a vacuum. Again, sound business relationships may obviate the need for functions like expediting. Creating an expediter function will delay that process.

A third consideration involves effectiveness. Buyers make the decisions on placing future business with suppliers. Future business is a major motivator for suppliers. If future business is disassociated from delivery performance, the relationship between performance and repeat business becomes blurred. If buyers feel the effects of delivery performance directly by becoming involved in any late deliveries that occur, they are in a position to tie future business to performance and resolution of performance problems. If buyers are responsible for supplier performance and for requisitioner satisfaction, the buying organization is poised to create effective and workable relationships with suppliers.

The ideal purchasing function is composed of three tiers: a manager, buyers, and a small clerical support staff (see Figure 1-1). The manager translates business goals to the purchasing staff, acts as a liaison to the other functions within the business, develops the staff's skill base, and administers the function. Buyers do the skill-based work of purchasing, which includes developing the supply base, setting up business arrangements with suppliers, and purchasing the materials and services required. The clerical support staff provides buyers with secretarial services and any data-entry support that may be required.

There may be a temptation to expand the clerical staff to off load tasks from buyers who are overburdened. The danger

Ideal

Majority of people in front-line value-added positions. Buyers have individual authority in their commodity.

Bottom-Heavy

Too many clerical support staff. Indicates bureaucratic administrative system. Becomes self-perpetuating.

Hierarchical

Too many layers leads to fragmentation of responsibilities and job scope. Difficult to expand job scope. Lower levels are more clerical than business-oriented.

FIG 1-1. *Organization of purchasing.*

of doing this is that once the tasks are off-loaded, there may be less urgency to work toward their elimination. Clerical staff members frequently do not have the power to make changes in the system. A clear vision of the direction in which the purchasing function is developing may be the best safeguard against institutionalizing tasks that should be eliminated.

ADMINISTRATION

The administrative tasks of purchasing include handling of requisitions and purchase orders, data entry, filing, contract preparation, and maintaining any regular communication vehicles with suppliers, such as EDI (electronic data interchange). While administrative duties will never disappear entirely, they can be reduced significantly.

The number of requisitions can be reduced through the use of systems contracts, pull signals for replenishment (such as kanban cards), and other automatic reorder systems. Every requisition that is removed from the work load also removes a purchase order and associated administrative tasks. Reduction of the volume of requisitions is discussed more fully in Chapter 6.

A purchase order is a contract between a buyer and seller that specifies the items to be purchased, the price that will be paid for the items, and the date that the goods or services are to be delivered. It may also contain other information regarding terms of purchase and specifications, such as quality levels. Generation of a purchase order begins when a buyer contacts a supplier and arranges the terms of price, quality, and delivery. That information may be written on a requisition form and passed on to a data-entry clerk to be entered into a computer system. The computer prints the purchase order and retains the data.

Examination of the effectiveness of the computer system may result in a further opportunity for reduction of administrative work load. If the data-entry process is simple and each buyer has a terminal, buyers can enter purchase orders while they are communicating with suppliers. Since the information must be written out clearly in order for someone else to interpret it, a simple purchase order data-entry system requires very little incremental effort on the part of buyers. The primary reasons a company may need a separate data-entry function for purchase orders are a laborious and time-consuming software system and limited availability of computer terminals. Enhancing the simplicity of transactions and providing greater computer access reduces administrative labor. Computers are also tools that can assist buyers in analysis of commodities and purchase patterns. This information is very useful in contract negotiations and in establishing sound business relationships. (For more information on software systems, see Chapter 19.)

A purchase order is a living document until the transaction has been completed. It is *the* legal agreement between the buyer's company and the supplier, and it is also the reference point for measuring supplier performance. Therefore, it is very important that any change to the original agreement is reflected by a change to the purchase order. If a purchase order is placed with deliveries scheduled into the future, it may be changed many times before it is closed. In some organizations, changes to purchase orders may outnumber the original orders by more than five to one. When examining the labor involved in the administration of purchase orders and any computer system that will be used, the *change-order process* must be considered. All change orders should also be retained for audit purposes.

Record retention and filing are major administrative tasks. Documents that must be retained and kept available include requisitions, purchase orders, change orders, quotations, contracts, and any backup documentation (such as a spreadsheet) that is key to the decision-making process regarding supplier and price. (For a more in-depth discussion of the documentation that must be retained, see Chapter 2.) Discussion here will focus on the administrative labor associated with record retention.

Keeping records in written form is more expensive and labor-intensive than keeping them in computer storage. Some documents can be generated, transmitted, and stored entirely by computer. Requisitions, purchase orders and delivery schedules to suppliers, and spreadsheets for price analysis will be considered here. The main reason for keeping paper records rather than storing them on computers is that authorization signatures are often required.

A requisition from an end-user to a purchasing department can be transmitted via computer if certain system conditions are present. The primary requirement is that users have secure personal system accounts so that messages originating from these system accounts are known to come from the owner of the account and no one else. A second requirement is that enough people within the company have access to the computer system so that a company-wide process is possible.

If personal account security exists, a requisitioner can fill out a form on the system with the information necessary to authorize the purchase, then mail it through "system mail" to the appropriate buyer (see Figure 1-2). This process occurs virtually instantaneously, whereas days might be involved in sending and receiving paper forms. When a buyer receives the system message, he or she may print it or simply use the information directly to create a purchase order. Confirmation is accomplished by replying to the requisitioner with the purchase-order number and date the purchase is due to arrive. Requisitions and purchase orders can be stored in a systems file for future access.

If an authorization signature is required, the requisitioner can mail the completed form via computer mail to the person who must authorize the expense. That person reviews the form on the system and if he or she approves the expense, forwards it from their account to purchasing. If systems-account security exists, receipt of the form from the authorizer's account is tantamount to receiving the authorizer's approval.

Use of a computer system to transmit requisitions to purchasing can result in significant cost savings. The time involved is lessened for both the requisitioner and approver and for the purchasing staff. The expense of printing requisition forms is eliminated. And the work and expense of filing paper records are eliminated.

Analysis tools used by the buyer to select suppliers may also be kept on the computer system. For example, some good programs are available that do spreadsheet analysis of quotations. Use of computerized tools for analytical work speeds the calculation process for buyers and, since the resulting information can be stored on the system rather than in hard-copy form, reduces the administrative labor of filing and retrieval.

ELECTRONIC DATA INTERCHANGE (EDI)
Transmission of purchase orders and shipment schedules to suppliers via a computer system has been termed "electronic data interchange," abbreviated EDI. Like other computerized systems, EDI is best used within a context that produces recognizable business results. The use of a computer system for its own sake is rarely productive, and this is especially true of EDI. The questions of what information will be transmitted to whom, how and when transmission will take place, and why, should all be considered before such a system is implemented.

As systems are developed that facilitate the automatic resupply of materials, easier and faster ways to communicate will

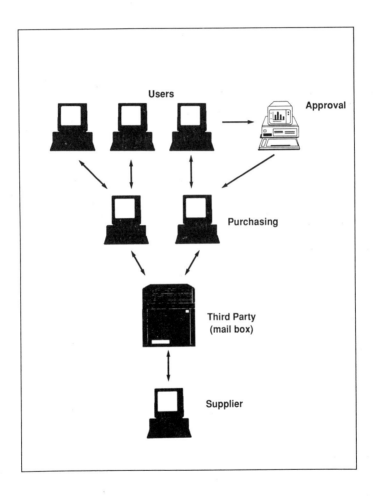

FIG 1-2. *Electronic mail system including EDI.*

develop in parallel. These can be manual. However, communicating long distances today is best done electronically. It is more cost effective to develop the business procedures *before* installing an automated communication system. What information must be transferred, and what format will evolve during the learning process. The defining of information and format should be driven by business requirements and not by software limitations.

Information that is commonly transferred between purchasers and suppliers includes schedules for shipments, purchase orders and/or contracts, acknowledgements, invoices, specifications, quality data, and problem-solving information. Not all of the types of information that will eventually be required are evident in the initial stages of a supplier partnership. As the partnership develops, communication needs will become clearer. For example, in the early stages, communication by telephone and fax machine may be sufficient. When they are no longer adequate, EDI may be a useful tool. The specific lines of communication must also be established before an electronic system is used: who is authorized to send certain information, and who is authorized to receive it and act on it. For example, if purchase orders or shipment schedules are transmitted with the intention that the receiver take action based upon the message, security against unauthorized access and a clear definition of responsibilities must be in place. This helps to prevent company employees without the proper authorization from making a transaction with a supplier. It also helps suppliers recognize unauthorized purchase requests.

The timing and frequency of communications must also be defined. One of the advantages of EDI is the speed with which the communication can occur. Fax and telephone are nearly as fast. Speed of transmission should support the speed at which business conditions and requirements change. For example, in many businesses the production schedule is updated at a regular interval, and new information must be passed to suppliers as soon as it is available.

When automation becomes necessary or desirable, technical considerations must be addressed. The first consideration is selection of appropriate software. Having already established clearly what information is transferred, and in what format, makes the selection of software a much simpler task. Once the software system has been chosen, system configuration, compatibility, and system security must be addressed.

Issues of configuration include whether to tie the EDI system into a mainframe computer or keep it as a standalone system. If the data transmitted and received ties in to data generated by the mainframe, integrating the EDI system is appropriate. This will avoid the duplication of data entry that may occur with separate systems. Another configuration issue is the translation of information into a standard format for transmission. Translation software can be used for this procedure, or it can be done by a third-party network.

EDI serves as a bridge between companies that may not have the same computer systems. If a purchasing department has many suppliers linked to its EDI system, there will most certainly be issues of incompatibility. One way these issues can be addressed is through the use of a third-party network company that specializes in electronic communications. These companies receive and retransmit data for businesses. They also reformat information to or from industry-standard formats so that it is system-compatible for either the sending or receiving company. Third-party networks also provide a measure of security: you can pull data from their systems as you need it, and you need not store sensitive information—and risk having it pirated or sabotaged—on your own computer system.

It takes care and work to establish an EDI linkage properly, and once established the link is not easily altered. This is another reason to make sure that the partnership with the supplier(s) to whom you are linked is proven and enduring. Contractual issues that are specific to EDI must be negotiated and resolved with the supplier(s). These include how the costs of the system will be shared, the specifics of the types of data transmitted, the configuration of the system, and the responsibilities and liabilities of each of the parties regarding the data received.

CHAPTER PERSPECTIVE

The first consideration in organizing the purchasing function is to define its contributions to value. The second is to organize the function so that valuable contributions are supported and the non–value-added work is marked for elimination. In general, the buyer role is broadened and enhanced through incorporation of related areas, such as planning, and through organization by commodity into areas of appropriate size. Certain clerical and administrative support functions are simplified or made unnecessary. Those tasks that cannot be eliminated can be reduced to their simpliest form and then automated. Automation should occur only *after* the purchasing function has been simplified. The process of automation has the effect of freezing transactions in automated form and makes further simplification much more difficult. Automation can also be extended to suppliers through the use of electronic data interchange (EDI).

Recordkeeping and Audit

INTRODUCTION AND MAIN POINTS

Because the purchasing function is responsible for a major portion of the cash flow of a corporation, it has responsibility for ensuring that those funds are properly administered. The purchasing function is a key area examined in an audit.

This chapter examines the audit process, what an auditor looks for, what constitutes appropriate records, and how a company can maintain those records with minimal bureaucracy. After studying the material in this chapter:

▬ You will know how to conduct an audit.

▬ You will be able to differentiate between essential records and needless bureaucracy.

▬ You will know what records are essential to retain.

▬ You will know how long they must be retained.

PURCHASING RESPONSIBILITIES

The purchasing function is responsible for obtaining quality goods and services as requested by the organization at the lowest total cost. This includes inventory material, capital equipment, expensed items, and services.

Purchasing establishes and maintains the supplier base, seeing to it that adequate capacity and quality are available and that the level of service and price are optimal. Fair conduct in the marketplace must also be assured for the purchasing function. An audit of a purchasing department first examines the organization, goals, and measurements of the function in order to determine its effectiveness, then follows the transaction flow into and through the purchasing process.

ORGANIZATION, GOALS, AND MEASUREMENTS

The first step in the audit process is to understand the organization of the purchasing department and its direction. An audit team usually requests the following information:

━ The organizational structure and resources available. (Obtain an organization chart.)

━ The measurements used by the purchasing function and how they are calculated. (Obtain the formulae for all measurements and both current and historical results.)

━ The goals of the function and the plans in place to attain them. (Obtain information on goals and plans.)

━ Purchasing policies and procedures currently operative. (Obtain a complete set of these.)

━ Job descriptions for individuals in the department that detail the responsibilities of each member. (Obtain job descriptions for each type of job in the department.)

Review of this information provides an auditor with a view of the purchasing function today and of its direction for the future. Data reviewed later should be examined in this frame of reference.

The following information also assists an audit:

━ Total annual purchase volume in dollars and a breakdown of that volume into categories if possible (inventory material, expense material, etc.)

━ Total annual volume of transactions by type (purchase orders, change orders, returns, etc.)

━ List of current contract agreements and their total dollar value.

━ Current level of signature authority for each member.

━ Any management reports that are routinely used to quantify operational effectiveness.

An audit team studies this information until a clear picture of the function emerges. They then interview personnel within the department. The following are questions that an auditor attempts to answer from the information provided and from interviews:

━ Are departmental goals clear to all personnel?

━ Are the goals integrated with the goals of other functions?

━ Are the goals integrated into the measurement of personnel?

━ Are people acting on the plans in place to achieve them?

━ Is each person clear about his or her job description?

━ Does the measurement system encourage individuals to perform at optimal levels? Does it encourage appropriate behavior, or does it reinforce bureaucracy and waste?

━ What do current measurement results indicate?

━ Do all personnel have the authority and responsibility to improve their operation within the function? Have they?

TRANSACTION FLOW

The second part of an audit is examination of the transaction flow to ensure integrity of the processes. A typical transaction flow in purchasing is as follows: The originator of the request communicates the need to purchasing. Upon receiving the request, purchasing determines if the required goods or services are already covered by an existing contract agreement. If not, the total dollar value will dictate whether competitive bids must be obtained, and whether they should be written or verbal. Purchasing selects the supplier and places an order for the required goods or services. The purchase order is maintained in an "active" file until the goods or services are received in full. After the purchase order has been completely closed, it is retained in a "closed" file. A typical flow chart of this process is shown in Figure 2-1.

In order to audit the requisitioning and purchasing processes, the audit team selects a random sample of purchase orders from the files. The sample is normally selected from the previous six months of activity, and from all types of purchases (inventory, expenses, capital, and services). The random sample should contain purchases whose dollar values range across the normal spectrum for the department. Each purchase order should have its requisition attached, along with any other documentation required. The whole package is audited, starting with the requisition.

REQUISITIONS

The purchasing process begins with a *demand signal* to obtain certain goods or services. The demand signal may take the form of a requisition or an automated demand signal, such as an MRP (material requirements planning) report. With either signal system, the following information must be present:

- A description of what is required
- The quantity required and its unit of measure
- The due date required
- The name of the person to whom it will be delivered
- The source of funds (normally an account number)
- The approval to spend those funds

The approval to spend the funds is normally conveyed by the signature of a person who has authority over the specified account or budget.

An audit of requisitions examines whether the required information is complete, whether they are mathematically correct,

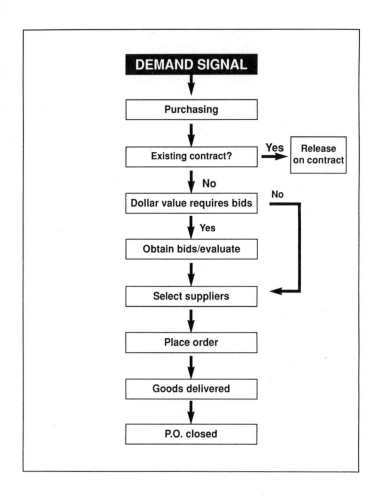

FIG 2-1.

whether they have been appropriately approved based on dollar value, and, if the purchase is capitalized, whether the appropriate capital approval documentation is attached.

If the requisitioner specifies the supplier, justification for that choice should be included on the requisition. Selection and management of the supplier base is the responsibility of purchasing and should not be circumvented without good reason.

The information required on a requisition can be obtained in a simple manner from a simple form—even sent electronically. An auditor attempts to ensure that the integrity of the signal to buy is maintained.

Automated demand signals such as MRP contain within them most of the information specified above. However, their use is audited to determine whether appropriate approval for the expense exists. By definition, an automated signal does not have an authorization signature for each purchase. Nevertheless, someone within the organization must be accountable for the signal and the expenditure of funds it generates. Normally, the person in charge of the process or in charge of the input to the system is also responsible for the subsequent expenditure. Approval of the master command is approval for all subsequent activity. For example, if an MRP report is the source of a demand signal, approval of the input to MRP (the master schedule) is also approval for the purchase of the necessary materials.

PURCHASE ORDERS

A purchase order (P.O.) is a legal document that authorizes a supplier to do something. It is similar in its use and impact to a check. If blank documents are misused, a legal and financial liability may be created. Therefore, control over purchase orders is always examined in an audit. An auditor checks for the following practices:

- Are purchase-order forms safe from unauthorized use?
- Are all purchase-order numbers accounted for?
- Are copies of all purchase orders available in the files?

Missing purchase orders or purchase-order numbers that cannot be accounted for indicate a process that is not in control and a potential for financial liability.

Each P.O. pulled from the files as part of the random sample is examined for the following:

▬ Is all required information complete?

▬ Does the purchase order agree with the requisition (items, quantities, etc.)?

▬ Has the purchase order been appropriately approved?

The dollar value of the purchase order is compared to the dollar value of the buyer's signature authority. If it is within the buyer's level of authority, only the buyer's signature is required. If it is greater than the buyer's level of authority, it must be cosigned by someone with sufficient authority for the total dollar amount.

Signature of approval on a requisition is the authorization to spend the funds by someone who controls that amount of funds. Signature of approval on a purchase order is finalization of a contract by an agent of the corporation who is acting within his or her authority to obligate the corporation. The limit of authority is the dollar value specified for each buyer.

Auditors also examine P.O.s for the following:

▬ Is the purchase identified as taxable or nontaxable?

▬ Is freight paid by the buyer or the supplier? If the buyer pays the freight, is it properly charged?

▬ Is the time between the receipt of the requisition and placement of the purchase order reasonable?

Two issues are examined in connection with the third item above. The first is the level of service provided by the purchasing department. Requisitions that were delayed may indicate a backlog of work or some other problem. The frequency and type of these problems are investigated.

The second issue is whether the requisition was submitted to purchasing before or after the goods or services were obtained. Submission of the requisition to purchasing *after* the goods or services were obtained indicates that someone within the organization contacted a supplier, authorized the expense, and incurred the liability for the corporation without purchasing approval or review. This is an "after-the-fact" purchase order— a dangerous practice and a breach of policy within most corporations. It creates a potential for misuse of corporate funds and the creation of a liability that the corporation may not be prepared to meet. It is a serious audit issue if it occurs with any degree of frequency. An auditor looks at how many times after-the-fact purchase orders occurred and what action was taken by purchasing to solve the problem.

Automated release systems such as EDI (electronic data interchange) and systems contracts are audited for the level of security. Who is authorized to transmit the demand signal to the supplier? Can unauthorized people access the system for private use? Is there an approval mechanism in place to authorize the expense? Do the people administering the process fully understand how the system operates, what the financial implications are, and what the security needs are? These types of systems are far more effective than individual purchase-order placement, and just as valid as long as system security is maintained.

SUPPLIER SELECTION

A major responsibility of a purchasing department is the selection and maintenance of a reliable supplier base and the assurance that corporate funds are being wisely spent. The purchasing function will be audited for justification of source and price. Purchase orders and their requisitions will be examined to understand the rationale for selecting the supplier and establishing the price paid. Each purchase order or contract should have source and price justification that an uninvolved third party can understand at a later date. Source and price justification need not be lengthy—just clear.

Purchase orders for items that are not covered by a contract should be individually source- and price-justified. The degree of justification should be commensurate with the dollar value of the order. Small-value "nuisance" orders require minimal justification, whereas larger-value orders need more thorough justification. The actual dollar limits and justification required vary from company to company but should be clearly defined by the company policies.

A simple method of recording the necessary information is by using the reverse side of the requisition to note the suppliers contacted and their prices. To simplify the process even further, preprinted boxes can be checked for standard selection criteria or for price ranges that do not require justification. Such preprinted information for price may include the following:

▬ Dollar value below limit requiring justification.

▬ Lowest price source. (Jot down the suppliers and prices.)

▬ Price established under contract agreement number _____ .

▬ Price compares to recent purchase. See P.O.# _____ .

The same type of preprinted information can be used for source justification. Categories may include the following:

▬ Lowest-priced source.

▬ Only supplier for item (single or sole source).

▬ Only supplier who can deliver in required time frame.

━ Established supplier per contract agreement number
_____ .

━ Factory-authorized supplier (for services, repair, or accessories).

━ Requisitioner-specified source. (Justification should be provided by the requisitioner.)

CONTRACTS

For contracts, quotations from all suppliers and, where applicable, a spreadsheet showing the analysis of the information and basis for selection should be kept in the files with the contract. Not only will this satisfy audit requirements, but it will also be useful when the contract is about to expire, providing comparison information for newer quotations. Once a contract is in place, individual releases against that contract need not have separate justification.

Contracts are audited for compliance with company policy and for financial soundness. This is an additional reason to retain backup documentation, especially spreadsheets showing comparisons and selection rationale. Questions that an auditor attempts to answer from the data in the files include the following:

━ Were competitive bids obtained? How many?

━ Were negotiations conducted with the final bidders, or was a bid accepted without question?

━ What concessions were made to achieve the end result? Do they appear reasonable?

━ What items were negotiated? Were negotiations limited to price, or were terms of business also considered?

━ Is the contract signed by someone with approval authorization for the total dollar value of the contract?

━ Was legal review necessary according to the company policy? If so, is there an approval signature from the legal staff?

Auditors also look for suppliers that have a repeat payment history. If significant repeat business has occurred and the total dollar value of this business is high, a contract should be in place or in preparation. Although audits do require that the process of bidding and selection be clear and that the contract be properly drafted and approved, subsequent releases require virtually no justification.

RECORD RETENTION

The critical records to retain include 1) purchase orders and corresponding requisitions, 2) contracts and backup data (especially spreadsheets). These records must be retained for the current year plus seven prior years. Not all of these records need to be immediately available. A common practice is to retain the current year plus one prior year in the office area and put the remaining records in secure storage. Only puchasing personnel and authorized personnel from security and finance should have access to the stored records. Only purchasing personnel should have access to the active files.

CHAPTER PERSPECTIVE

The audit process is intended to ensure the integrity of the purchasing process. It does not necessarily require that a purchasing department equip itself with additional layers of bureaucracy. In many cases, heavy bureaucracy leads to less control of processes, not more. What is important is that the rationale for a purchase and for the selection of supplier and price be clear to an uninvolved third party. Simply designed forms and educated staff can accomplish this with a minimum of effort. The most important ingredient for passing an audit is ongoing education of purchasing personnel. If all buyers know *what* information is needed for audit purposes and *why,* increasingly simpler ways of retaining that information can be devised.

Purchasing Strategies

INTRODUCTION AND MAIN POINTS

It is easy to become caught up in day-to-day purchasing activities and not consider how the function will perform in the future, or even what those duties may be. Economic and political events the world over have an impact on the availability and cost of raw materials, capital, and labor. The creation of new technologies and products, changes in market conditions and demand patterns, and changes within the buyer's company all affect purchasing's short- and long-term roles. Purchasing must learn to anticipate and respond to these changes.

Two distinct types of purchasing strategies must be developed: those for the internal organization and related purchasing duties and those for the external marketplace.

After studying the material in this chapter:

■ You will recognize the key components of a strategy.

■ You will be better prepared to address the environment in which strategic planning takes place.

■ You will be able to identify strategies that are appropriate for your company.

THE IMMEDIATE ENVIRONMENT

Before considering purchasing strategies, a buyer must know the environment in which he or she currently operates. A buyer or purchasing manager must recognize and deal with the existing managerial structure and attitudes.

Purchasing should ask itself the following questions:

■ What is management's present attitude toward purchasing?

■ Is purchasing perceived as an overhead expense, a profit contributor, or something in between?

■ To whom does purchasing report within the organization?

■ Is purchasing an "equal" of manufacturing, finance, sales, and engineering in the eyes of management? Is stature, pay, and involvement in company decisions equivalent to those of other functions? In service industries, these other functions are doctors, lawyers, consultants, sales personnel, and the front-line deliverers of services.

Unless purchasing is considered by top management to be an integral part of the management team, purchasing's strategies, plans, and advice will go unheeded.

DETERMINING PURCHASING'S STATUS
Look around and survey the political landscape. If you do not know how purchasing is perceived or if you are new to the function, there are some quick questions that will begin to categorize and evaluate perceptions:
1. Purchasing reports to whom?
   a. a person who is no more than one level below the president
   b. a person who is more than one level away from the president
   c. a finance or a materials manager

The preferred position is (a), reporting to the president or an officer removed by only one level of management. If purchasing reports to finance, the function may be seen as an expense and be measured by adherence to predetermined goals and budgets. If purchasing reports to a materials manager, purchasing's contribution may become diluted and inventory levels and delivery schedules may become the prime measures used to evaluate it.
2. To which meetings are purchasing personnel invited?
   a. factory-floor schedules and expedite meetings
   b. supplier quality and factory process yield reviews
   c. budget reviews
   d. company financial-performance reviews
   e. product-planning sessions with sales, engineering, and manufacturing

Purchasing is usually always involved in meetings a, b and c. But if purchasing personnel make contributions to financial reviews and product planning sessions, they can be considered key members of management.
3. Is purchasing's advice sought by top management prior to the commitment to add a new product or significantly expand production capacity?

Often, purchasing is not included at the planning and decision stages of plant and product changes that will have a large impact on purchasing. It is only after final decisions are made that purchasing is asked to find additional capacity for purchased items, find sources of new technology, and evaluate the impact of changes on existing suppliers.

STARTING FROM WHERE YOU ARE

If the purchasing function is not currently held in high esteem within the organization, purchasing must change the perceptions of others by changing itself. Credibility is built over time. The purchasing department can start by doing the following:

1. Provide proper training for department personnel (even if it is a department of one). Training and preparation are fundamental strategies (see Chapter 4). Make the commitment to training permanent, and keep training and retraining.

2. Set goals for the department for cost and lead-time reductions, supplier development, improved supplier quality, etc. Work toward these goals. Record and report the results.

3. Offer services to other departments, including the following:

Engineering—for locating new technologies, supplying samples, etc.

Finance—for negotiating preferred terms of payment and helping to resolve problems with discrepant invoices and problems with standard costs.

Maintenance—for resolving problems such as availability of repair parts, supplier technical assistance, and quality of materials and tool life.

Inventory—for reducing inventory levels and assuring proper inventory mix. Suppliers can assist in this effort.

Sales—Purchasing has access to many external sales personnel and resources, which can be a valuable source of marketing information. Purchasing is often aware of new products and trends before they are made public.

Quality—Meet with quality-control personnel to learn of quality requirements for purchased components and supplier performance. Know how purchased components perform in the finished products and understand current process yields. Volunteer to assist in supplier quality evaluations.

4. Volunteer your services to all company functions and become a resource of information and assistance that is sought and valued by these functions. This may initially be an added

burden for which purchasing has little time, but start small. As your services become valued, your requests for added resources may be granted more readily. Also, smart purchasing will cut the work load for all functions.

5. Toot your own horn. Publish results of financial, lead-time, and quality efforts.

6. Ask to be invited to management meetings that address issues such as the financial status of the company, new product developments, sales meetings, and plant expansion. Come to these meetings prepared to contribute. Get agendas in advance and brainstorm with the chairperson prior to the meeting.

7. As word of your comments, questions, and contributions during these meetings spreads, you will not have to ask to be invited. You will be regarded as part of the team.

8. Continue to develop networks of supporters in your organization. Broadcast purchasing's accomplishments in contributing to profit, penetrating new markets, responding to customer needs, and improving product quality.

9. Make sure full credit is given to all people and departments who have assisted purchasing in achieving improvement and its goals.

KNOW THYSELF

To be a team player and develop effective strategies, purchasing must understand and incorporate top managements's goals. Sales forecasts and annual planning sessions alone do not provide the long-term vision and corporate objectives purchasing needs to form effective strategies. To form meaningful strategies, purchasing must know the products and markets of the future, the company's financial and growth plans, current and projected competitors, the new technologies required for future products, and even management's political and economic views. Armed with these insights, purchasing can plan for the material resources required to support the company's long-term objectives.

INFORMATION GATHERING

In order to have the necessary information base, purchasing must answer a myriad of questions:

■ Who are our competitors today and who will they be in the future?

■ What will our future products be and what technologies will be required to support them?

▬ Can today's suppliers grow with us and supply the technologies and capacity required for our future products?

▬ What product technologies and manufacturing techniques must be protected and which can be sourced outside the company?

▬ What are top management's views about sourcing components and technologies to companies located in foreign countries?

▬ What strategic alliances with suppliers will be required in the future?

▬ What roles will price and quality play in the product sourcing decisions of the future?

▬ How will purchasing ensure that key technologies are protected in the future and how will buyers obtain suppliers that allow us to meet our quality and pricing objectives?

These are some of the issues purchasing must address when planning and executing strategies. Top management can add to this list—another reason for purchasing to ally itself with management and management's concerns.

IDENTIFYING RESOURCES

Consider the available suppliers and the projected needs. Which suppliers are star performers and are likely to be key contributors in the future? These should be retained and developed further. Identify those suppliers who are not living up to their potential, those who are worth saving, and those who will join the ranks of star performers in the future. Make a list of the voids—those commodity areas in which there are inadequate or nonexistent suppliers.

List those materials that are at geopolitical risk. Examples include rare metals whose sources are found in politically unstable areas of the world, foreign monopoly technologies, and oil-dependent materials. Make your concerns known to top management, seek alternative materials, and enlist the assistance of engineering personnel in developing alternative materials and designs.

AVOIDING THE CREATION OF COMPETITION

Be as certain as you can that today's supplier is not tomorrow's competitor. Little did many U.S. companies suspect that when they were sourcing parts and assemblies in Japan in the 1960s, they were developing and funding their competitors of the 1980s.

These competitors came to dominate world markets once held by their former customers.*

There have been numerous examples of deliberate but well-meaning transfers of technology to companies that would later use this information to compete with the originators and funders of the technology. Purchasing personnel cannot always prevent such transfers, but they can alert top management.

EXCLUSIVE TECHNOLOGIES

Work with engineering personnel in the product-design stage to help them avoid specifying components or technologies controlled by competitors or organizations that do not have a vested interest in your company's success. Where exclusive technologies cannot be avoided, explore the possibility of developing the capability in-house. This effort will require the assistance of engineering, manufacturing, and top management. If in-house capability is not practical, search for an external supplier of this technology with whom you can develop a noncompetitive relationship. Whenever an exclusive technology is key to a company's product or survival, purchasing must be on guard to carefully source this technology with a friendly supplier.

SUPPLY-BASE MANAGEMENT

Chapter 8 covers this subject in detail. However, a brief summary of supply-base management as part of purchasing's long-term strategy is in order here:

1. Reduce the number of suppliers.
2. Focus on quality improvement and lead-time reduction.
3. Foster long-term relationships.
4. Be continually on the alert for new suppliers that will support future technologies and products.

LONG-TERM SUPPLIER RELATIONS

It has been common practice for buyers to develop short-term relationships with suppliers who can provide opportunities to reduce price or take advantage of temporary market situations.

---

*In the late 1980s, the United States agreed to transfer all the avionic and semiconductor technologies of the F-16 fighter aircraft to Japan in a co-production agreement to build FSX aircraft. Only the last-minute intervention of the President of the United States prevented this transfer of technology, which could have spawned a Japanese industry capable of competing with commercial aircraft builders in the United States.[1]

This opportunistic approach does not encourage the formation of lasting relationships with suppliers.

The importance to a buyer of a long-term relationship with a supplier can be seen in the following benefits:

- Suppliers develop loyalty that manifests itself in
1. investments in product and process development
2. closer liaison to the buyer's product-development process
3. a shared responsibility to protect exclusive technologies
- Suppliers have greater assurance of participation in the business. Business and resource planning is thereby made easier and more accurate.
- Suppliers are more willing to invest in customer service and satisfaction.
- Long-term costs tend to be lower both for the supplier and the buyer, because processes are more productive, material quality is higher, and better business decisions are made with the availability of more information.

These may seem like intangible benefits, but they have a lasting impact on the value the buyer ultimately receives.

At first glance, long-term buyer-supplier relationships may appear to be exclusionary and collusive, and to an extent they are. A buyer must steer a course between fostering long-term relationships and providing an opportunity to newcomers in the market who may offer future competitive advantages.

SUPPLIER DEVELOPMENT

There is no such thing as a perfect supplier. Good suppliers must be developed and nurtured by purchasers. Purchasers must spend time, energy, and money to assist suppliers in achieving the level of performance required.

Training for suppliers in quality and process-control practices, process refinements, product development, and attainment of needed service levels may have to be provided by purchasing. This is one of the reasons why a purchasing department cannot afford a large supplier base; there simply aren't enough resources to work this closely with all suppliers. Investment in supplier development is one method purchasing can use to obtain the supplier base required for the future needs of the company.

LIFE-OF-PRODUCT SUPPLY

A long-term supplier-buyer relationship must be supported by commitments to buy and sell; otherwise, there is no reason for the relationship to continue. Furthermore, since both parties have made significant investment in developing the relationship, both have an interest in each other's long-term financial success.

A purchasing department should consider life-of-product and life-of-technology business agreements with suppliers. These long-term commitments are contrary to the practices of the past fifty years. It is also the area in which purchasing will find the most resistance from top management and even from those within their own ranks. In the past, the existence of many suppliers has given comfort to those who believe that more is better; that adversarial conditions produce lower prices; and that the less suppliers know about a business, the less likely they are to take advantage of its weaknesses.

Chapter 16 discusses the written contractual forms such an agreement may take. The true test of a *bilateral agreement* is that the relationship be capable of surviving without a formal agreement. A buyer should determine if the business agreement shares the benefits and risks of business to the extent that a contract is unnecessary. If a contract cannot survive on a handshake, the agreement is not perfectly balanced and may ultimately break down. If an agreement cannot survive this test, the buyer should reconsider and renegotiate the agreement.

TRENDS AND FORECASTS

Even if a small, flexible, and reliable supplier base is or will soon be in position, purchasing must keep an eye on market and product trends to be sure that materials will continue to be available and that the proper suppliers are in place to support future needs. Internal forecasts should be compared with external economic forecasts and tempered by human judgment. In this process a course is set for the company and for purchasing in its supporting role. The course is continuously monitored, new information is ceaselessly added, and midcourse corrections are regularly made. *Forecasts* provide purchasing with the direction to prepare for changes in products, volumes of purchased material, requirements for new technologies, and to assist in aligning suppliers to meet the company's future needs.

Large corporations may have the luxury of staff economists. Small and mid-size companies have a more difficult time gaining insights into economic projections. Fortunately, some professional and government organizations provide economic forecasts. The Chamber of Commerce, the Bureau of Labor Statistics, the Department of Commerce, and the National Association of Purchasing Management are a few. There are also econometric services offered by the Chase Manhattan Bank, Data Resources, and Wharton. Economic forecasts and trends appear regularly in business newspapers and magazines. A buyer cannot possibly assimilate all the available economic information. Therefore, a few key indicators must be developed and followed. For example, a manufacturer of home appliances may want to follow the projections for new homes. Manufacturers of printed circuit boards may want to follow the futures markets in copper and gold, as well as market trends that involve their customers (computer manufacturers, for example). Those involved in health care may follow statistics on demographics, health-care legislation, and construction costs. Retailers may be interested in disposable-income figures and demographics.

Develop a few indicators that will track your business and are good indicators of trends. Work with your marketing department, which may be using such indicators already. Offer to supply market information to which you regularly are exposed.

Plot and react to changes in forecasts and trends. You may decide to stockpile raw materials to allow engineering sufficient time to develop alternative materials, advise marketing of significant price changes, or pass on to top management impending allocations of material. Share this information with your suppliers so that they, too, can be more responsive to changes in your needs.

THE WORLD

We live in a global economy. Political unrest in the Soviet Union, aggression in the Middle East, monopolies in Japan, significant negative balances in U.S. trade, commodity cartels, major labor unrest in the transportation industry, global inflation and recession, new technology discoveries in Germany, and world embargoes are all concerns of the buyer. Global forces can and do affect the price and availability of everything from bauxite ore to energy. Tariff agreements such as GATT (General Agreement on Tariffs and Trade) also influence prices on world markets.

Some events are gradual and predictable. Others are sudden and require an immediate response by purchasing. At best, purchasing can forecast and prepare for the likely and react to the unanticipated. Long-term trends offer a purchasing department the best opportunity to plan its long-term strategy. There are forces at work in the world today that will shape the economic and political realities of tomorrow.

EUROPE

The European Economic Community (EEC) will begin to realize its combined economic force in 1993. Eastern Europe will open new markets as each country begins to reclaim its national identity, but first they must stabilize their respective governments and economies. They will offer cheap labor and the opportunity for joint business ventures. Initially, they will offer raw-materials and high-labor value-added items such as textiles. With Western investment, the sophistication of their products will increase. Ultimately, they will be incorporated into the economy of Western Europe.

THE SOVIET UNION

The Soviet Union must pass through tremendous political and economic change before it is able to join the Western economic community. The ruble is next to worthless both within and outside the country. The fifteen republics each want political and economic independence. The Soviet Union is rewriting its commercial laws to provide for private enterprise and foreign ownership of business entities. It has even passed antimonopoly laws fashioned after the Sherman and Clayton acts of the United States.[2]

At the moment, the Soviets are unwilling to sell off natural resources to generate foreign capital. They see United States companies as natural partners to build new Soviet businesses. They do not trust the Japanese or believe that Japan is valuable as a long-term economic partner.[3] The Soviet Union is a market of 280 million people, but its industries, communications, and banking systems are thirty to fifty years out of date. However, within twenty years they could become a potent economic force.

THE FAR EAST

The effects of Japanese economic savvy on the U.S. economy are well known. But there are other contenders in the Pacific Rim, including South Korea, Taiwan, Singapore, India, Malaysia, and China. Any one of these countries could be the next Japan.

In 1997, Hong Kong will be released from the British Commonwealth of Nations and will become part of mainland China. Taiwan recently voted for its first native-born president since the end of World War II, and there is a new freedom of trade between Taiwan and the mainland for the first time in forty years. North and South Korea have begun discussions on the reunification of their country. Singapore is a small but dynamic productivity powerhouse. The Japanese are not particularly liked in the Pacific Rim because of their military adventures from 1900 to 1945, but they do have the capital to fund further development in the area.

Picture a united economic states of Asia, with their human (1.1 billion population) and material resources, Japanese capital, the financial institutions of Hong Kong, and the manufacturing acumen of Taiwan, Korea, and Singapore. Their combined economic power would be awesome. The biggest obstacle to achieving this economic might is China's dogmatic leadership. However, the turn of the century could find a new economic and political force in the world.

THE UNITED STATES

By the year 2000, the United States could find itself caught between two economic juggernauts—one in Europe and one in the East. The mounting trade deficit of the United States is unlikely to subside or be reversed. The U.S. government has not yet come to the conclusion that national economic security is more important than military security or political stability. Economic survival is not a priority, so it is unlikely that the federal government will promote or even encourage domestic industries competing in the world arena.

Not only can domestic industries not count on assistance from the government, we are likely to see further deterioration of industrial America, more export of technology via government programs, and no assistance in combating unfair trade practices with foreign powers. In short, tougher times are coming to industrial America.

Purchasing managers must consider the effect of all these factors on long- and short-term purchasing practices, and on the availability of raw materials and products. They must take these factors into account as they assess their ability to support the growth plans and new products of their company.

CHAPTER PERSPECTIVE

One strategy is training and constant retraining of staff. A second is to become of value to company management through goal alignment, active contribution to company goals, and networking with other departments.

A third strategy is to be perceived as a valuable contributor and to be in the management information loop. A fourth is to align suppliers toward company goals. A fifth is to locate sources of technology and capacity for the company's continued growth. A sixth is to be a valuable source of feedback information from the outside world to the company. A seventh is to implement a global strategy that encompasses all sources of information and materials, and that assists purchasing to anticipate external influences on the company's future viability.

REFERENCES

1 Clyde V. Prestowitz. *Trading Places,* (Basic Books, Inc., New York, 1988), pp. 5–58.

2 Based on the author's discussions with the director of the Institute of Small Business Development at Moscow State University on May 21, 1990.

3 Based on the author's discussions with Oleg Belorus, Director-General of the International Management Institute in Kiev, Ukraine, S.S.R. on May 30, 1990.

Training

INTRODUCTION AND MAIN POINTS

Skilled buyers are made, not born. Where do people in the buying profession come from? How do they learn to do what they do? How to create a staff of competent buyers is the subject of this chapter.

After studying the material in this chapter:
- You will know the relationship between expectations and performance.
- You will know what training a buyer entails.
- You will know what vehicles for training exist and which are appropriate for each topic.

EXPECTATIONS

Expectations determine behavior. In purchasing, this is reflected in the expectations that a manager has for each of the people in the department and his or her vision of the department's function. Does the purchasing function exist to process the paperwork for an order, or to manage a major section of the company's cost structure? The view a purchasing manager holds of the purpose and value of the function plays a big part in establishing the role of a buyer and therefore what skills a buyer needs.

Viewing purchasing as a clerical function that exists to process orders translates into a buyer job description that values attention to detail, patience, stability, and a tolerance for heavy work loads. To be sure, these are admirable traits. However, viewing purchasing as a section of business management that controls a major portion of the corporate cost structure translates into a buying function that requires an additional set of skills: business and financial analytical skills, knowledge of law and markets, and technical knowledge of the products and commodities. This latter view of buyers that will be addressed here.

BUYER SELECTION

The way purchasing is viewed within a corporation influences who is hired for buyer positions. Many companies hire buyers through newspaper advertisements and through employment agencies. These companies simply choose the candidate for the position whose skills most closely match the requirements. However, companies whose policy is to hire buyers from within face a more difficult task. An internal hire may come into the purchasing function with no knowledge of purchasing at all. Different selection criteria must be used in the hiring process, and more extensive training is needed.

Key attributes to look for when interviewing candidates for a buyer position are basic business sense, financial analytical skills, and interpersonal skills that include a desire to be self-managing, a desire for measurable success, a desire to learn, and the ability to work as part of a team.

THE TRAINING PLAN

Every member of a purchasing department should have a training plan that points up the areas where additional skills are required and outlines a general approach to obtaining those skills. The formality of the plan is not important. It may be a formal plan with specific training or an informal plan on a piece of scratch paper. What matters is that the direction of training is clear and agreed upon by both buyer and manager and that time and money will be provided as necessary to help the buyer achieve the needed skills.

MAJOR AREAS OF KNOWLEDGE: COMMODITIES

To be effective, every buyer must master certain areas of knowledge. The first that will be considered here is knowledge of the commodity or commodities that are being purchased. This encompasses both technical understanding and a knowledge of the market. Rarely are there specific courses available in which a buyer can get this type of information. The suppliers and the market become the best teachers.

Technical understanding of a commodity starts within the buyer's organization, with the users and the technical staff. Every buyer should spend time with technical personnel learning why the commodity is used, what dimensions or specifications are critical and why, how quality is defined and what levels of quality are required, what alternatives or substitutes exist, and what performance results are important to the final product.

This information not only helps the buyer do a better job, but also leads to a better relationship with the users of the commodity based on a common understanding and language. Specific time to train with the technical community should be set aside and be both monitored and supported by purchasing management.

After the buyer has a solid understanding of how the commodity is used, he or she should visit the suppliers of the commodity and learn how it is manufactured. Suppliers are usually quite willing to have a buyer visit their facilities and talk to staff members. Buyers can learn how the items are made, what are the critical factors, what are the quality levels and limiting issues, and where the leading-edge research is going in this commodity.

Some understanding of the market and the supply base for the commodity comes with technical training. But additional information should be sought as well, including possible suppliers, current position of suppliers in the market and why, and trends in the market for price and supply. A buyer should know whether the commodity follows cyclical trends, whether it is a buyer's market or a seller's market, and what position the buyer's company holds as a consumer. This information can come from several sources, including trade publications, suppliers, and professional contacts such as commodity committees within the National Association of Purchasing Management. Market knowledge should be specifically addressed in a buyer's training plan, and an appropriate method for obtaining the knowledge should be detailed.

MAJOR AREAS OF KNOWLEDGE: PURCHASING

Every buyer should have a firm grounding in the skills of purchasing, including law, finance, and negotiations. Legal training for buyers should include instruction in the law of agency, the Uniform Commercial Code, and contract law. Ethics and the laws governing business conduct may also be included. If the company has significant business with the United States government, federal regulations governing procurement should also be covered. Courses in purchasing law are offered as regional seminars, as academic courses, and as video-based courses. Since there is a significant amount to learn in this area, training should provide for ongoing re-education. Information that is used promptly will be retained more easily. Information that is not used promptly may need to be refreshed later. Course texts, videos or other vehicles may serve this purpose. The company's legal staff should be available to educate buyers as specific issues arise.

Financial training should encompass total-cost analysis, the time value of money, and how to assess the financial health of a supplier. Administration of company assets that are spent on materials and the value received for those assets is the primary responsibility of purchasing. That responsibility can be met only insofar as the skill level of the purchasing staff permits. Financial analytical skills are of primary importance to effective purchasing and should be among the first areas addressed in a training plan.

The training of buyers should include the introduction of basic accounting principles. Beyond basic math skills, a buyer should know:

- Preparing and analyzing spreadsheet to compare quotes.
- How to analyze total cost.
- How to assess the cost of administration.
- How to calculate the time value of money.
- Calculating the impact and hidden costs of defective materials.
- How to read an annual report.
- How to determine the financial strength of a supplier.

Good academic training in purchasing will cover most of these areas. Those that are not covered in formal courses have to be taught by knowledgeable people within the organization. If there are buyers with specific areas of expertise within the company, it is beneficial to have them available when a similar purchasing task arises that requires the skill so that a buyer can be coached with a real task before him or her. Experienced buyers can teach those less knowledgeable. Finance personnel may also be available to teach or coach novice buyers.

Negotiation is an area that requires both formal training and experiential learning. Formal training in negotiation strategies and techniques can be obtained from seminars, books, and from academic courses. However, no amount of formal training will completely prepare a student for the real thing. Experience is essential.

Experience can be gained from practice exercises and actual negotiations. Practice exercises give the buyer an opportunity to experiment in a low-risk environment. He or she can determine how comfortable they are with various techniques, how to prepare for and conduct negotiations, and how to assess success afterward. Some of the better books and seminars on the subject contain case studies that can be used as practice exercises. It is also possible to create your own, which has the advantage of allowing you to tailor the scenario toward one that is encountered in your purchasing environment. In setting up practice negotiations, it is important that the information given to the "buyer" and to the "seller" be significantly different and that the students not allow the other party access to their information.

Statistical process control (SPC) is becoming so important as a measure of quality that all buyers should have an understanding of it. Increasingly, SPC is being used to improve purchasing processes themselves. Buyers may eventually use these tools to generate measurements of their own performance. SPC can be learned from texts or from seminars. However, if these principles are being taught within your company to other departments, buyers should be included in this training. The addition of purchasing personnel into classes intended for manufacturing or quality personnel will not only accomplish the learning, but will also insure a common process and language within the company as well as cement a bond between these functions.

TIME FOR TRAINING

Finding the time and the resources for training of buyers can be a challenge. To develop a training plan that works for both the buyers and the department, the content and vehicles for training should be considered together. Some vehicles are more time-consuming or more expensive than others. After individual training plans have been developed, you will begin to see the types of training that are required and the number of people who need each type.

Where formal training is appropriate, either seminars or academic courses, time and money should be allocated for it. If a significant number of people need the same training, it may be worthwhile to bring the seminar or course inside your facility. If only one or two people need this training, they can attend a public seminar or an academic institution that offers appropriate programs of instruction.

Once the time and budget for formal training has been established, other vehicles of instruction can be added to expand training opportunities. The training budget should allow for books, videotape rentals, publication subscriptions, and other instructional materials.

Informal techniques for training can be a useful addition to the formal training plan. The following are some suggested informal training techniques:

▬ Practice negotiation exercises, with prizes for the winners.

▬ Study sessions in which each person in the group studies a section of a book and then "teaches" the others.

▬ Videotape rentals shown at a staff meeting or in another session that is a break from the routine daily work. (The National Association of Purchasing Management has an extensive video library for the purchasing profession.)

▬ Trade publications are excellent vehicles for information on market trends. These can be circulated through the group.

▬ Actual events are a good tool both for training and for group cohesion. For example, if a major contract is being renegotiated, or an issue surfaces with internal departments, or a supplier partnership is being established, you can explain exactly what is happening and why. Input and discussion among the members of the group will also provide an additional check for the staff members actually working on the issue. Sharing of information will allow the group to support the people directly working on the issue and allow their successes to be known and appreciated when the work is finished.

When the belief that training is important and a never-ending process becomes established, more vehicles will become available because they will be actively sought out.

CERTIFICATION

Certification by an external agency is unbiased testimony that an individual has achieved a significant career milestone. Professional certification accomplishes two very important benefits. One is a rise in a sense of professionalism among staff. The second benefit is the education and training in which an individual participates on the way to certification. Although the certification process is not a guarantee of wisdom or success, it does produce at least a minimum level of competence in the field. Seminars or study sessions in preparation for the certification exams may be available through the professional societies that offer the certification.

Certification in purchasing is offered by the National Association of Purchasing Management. It requires the successful completion of a four-module examination covering the general disciplines of purchasing and a certain level of experience in the field.

Another certification is offered by the American Production

and Inventory Control Society. This certification covers the fields of Material Requirements Planning, Inventory Management, Master Planning, Just-In-Time, Capacity Planning, and Production Activity Control. Certification is granted after successful completion of examinations.

REACHING OUT

Just as buyers can be trained in a commodity by the technical staff of the company, buyers can train people in other functions. Especially important for the user community within the company is an understanding of the legal ramifications of dealings with a supplier, negotiation strategy and the user's role in the process, and total cost analysis.

CHAPTER PERSPECTIVE

Training is key to maintaining a professional purchasing staff. Major areas of training are the use and manufacture of commodities, finance, law, negotiations, and the processes of the purchasing function. A plan for training should be developed and maintained for all personnel. Many vehicles can be used for this purpose, including formal courses, books, videotapes, and exercises. Training should be viewed as an ongoing process.

Ethics

INTRODUCTION AND MAIN POINTS

Ethics as discussed here refers to the rules of conduct recognized in a particular area of endeavor or by a profession. There are operating guidelines for all areas of business; this chapter will address those that affect people who buy or sell goods. The definition of ethics also encompasses individual moral principles, which cannot be totally separated from the discussion of business guidelines, since all business is conducted by individuals.

Several types of ethics questions will be addressed: laws governing behavior in business, issues that while not illegal are damaging to individuals and to businesses (called "sharp practices"), and rules that organizations establish to guide the behavior of members. There is a degree of latitude in the behavior rules and policies that organizations establish. In this book, the issues underlying corporate policy and rule formulation will be examined, and recommendations made, so that you can determine how these issues are best addressed within your business environment.

After studying the material in this chapter you will:
- understand the issues behind ethics guidelines.
- understand the need for corporate ethics policies.
- understand what areas of corporate ethics should be addressed by the purchasing function.
- understand how questions of ethics can be addressed.
- understand some of the legal limits of behavior that apply to buying and selling.

GENERAL ISSUES CONCERNING ETHICS

Every business should have explicit rules of conduct for its members. By establishing these rules and making them clear to all members, a company can deal with many difficult issues before they become full-blown problems. Establishing rules after a problem has arisen is much less effective, since the heat of the problem may affect perception and judgment.

The rules of conduct by which a business operates should be published and made available to all purchasing employees and also to suppliers. There are simple mechanisms for informing suppliers, such as posting company ethics policies in the lobby or reception area, sending a general informational letter, and requiring that buyers explain the policies to suppliers.

An informational mailing on behavior guidelines need be done infrequently. It may be done for specific policies such as before a period of expected challenges. Suppliers of the company can be notified of the company policy toward gift-giving prior to a holiday season.

The purpose of publishing ethics policies is to make limits clear. If a buyer violates an ethics policy, a supplier can react accordingly. Conversely, suppliers may be more careful in their behavior toward buyers and make an effort not to embarrass either the buyer or themselves by breaching the company's standards of conduct. Many awkward situations arise because one of the parties was unaware that the behavior in question was not acceptable. If a breach of conduct does occur, the prior efforts at education can help to establish whether it was intentional misconduct or a result of ignorance.

It is important to have *one* set of standards for behavior within a corporation. There may be a temptation, for example, to allow sales to do whatever is necessary to get business while holding purchasing to rigid standards of behavior. If a company establishes one set of standards for purchasing and another set of standards for its sales organization, it is asking for disrespect and disregard. A double standard is no more legitimate in a business context than it is in a social context, and it can be just as damaging.

It is also important to publish policy on behavior to *all* employees of the corporation. Employees outside of purchasing who deal with suppliers may be just as open to influence and much less trained or aware of ethical issues than their purchasing counterparts.

Consider the following example. Fred is an engineer who tests and approves parts for a new product. A supplier of one of these parts visits Fred regularly in the normal course of the qualification process. He knows that Fred is an avid sports fan. One day he tells Fred that he has two tickets to an upcoming professional football game. He "cannot attend," but asks Fred if he can use the tickets. Fred jumps at the chance and thanks his benefactor profusely. When the new product is released, the supplier's parts are specified on the prints in such a way that they are effectively sole-sourced. The price for those parts undergoes a sudden price increase. When Fred is pressured by company executives to qualify another source, he adamantly refuses since his reputation is now at stake, and he defends his original selection with all the resources at his disposal. No other supplier is ever qualified. The price differential between what is paid for the parts and what was available elsewhere in the market amounts to $600,000 per year for the years that the product is in production.

Although the name is fictitious, the details of Fred's story are true. The engineering and technical community of a company is especially at risk in a situation such as this, because they deal with suppliers so frequently in the course of their work, because they have control over specifications, and because they normally are not trained in ethics issues or cost issues.

Three questions that help in the evaluation of behavior are: Is it legal? Is it moral? Is it good business over the long term? Each question will be examined by looking at root issues, business considerations, the options available, and recommendations for sound policies.

GIFTS

The giving and receiving of gifts is an area in which behavioral limits must be specifically addressed by corporate policy. The ethical question is whether to allow personnel to receive gifts from those with whom they do business. If the chosen answer is "Yes," a second question is "How much is acceptable, and how much is too much?"

The root issue with the giving and receiving of gifts is the creation of influence or obligation that may affect a person's judgment in a later business deal. Gifts are offered for a reason. Even token gifts or advertising, such as pens and calendars, are given with the expectation that they will yield a result for the giver. Advertising is a significant expense in many corporations; the money is spent by a company in order to keep its name in front of those who make judgments about buying their products. Name familiarity and easy access to telephone numbers have business value.

The question then becomes whether buyers are actually

influenced. The degree of influence from token items is subtle and difficult to measure. However, token gifts *do* persuade. A discussion with the sales division of your company about how gift-giving fits within their sales strategy and what results they have derived from it would assist in the effort to set a sound corporate policy in this area.

Gifts of greater value are usually given with a more explicit intent to create obligation. Reciprocation is a strong trait in our culture. If we receive a gift or a favor, there is a natural desire to repay and a sense that we somehow owe something to the giver. As in the story of Fred, this sense of obligation can have a significant financial impact on a corporation. It is very difficult to prove or to overcome once it has become an acceptable practice. Allowing *anyone* in the corporation to receive gifts of more than token value from those with whom they do business creates a climate that can adversely affect the corporation. Areas outside of purchasing are not immune to this issue. Even upper management is a favorite target of gift givers. Engineering or design people who often qualify or specify suppliers are also targeted. A carefully considered policy on this issue should be developed and applied to everyone.

Special provisions may have to be made when dealing internationally. Some cultures outside of the United States consider gift-giving an integral part of doing business. If your corporation deals internationally, provide for those special circumstances where gift *exchange* is appropriate and define the limits of appropriateness. Keeping in mind the underlying issue of influence on business judgment may help in the establishment of a sound policy.

Bribery is the outright and deliberate exchange of something of value for the favor rendered. Intent is the essence of bribery; one cannot take a bribe by accident. Laws prohibiting commercial bribery vary from state to state; check the laws in the state in which your corporation operates. The law for New York State (Article 180) defines bribery as follows:

> A person is guilty of commercial bribing when he confers, or offers or agrees to confer, any benefit upon any employee, agent or fiduciary without the consent of the latter's employer or principal, with intent to influence his conduct in relation to his employer's or principal's affairs.

Bribery is sometimes difficult to prove, and many companies do not want to deal with the publicity that comes from a legal prosecution. This is additional reason for having a well-considered corporate policy that defines the limits of acceptable behavior and states the penalty for a breach.

The following are examples of corporate policy statements regarding acceptance of gifts or gratuities:

Contractors shall not give or offer gifts or gratuities of any type to employees or members of their families. Such gifts or offerings may be construed as Contractor's attempt to improperly influence our relationships.

No employee or member of employee's immediate family shall accept (or receive) any gifts or accommodations of more than nominal value from anyone with whom the employee does business on behalf of the company which might place him in a difficult, prejudicial or embarrassing position or interfere in any way with the impartial discharge of his duties. Nominal value is defined consistent with the Internal Revenue Service regulation which restricts gifts by corporations to $25.00 per year to any individual (to be deductible).

Neither seek nor accept any gifts, gratuities or other form of compensation, benefit or persuasion from suppliers, customers or others doing, or seeking to do, business with the company. Personnel violating this policy may be subject to disciplinary action, up to and including dismissal.

No display of advertising matter (such as calendars, pens, note pads, desk accessories, etc.) is permitted.

The last example, which deals with display of advertising material, may at first seem unnecessarily harsh. However, the purchasing function is in a unique position with respect to gift-giving. If engineers or other requisitioners visit the purchasing department and observe what buyers have been given, will they also want to deal with suppliers? What will be the result? If backdoor selling is a problem in your company, or if the user community is not working as closely with purchasing as it should, it may help business goals if receiving and/or display of any gifts by either purchasing or the users is discouraged.

If a supplier visits a buyer and observes gifts or advertising tokens from a competing supplier displayed in the buyer's office, is the relationship with the buyer helped or worsened? If your organization is working toward partnerships with suppliers, then gift-giving and display should be discouraged.

One type of gift-giving that deserves separate consideration is payment for business lunches and entertainment. There is often valid reason for business to be conducted outside of the office—over a meal for example. The issue of creation of obligation is the same, however. If the supplier pays for lunch on a repeated basis, there may be a shift in the balance of power that favors the supplier. This can have an impact on the buyer's self-perception and may affect any subsequent business dealings, especially negotiations where establishment of power is a significant factor. A company's policy for business lunches should seek to avoid the creation of obligation on the part of the buyer. There are several proven ways of doing this: provide for buyers to pay for lunch on an alternating basis; stipulate that each party pays for his or her own meal; provide a place within the buyer's facility for a business lunch or a confidential meeting.

Entertainment should be allowed only as an incidental part of a legitimate business trip or meeting—for example, a trade show or convention that provides entertainment for all registrants. However, entertainment for its own sake serves no business purpose and may compromise a buyer's judgment. The story of Fred is an illustration of this. Entertainment can be a method of creating obligation that leaves no tangible trail of evidence.

The following are recommendations for policies regarding gifts:

1. Discourage the receiving of gifts from suppliers, even low-value advertising.

2. If your sales department gives such gifts and considers it a valuable part of its sales strategy, seek to understand why and what they expect to gain from the practice. Then agree on a value limit for gifts that both sales and purchasing can live with, and prohibit gifts of higher value for all employees.

3. Teach all purchasing personnel about the impact of advertising and the creation of obligation so that they are aware of the issue and its implications. Once they are aware, extend the awareness to others within the company who are likely targets for influence (such as engineering or the product design groups).

4. Provide for bilateral payment for business lunches.

5. Discourage entertainment unless it is incidental to a larger business function.

INFORMATION
The handling of information is an area that frequently gives rise to ethical considerations. The primary ethics questions are

whether and with whom it is appropriate to share a piece of information. The underlying issue in the handling of information is betrayal of trust. Inappropriate sharing or withholding of information can damage a relationship with a supplier or relationships within your own organization. Since betrayal of trust is the root issue, maintenance of trust is also the root solution. A corporate policy for the handling of information should address three points:

■ define which information is sensitive
■ agree among all involved parties how it will be handled
■ keep that agreement

These guidelines will become more and more useful as purchasing evolves into closer supplier relationships, into use of new transmission technologies such as electronic data interchange (EDI) and fax, and into use of increasingly sophisticated technology in the manufacture of products. More information is being exchanged, and at a faster rate, than ever before.

An area of particular concern is the quotation process. In commercial purchasing, buyers are reluctant to release quotation information, even when it is in their best interest to do so. In the public sector, quotations are opened in a public forum and are posted for all to see. To determine the best policy for your organization, use trust, integrity, and good business judgment as fundamental guides. Legally, a submitted quotation becomes the buyer's property. Integrity and trust dictate that a supplier's expectations regarding the handling of quotation information are not betrayed.

Should quotation information ever be made available to parties outside the direct purchasing process, and if so, under what circumstances? The primary fear is that price information submitted by one supplier will be used to help another supplier obtain the order unfairly. Clearly, the careless handling of quotation information between suppliers will violate all the guidelines discussed earlier: trust, integrity, and good business judgment. Regardless of the outcome on any particular purchase order, such activities will have a negative effect on long-term supplier relations.

Even so, there are occasional circumstances in which such use of quotation information may be indicated. Suppose, for example, that Jack is the buyer for a very large manufacturing company, and Supplier A and Supplier B are bidding for their annual contract on a sophisticated subcomponent. Also suppose that for capacity, both suppliers will be needed for the foreseeable future. Supplier A has a term in the contract that is much more favorable to Jack than Supplier B. Supplier B's negotiating team indicates that such terms are governed by their corporate legal staff and are not easy to change. However, if they can show their legal staff what the competition offers for that term, there is a better than even chance of getting it changed. Based on his knowledge of Supplier B from prior dealings, Jack believes them. Supplier A's contract is already settled, and such a disclosure would not affect their allocation of the volume or the selling price. Should Jack:

1. give Supplier B a copy of Supplier A's quotation,
2. give them a copy of only the term in question, or
3. refuse to give Supplier B anything and forfeit a potential gain for his company?

If Jack wanted to use the second option, how could he do so without violating the guidelines for trust, integrity, and good business judgment? Much depends on the policy of his company regarding quotation information. If Jack's company bans release of any information, Jack has no viable option except to ignore the opportunity. If release of information is allowed under special circumstances, Jack can take that course of action. If suppliers are routinely informed that quotation information becomes the property of the buying company and may be used by them as they see fit, Supplier A's trust and expectations will not be violated.

Allowing suppliers to requote and accepting late quotations are other areas of controversy. The guidelines of trust, integrity, and good business judgment can be used here to determine what is ethically proper for all concerned. For example, if a trustworthy supplier has made an honest error and asks to correct it and requote, good business judgment and integrity will most likely decide in favor of the correction. However, if a supplier has gotten information about a competitor's quote and wants to use it to favorably position his own quote, the integrity guideline would dictate that the original quote stand unaltered.

It is important to educate buyers regarding company policy and the underlying guidelines of trust, integrity, and good business judgment. The best safeguard against any of the ethics violations discussed in this chapter is a well-educated and highly valued buying staff who have clear company policies to rely on.

The emergence of fax, EDI, and other electronic forms of information transmittal have raised other ethical issues. Normally, information faxed to another company is not secure, and the use of fax should be tempered accordingly. EDI requires security protection for access to the system, especially since transmitted information is frequently the signal to authorize production or purchase.

As long-term relationships with suppliers become the norm, sensitive information is transmitted routinely. Sales and production forecasts, new-product design information, and future development plans are examples of such information. Security becomes particularly essential if the information is potentially patentable or copyrightable. Definition of *sensitivity* and *agreement* on handling are critical, both to safeguard the information and to preserve the relationship.

The following are recommendations for policies regarding the handling of information:

■ Specify all information that is considered confidential in nature and clearly mark it as such. Request that suppliers do so.

■ Define how such information will be handled.

■ Specify that ordinary information, such as quotations, becomes the property of the buying organization and may be used by the buyer consistent with company policy and good business judgment.

■ Establish a check-and-balance system (such as a review or approval requirement) for potential release of information to any organization other than the buyer's.

■ Educate buyers in the issues surrounding the handling of information so that they are prepared to deal with these issues in a professional manner.

■ Make company policy with respect to information transfer known to all suppliers and clarify any questions that arise.

CONFLICT OF INTEREST

Conflict of interest may arise whenever a buyer has a vested interest in the advancement of a company other than his or her employer. Such vested interest may be a consequence of stock ownership, relatives employed with the other company, or extra discounts or benefits offered to the buyer individually rather than to his or her company. Most companies require buyers to disclose any circumstance that may be considered to be a conflict of interest. The buyer and his or her manager can then decide upon the proper course of action.

PERSONAL PURCHASES

Company employees should be strictly forbidden from making *personal* purchases through the purchasing department. At the very least, this practice drains resources away from legitimate activity and promotes back-door selling. And it does nothing to enhance the legitimacy and professionalism of the purchasing function.

The question of allowing buyers to make *personal* purchases from suppliers is a bit more complicated, primarily because what a buyer does in his or her own time is difficult for an employer to regulate. But buyers should be discouraged from engaging in this practice—and the dangers explained. It opens up opportunities for undue influence through gifts and deep discounts. It may set up circumstances that lead to conflict of interest. It may create at least the perception of favoritism and thereby affect the buyer's performance on the job. Education and valuing buyers as professionals is a way of addressing this without resorting to policies which may be very difficult to enforce.

SHARP PRACTICES

Sharp practices are activities that, while not illegal, are not in accord with the principles of trust, integrity, and good business judgment. They are to be avoided by organizations seeking integrity for themselves and stable relationships with suppliers.

One of these practices is "bait and switch," which is the offering of one item for quotation when in fact another item is needed. Once the quotation is submitted, the item actually needed is substituted, and the supplier feels pressure to hold to the price originally quoted.

Lying to a supplier is another sharp practice. This harms both the individual who engages in it and the relationship. Eventually, truth will come out, and when it does, trust is shattered and doubly difficult to ever rebuild. Lying is the most damaging thing that can be done to a relationship—business or personal.

Many sharp practices are various forms of lying. Another is inflating the desired quantity in order to obtain a better quote price, then attempting to hold the supplier to this price for the actual quantity needed. Frequently, the actual quantity is not known precisely at the time price quotations are requested. There is a range of probability in the quantity that will ultimately be used. How far is it reasonable to reach for a higher quoted volume in the hope of achieving both a lower price now and perhaps the higher volume over the life of the contract? A general guideline is that if the odds are 50/50 or better that the higher volume will actually be needed, then quote the higher volume. The surest guide is integrity and intent.

In the purchasing profession, questions often arise regarding how honest one must be in setting the stage for a negotiation. Of course, there are different types of negotiations and negotiating relationships. But if the negotiation is with a supplier of long standing, it is of mutual benefit to be as forthright as possible on both sides. Mutual honesty and trust is the foundation of the relationship.

However, if the negotiation is with an enterprise with whom you have no history and no plans for long term future business, more caution is called for. A good analogy is the game of poker; you play with all your cards on the table, but not with all your cards faceup. What constitutes cheating is well defined. Dishonesty (such as a card up the sleeve) is considered cheating, but allowing someone else to guess what you have in your hand and play accordingly is a legitimate part of the game. A good negotiation has similar characteristics. There is an ethical and business obligation not to lie, but allowing the other party to learn those things that it is in your interest for them to know, while not revealing those things that are not in your interest, is a legitimate part of negotiating. (See Chapter 11.)

CHAPTER PERSPECTIVE

The best safeguards against unethical behavior are education about issues and clear corporate policies that demand integrity and good business conduct from all employees.

Mutual understanding of what is appropriate behavior—between buyers and suppliers, between purchasing personnel and other company employees—stops many issues before they arise.

A staff that is treated with respect for its knowledge and abilities will, in turn, respect those with whom they deal. A staff treated as if it cannot be trusted will most likely become untrustworthy employees. A corporate manager has an opportunity to shape the ethical climate of the organization, since people frequently behave in a manner that reflects the regard in which they are held by their superiors.

The Demand Signal

INTRODUCTION AND MAIN POINTS

This chapter will look at the various methods for transmitting a signal to purchasing for the procurement of goods or services. These methods include requisitions (both single-use and traveling), material requirements planning reports, kanban and pull signals direct to suppliers, and systems contract releases.

The demand signal has two basic purposes. The first is to communicate enough information that a buyer knows what to purchase. The second is to authorize the expense. Both of these functions must be fulfilled by the signal you choose.

After studying the material in this chapter, you will be able to:

■ Determine which signal systems work in which situations.
■ Determine which systems are appropriate to your functions.

REQUISITIONS

The most commonly used demand signal is a single-use purchase requisition. This is a standardized form, usually with attached carbons. An employee who wants something purchased simply fills out the form, gets an authorization signature, and takes the form to purchasing. A sample requisition is illustrated in Figure 6-1.

However, the single-use purchase requisition also requires a fair amount of legwork and generates more paper than do other demand signals. After the material or service has been purchased, the purchase-order number and delivery date are entered on the requisition by the purchasing department. One copy is retained with the purchase order; another is returned to the requestor so that the person or department will know when the purchased item is due to arrive.

A single-use requisition is appropriate in situations where many people are requesting items on a one-time basis. For example, requisitions are often used for employee needs such as

PURCHASE REQUISITION

Purchase Order
____

Recommended Supplier:

Accounting Information:
Cost Center ________
Project # ________
Taxable Y___ or N___

date	req # 00000001	delivery	ship via:	F.O.B.	terms:

item#	quantity	unit	description	unit price	amount

________________ Requisitioner

________________ Approval

Confirming to:	Promised Delivery:

FIG 6-1. *Purchase requisition.*

supplies. There is no information on a requisition that tells the buyer whether the item is a one-time buy or not. Consequently, if the buyer does not contact the requisitioner and ask if further orders for the item are anticipated, the opportunity to take advantage of volume pricing is lost. Where the single-use requisition is the primary demand signal, visibility of future demand is limited and the purchasing function is primarily paperwork.

When the same items are ordered repetitively, a simpler demand signal is the *traveling requisition.* It is formatted like the single-use requisition and is usually made from heavy card stock. A separate requisition card exists for each item to be purchased and it has many lines for repeat purchase information (see Figure 6-2).

When another purchase is required, the requisitioner fills in the next available order line with the new amount and need date, obtains approval signatures if necessary, and forwards the card to purchasing. After a buyer has placed the order, he or she completes the information on the requisition by adding a purchase-order number and due date, then sends it back to the requisitioner. The card serves as an acknowledgement to the requisitioner that the order has been placed, and as a purchasing history for the buyer. One form may circulate from requisitioner to buyer and back many times.

Of course, this type of requisition form simplifies paperwork and provides the buyer with the purchase history for the item. However, like the single-use requisition form, it does not provide any information about future demand.

MATERIAL REQUIREMENTS PLANNING

Material Requirements Planning (MRP) is part of a business management system called Manufacturing Resource Planning (MRP II) in which forecast and production plans are used to drive requirements for both purchased materials and production capacity. MRP is a time-phased scheduling process. Its primary output is a material-requirements plan that provides a network of supporting schedules to manufacturing for those items that are made and a part-by-part sequence of schedules to purchasing for those items that are bought. These schedules result in the manufacture of the quantity of finished products specified in the master production schedule.

Inputs start at the top (see Figure 6-3). The business plan, the sales plan, and the production plan are synchronized by the

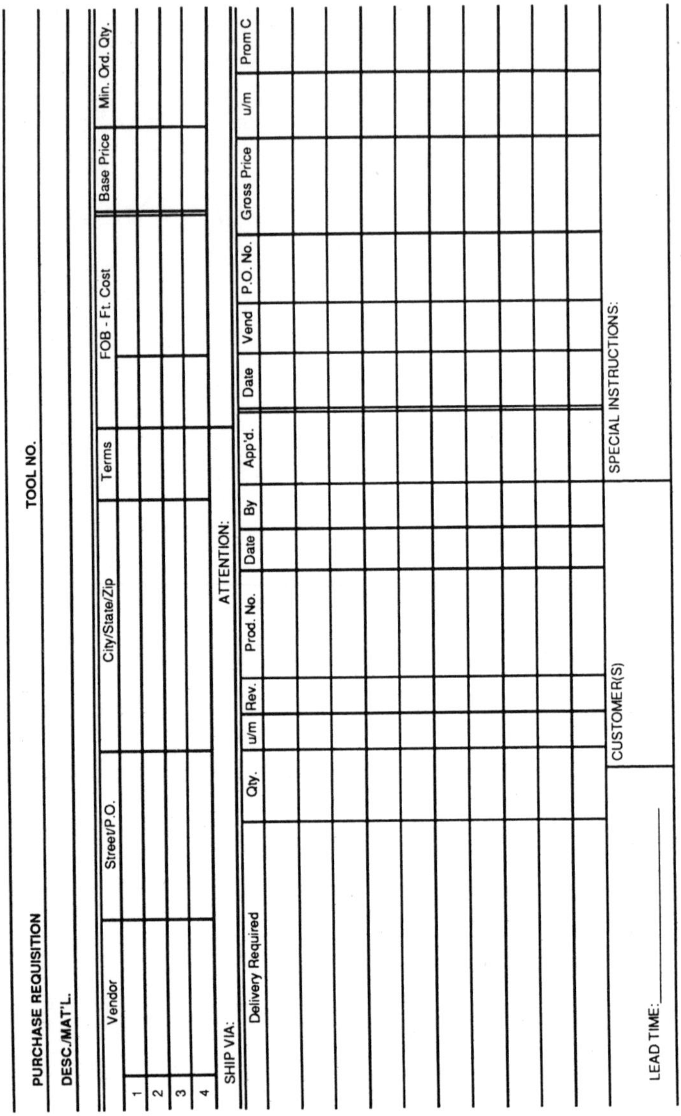

PURCHASE REQUISITION   **TOOL NO.** _____

DESC./MAT'L. _____

Vendor	Street/P.O.	City/State/Zip	Terms	FOB - Ft. Cost	Base Price	Min. Ord. Qty.
1						
2						
3						
4						

SHIP VIA: **ATTENTION:**

Delivery Required	Qty.	u/m	Rev.	Prod. No.	Date	By	App'd.	Date	Vend	P.O. No.	Gross Price	u/m	Prom C

CUSTOMER(S)   **SPECIAL INSTRUCTIONS:**

LEAD TIME: _____

FIG 6-2. *A traveling requisition.*

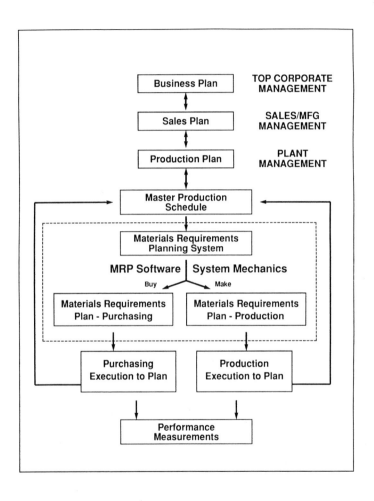

FIG 6-3. *Flow of information in MRP II.*

appropriate levels of management. After the production plan is prepared and released, a master schedule is prepared and entered into the material-requirements planning system. Within the system, the master schedule is multiplied by the bills of material for master scheduled products which yields the gross requirements for all components needed to build the end products.

The next step is to determine which of the components are available from inventory or are already on order. Gross requirements are deducted from available inventory and the net requirements are calculated (see Figure 6-4). The net requirements are scheduled based on when they will be needed to complete the finished product on time. Each item, starting from the finished product, is scheduled by backing off its lead time so that it is completed just as the next level of assembly requiring that item is scheduled to begin.

The major output of the MRP system are part-by-part schedule reports to purchasing and to production showing the quantity balances for items that must be acquired in order to complete the manufacture of a product. Such a schedule commonly encompasses a time horizon that is six to twelve months forward (see Figure 6-5.)

Since the production plan and the master schedule are usually reviewed and approved by senior management, all required materials are automatically authorized. In many businesses, the output of MRP goes directly to purchasing, where orders are placed for the required materials without any formal requisitions or written approvals.

In purchasing, the effects of this system include the benefits of forward visibility provided by the schedule, the opportunity to plan delivery of materials in a more organized manner, and freedom from the volume of paperwork involved in requisitions processing.

The validity of the MRP schedule also depends on the accuracy of the master schedule and the inventory and bill-of-materials databases. If the master schedule and databases are accurate, MRP presents a significant opportunity to purchasing. Because it forecasts demand, MRP can be used to manage the flow of material from suppliers and to determine the likely quantity for contract negotiations. For example, purchase orders can be placed far enough in advance to cover supplier lead time. Depending on the strength of the relationship with the supplier, it may be possible to send the MRP schedule directly to a supplier

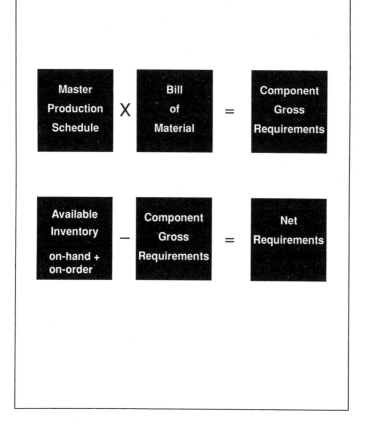

FIG 6-4. *MRP calculations.*

PRINTED 19-Jan-91 05:11 PM

PART NUMBER	E R A	PART DESCRIPTION	UM EA	LEAD TIME PUR KIT MFG YLD FACT 100.0 0	SHRK 0	QTY PAST DUE 0	BAL ON HD 29	MIN SS 0	ORD QTY 1
1015									

ENG CHANGE DATE: 08-Aug-90
ENG CHANGE NO.: 18

STANDARD COST: 9.59
STANDARD LABOR HOURS: 0.00
PURCHASE PRICE STANDARD: 9.59

Lead Times:

	WK 21-Jan-91	WK 28-Jan-91	MON 04-Feb-91	WK 11-Feb-91	WK 18-Feb-91	WK 25-Feb-91	WK 04-Mar-91	WK 11-Mar-91	WK 18-Mar-91	WK 25-Mar-91	WK 01-Apr-91	WK 08-Apr-91
GR. REQ.	11	7	10	10	11	9	6	3	6	9	6	7
ON ORDER	0	0	0	0	0	0	0	0	0	0	0	0
FRM PL OR	0	0	0	0	0	0	0	0	0	0	0	0
AVAILABLE	18	11	1	0	0	0	0	0	0	0	0	0
REC ORDER	0	0	0	9	11	9	6	3	6	9	6	7
REMNG QTY	18	11	1	-9	-20	-29	-35	-38	-44	-53	-59	-66
DAY CNT	11.00	6.00	1.00	0.00	0.00	0.00	0.00	0.00	0.00	0.00	0.00	0.00

	MON 15-APR-91	MON 29-APR-91	MON 28-MAY-91	MON 01-JUL-91	MON 29-JUL-91	MON 26-AUG-91	MON 30-SEP-91	MON 28-OCT-91	MON 25-NOV-91	BAL 29-DEC-91	TOTALS
GR. REQ.	16	29	29	24	24	30	27	30	32	204	540
ON ORDER	0	0	0	0	0	0	0	0	0	0	0
FRM PL OR	0	0	0	0	0	0	0	0	0	0	0
AVAILABLE	0	0	0	0	0	0	0	0	0	0	
REC ORDER	16	29	29	24	24	30	27	30	32	204	511
REMNG QTY	-82	-111	-140	-164	-138	-218	-245	-275	-307	-511	511
DAY CNT	0.00	0.00	0.00	0.00	0.00	0.00	0.00	0.00	0.00	0.00	

FIG 6-5. *Detailed MRP report.*

so that they can forecast their own material requirements and work load.

The risk of using MRP is that the databases or master schedule may be inaccurate or unstable. As a result, purchasing may be bombarded with information that is wrong or that fluctuates wildly from week to week. If your business is considering the implementation of material-requirements planning, purchasing should volunteer to participate in the project and help to shape the business practices that will lead to a useful implementation.

There are three major data inputs to MRP that purchasing owns for those components that are bought, not made: lead time, lot size, and safety stock. It is important to understand the impact that they have on the system and on the validity of the MRP output schedule.

Lead time for purchased items is the time from the recognition of need to the time that the items are available for use. This includes time to read the MRP, analyze the requirement, and place the order; the supplier's lead time; transportation time; and any time that is required to receive and inspect the goods (see Figure 6-6). In MRP, the lead times for each of the levels of assembly and purchase are cumulative. Since purchased items are normally required to start the manufacturing process, they are the farthest removed from the date the finished product is required (see Figure 6-7).

The further into the future one forecasts, the less reliable the forecast becomes. Consequently, purchasing is most vulnerable to forecast changes, since they are first in the manufacturing process. Because long lead times exacerbate this problem, buyers should work with suppliers to *reduce lead time.*

Lot size is the quantity multiple in which materials are ordered. It is determined by various factors, including packaging and use considerations, cost to order versus cost to carry, and length of lead time, and transportation pipeline. A common purchasing material is ordered less often and is therefore less work to manage. In an MRP environment, large lot sizes have other ramifications: they create a "lumpy" demand signal to purchasing and to suppliers, which can lead to delivery delays. They lengthen lead time from suppliers. They lengthen the time required to solve quality problems and increase the consequences of those problems. MRP functions better when lot sizes are small and delivery is frequent. Adjustments to the schedule have less impact on suppliers and on the manufacturing process.

Safety stock is "just in case" inventory put in place to protect

Read MRP	Place Order	Supplier Lead Time	Transit Time	Receive	Inspect

FIG 6-6. *Components of purchase lead time.*

against uncertainty of supply or demand. MRP protects safety stock by scheduling as though it were not there. If a near-term increase in the production schedule requires safety stock to be used, MRP schedules its replenishment in the first available period. If safety stock is never used, it simply consumes space and money. If safety stock is used, it will increase the normal schedule in MRP to cover its replacement. It is possible to have an MRP schedule driven by safety stock, which masks true demand and allows the root cause of problems to remain unaddressed and unsolved. Safety stock should be used with great prudence and reviewed often—if it is used at all.

Properly understood and administered, MRP can provide great benefits to the purchasing function. If it is used without understanding and in a business that is not well managed, it can result in inaccurate information that changes so often that it is more a detriment than a benefit. Therefore, purchasing has a strong vested interest in ensuring that the implementation of MRP into a business is smooth.

KANBAN

The term "kanban" is Japanese for "numbered card." The term is used in business to designate a system in which materials are replaced as they are used. A card that travels with the materials is the resupply signal. Each card represents one container or standard unit of measure of material (see Figure 6-8).

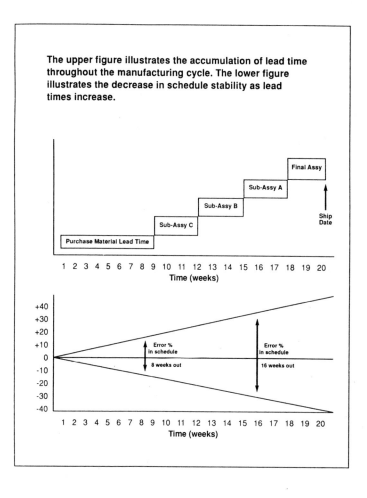

The upper figure illustrates the accumulation of lead time throughout the manufacturing cycle. The lower figure illustrates the decrease in schedule stability as lead times increase.

FIG 6-7. *Cumulative lead time in MRP.*

For a kanban system to work, the following conditions must exist:

■ Quality problems have been solved to the point that the material resupplied by a kanban system has a very low probability of being rejected as defective.

■ The schedule by which materials are consumed and resupplied is relatively smooth and predictable.

■ Lead time to make and resupply the material is stable.

■ Approval to purchase resupply materials is unnecessary.

■ A contract exists with the supplier that covers the business aspects of material supply and details the process by which the kanban will be used so that no purchase orders are required (or a single P.O. number can be used as a reference for deliveries).

■ The supplier administers its side of the system.

A kanban pull system for resupply works as follows: Supplier X delivers a box of materials to the customer's receiving area (or directly to the point of use). The box also contains a kanban card. The kanban card from the previous box or boxes of materials is then picked up by the supplier. These cards are the authorization for the supplier to build and deliver more material. The buyer controls the level of inventory by controlling the number of kanban cards in the cycle. A simpler method is to use the shipping container itself as the resupply signal. Adding cards to the process will increase inventory either in manufacturing or at the supplier. Removing cards from the cycle will reduce the level of inventory.

With a contract and trained personnel in place, the kanban system should work with a minimum of paperwork and effort on the part of purchasing. However, inventory levels and the system itself should be monitored to ensure that any problems are caught early.

A kanban system is very useful in a manufacturing process as a way to schedule production material and regulate inventory. It is also useful in any non-manufacturing process where regular smooth flow of material is required.

REORDER POINT

Reorder point systems use the actual goods on hand as the resupply signal. A prerequisite for a reorder point system is that the materials be stored in a single location or a small number of locations. At the storage location, a physical indicator of stock level is established. It may be a mark on a bin, a standard container, or whatever is appropriate for the type of material

Part Number:	Z40795

Supplier: Pagehill Suppliers, Inc.

PO: A 093746

QTY:  **10**

Deliver To: Production Line B

Delivery Frequency: **4 Hours**

Floor Location: **60 — A**

Location Desc: **Conveyor**

Product Code: **LO 71**

KANBAN #

||||||||||||| |||| ||| ||||| |||| |||||||

3000008071

FIG 6-8. *Example of a kanban card.*

being monitored. A visual inventory of the stock level is taken frequently. Whenever the level of material falls below the indicator, a signal is passed to purchasing to resupply the item.

A reorder point system is a good way to regulate and monitor materials usage and minimize administrative labor—especially for items whose usage is relatively predictable and items that are replenished frequently. A major drawback to reorder point systems is that they do not permit the forecasting of usage. They trigger a resupply signal only after the material has been consumed. If the ability to forecast is important to a smooth flow of material, as is the case with items that have a long lead time, then a reorder point system may not be appropriate.

THE BREADMAN

A variation on the reorder point system is "the breadman," so called because it is copied from the resupply system used in the grocery industry. In large grocery stores, the supplier for a certain type of goods sends a representative to the store on a regular cycle. This person visits the area in the store where that item is sold, takes inventory of what is on the shelf, checks the date codes, removes any outdated items, resupplies the shelf to an agreed-upon maximum inventory, and takes a slip to the store office that indicates how many items have been restocked so that payment can be made.

This type of system also works well in business, especially when suppliers are geographically close. The items should be kept in a stock area (such as a reorder point area) and should be standard industry merchandise (not materials made to custom order). A contract that specifies the prices for all items and the system for delivery and billing should be in place.

Control of the inventory and the associated expenses resides with the department responsible for maintaining the stock area(s). Inventory is controlled by adjusting the maximum level to which the supplier restocks.

SYSTEMS CONTRACTS

A systems contract is the type of agreement that is required to support the resupply systems described above. It specifies price and terms for standard merchandise and spells out the mechanism for resupply and billing. Its purpose is to arrange for a resupply mechanism that does not involve individual purchasing requisitions. It is used for standard merchandise (such as catalog items). Systems contracts are discussed in Chapter 16.

CHAPTER PERSPECTIVE

There are many ways in which resupply signals are passed to a purchasing department. To determine which is the best for a given situation, the following questions should be asked:

▬ On what tasks should purchasing be spending its time in order to be most cost effective for the company?

▬ Should the resupply signal come to purchasing, or go directly to the supplier under defined conditions?

▬ If the signal must come to purchasing, what is the most simple way to do that?

▬ Which items require supply forecasting?

▬ How can that information best be obtained?

The primary considerations in any signal system should be satisfaction among requisitioners and the minimization of paperwork in the purchasing function. Well-run signal systems also allow for good fiscal and auditing control, as well as more direct control by users.

Inventory Management

INTRODUCTION AND MAIN POINTS

Inventory represents a major portion of a company's cash investment and is an area that purchasing influences significantly. Consequently, a buyer should be aware of the major categories of inventory and the various options for managing them. This chapter will explore the purposes of inventory, its place in the production process, the impact of cycle time, and management of the inventory pipeline.

After studying this chapter, you will be able to:

■ Determine the reasons that you have inventory.
■ Analyze where inventory serves a legitimate purpose.
■ Understand how cycle time affects inventory.
■ Define the inventory pipeline, and how you can affect it.

THE PURPOSE OF INVENTORY

Inventory is all the material goods that are consumed in the performance of a company's service or in the manufacture of a company's products, including the products themselves. Inventory is commonly subcategorized to identify where in the process it is kept. *Raw material* inventory is material that has been received from suppliers and will be put into the manufacturing process, but at present is stored as it was received. *Work-in-process (WIP)* inventory is material that is in the manufacturing process in some stage of transformation, as well as material that has been partially completed and placed in storage, such as subassemblies. *Finished goods* are those materials that have passed through the manufacturing process and are ready to be sold or shipped to a customer. *Maintenance, repair, and operating supplies (MRO)* inventory is material that is consumed in the course of daily business but does not go into the product itself. Examples are office supplies, lubricants used to keep production equipment running, rubber gloves, and tools.

In service industries, inventory includes MRO supplies as

defined above, plus those items that are consumed in the performance of the service. For example, the inventory in a hospital includes such items as X-ray film, saline solution, bandages, surgical tools, and pharmaceuticals. A cleaning service regards as inventory the chemicals and supplies used in the performance of the service, such as cleaners, soaps, cloths and scrubbers, etc.

The only good reason for maintaining inventory is that conditions exist that make it less costly to have it than not to have it. Focusing on this belief forces attention on the conditions that drive inventory and on the costs of carrying that inventory. (For a discussion of the costs of carrying inventory, see Chapter 17.) When the conditions that drive the necessity for inventory are clear, better business decisions can be made regarding whether to carry the inventory or change the conditions that drive it. What are those conditions?

Inventory can be used as a buffer, a decoupler, or as insurance. A *buffer* protects the process against changes elsewhere in the supply/demand cycle. If the forecast is subject to significant changes on short notice, then some finished product inventory will insulate the production process from those changes and allow smoother operations. *Decoupler inventory* allows different parts of the production process to operate independently. If certain steps of the production process run at speeds significantly different from the remainder of the process, inventory accumulates after that step (if it is faster) or before it (if it is slower). *Insurance inventory* covers just-in-case concerns. For example, if a supplier doesn't deliver on time, extra inventory compensates for the problem and allows operations to continue.

These categories can be further defined based on their specific use. *Anticipation inventory* (also known as Hedge inventory) covers a known future event that will disrupt the normal flow of material. Examples of such events are the following: A supplier plant will shut down for a two-week vacation period; a special sale will increase demand for a product; production is planning a shutdown of its equipment for a major technical upgrade.

Fluctuation inventory (also known as *safety stock*) covers random or unpredictable changes in demand or supply. Examples are supplier delivery problems, quality problems, and normal sales fluctuations.

Lot-size inventory is determined by the batch sizes in which goods are manufactured or shipped. If an item is sold or shipped only in a certain unit multiple, the minimum lot is one unit multiple. An example is small electronic components that are sold on a reel for automatic insertion. The minimum quantity is one reel, which can be 2,500 parts.

Transportation inventory is all material in transit.

Each of the examples above presume that the reason for creating the inventory cannot be changed or fixed. In reality, there are alternatives to carrying inventory. In American business, however, inventory has been accepted as a necessary part of doing business for quite some time.

Inventory is a result. It is also very expensive. Keeping these two principles in mind will help in analyzing why inventory exists and where it should be kept. Inventory hides problems; by carrying inventory, a company can function in spite of its problems. However, the problems persist. One way to identify problems is to slowly lower the level of inventory. The problems that are being concealed will surface as the level of inventory drops, and each problem can be addressed. When these problems are resolved, inventory can be lowered again and the next layer of problems exposed. Table 7-1 shows some of the problems concealed by inventory buildup.

Inventory carried close to the finished-goods end of the production process often conceals problems related to customer demand, forecasting, customer returns, and production. Finished-goods inventory means that a company can respond to a customer sooner than its production lead time allows. Carrying finished goods, is the inventory alternative to solving problems.

Work-in-process (WIP) inventory is often carried as protection from problems related to production, such as yield prob-

TABLE 7-1
PROBLEMS COVERED BY INVENTORY

PROBLEM	Raw	WIP	FG
Unpredictable customer demand	X	X	X
Inaccurate forecasts	X	X	X
Low process yields, scrap, rework	X	X	X
Incoming material rejects	X		
Unreliable supplier deliveries	X		
Equipment availability, downtime	X	X	
Missed production schedules		X	X
Field failures, customer returns			X

lems, scheduling problems, equipment availability problems, and disorganization in the production process. If the final stages of production are short, and the final product is customized or assembled into different variations, inventory is carried as WIP and finished as specific customer orders are received.

Raw material inventory is carried as protection from problems with suppliers, either in quality or delivery. It may also be carried as extra protection against problems in production. If lead times are long, it may be carried as protection from forecast changes, or customer demand or schedule increases.

Inventory increases in value as it moves through the manufacturing process. Carrying inventory any place in the process other than the raw state is carrying the labor that has been invested in it to that point. Inventory can also be considered stored labor.

THE INVENTORY PIPELINE

The inventory pipeline contains the movement of both the physical materials and the information that creates it:

INFORMATION

SUPPLIER SCHED < P.O. < PRODUCTION SCHED < ORDERS < FORECAST

MATERIAL

SUPPLIER > TRANSIT > RAW > WIP > F.G. > CUSTOMER

Considering both the flow of goods and the flow of information as part of the pipeline of inventory allows more freedom in the search for ways to reduce it. If a demand signal decreases, but that information is not passed on, the information part of the pipeline is directly responsible for creating additional inventory. Reduction of the information pipeline is a good place to begin an inventory-reduction program. How fast does information get transmitted through your business and to your suppliers? If that information channel can be improved, the inventory level will begin to come down and better information will support better business management at all levels.

THE EFFECT OF CYCLE TIME

Time is a significant driver of inventory, both at the information level and at the physical goods level. For example, if Bob Buyer keeps safety stock on hand because Sam Supplier sometimes ships defective material, and the lead time to get material from Sam Supplier is four weeks, Bob will probably keep enough material on hand to cover four weeks of production operations. If Sam Supplier's lead time is eight weeks instead of four weeks? If the time to replace the material is twice as long, then Bob will probably carry twice as much because the safety stock will have to cover eight weeks of production, not four weeks.

The effect of time on inventory is magnified through the production process. The demand signal to production comes from customer orders and from forecasts. As forecasts and customer orders extend further and further into the future, they naturally become less and less accurate. This increase in forecast error is represented graphically in Figure 7-1.

Yet the demand that is in the future more than the combined lead times of your production cycle plus the supplier's lead time is what is driving you to order today. (For a graphic representation of this cycle, see Chapter 6, Figure 6-7.) If production lead times and supplier's lead times are long, the signal that is causing you to act comes from a forecast so far in the future that it is almost certainly inaccurate.

But when lead times are less than the customer's desired lead time, demand becomes much more stable. This is because production is driven from customer orders rather than from a forecast. Figure 7-2 illustrates the period into the future for which a company has orders for its products and the effect of lead-times longer or shorter than the bookings horizon. If the bookings horizon is much beyond what customers want and will accept, lost market share may result.

THE EFFECT OF LOT SIZE

In production operations, an increase in lot size has the effect of increasing both inventory and total lead time proportionately. For example, if the production of one unit of an item is a four-step process that takes ten minutes per step, the entire process will take forty minutes. It will take 400 minutes to produce a lot of ten pieces.

PROCESS STEPS:	1	2	3	4
PROCESS TIME PER OPERATION PER PIECE	10 MIN	10 MIN	10 MIN	10 MIN

LOT SIZE = 1   10 MIN + 10 MIN + 10 MIN + 10 MIN
TOTAL TIME = 40 MINUTES
TOTAL WIP INVENTORY = 4 PIECES

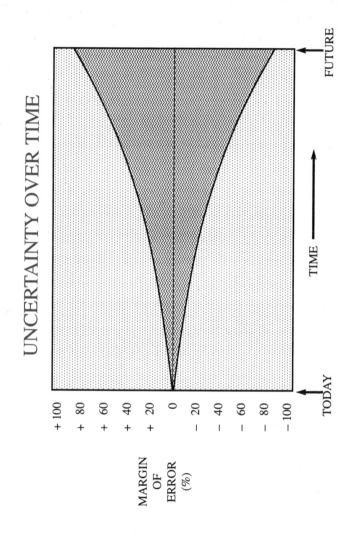

FIG 7-1. *Uncertainty over time.*

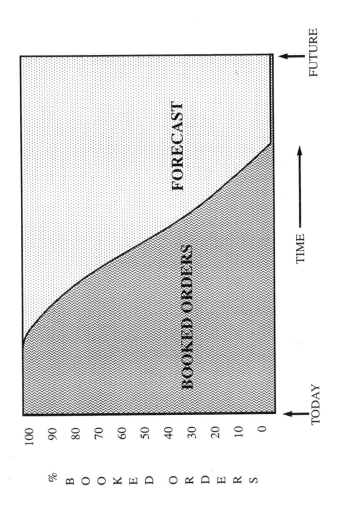

FIG 7-2. *Bookings vs. forecast.*

LOT SIZE = 10   100 MIN + 100 MIN + 100 MIN + 100 MIN
TOTAL TIME = 400 MINUTES
TOTAL WIP INVENTORY = 40 PIECES

In normal production processes, all ten pieces of a lot of material are completed before the lot is passed to the next step. This creates a multiplier effect that increases lead times and creates an unstable demand. Decreasing the lot sizes can reduce the manufacturing cycle time dramatically and make the demand signal more reliable.

Lead time from suppliers can also be reduced significantly by use of direct release mechanisms (described in Chapter 6), by simplifying the information pipeline, and by simplifying the administrative processes between the buying and supplying companies. If a supplier is producing an item to your exact specifications, the suppliers lot sizes will have the same effect on the supplier's lead time as that described above.

ANALYTICAL TOOLS

Two tools that have been developed to analyze and measure inventory are the ABC system, the measurement of inventory turns, and weeks-on-hand.

The *ABC* system of analysis is based on the presumption that inventoried items follow Pareto's Law for the distribution of value in the population. Also known as the 80/20 rule, Pareto's Law states that a majority of the cost of inventory is in a small minority of the items. Typically, 80 percent of the cost of the inventory comes from 20 percent of the items, and conversely, 80 percent of these items represents 20% of the cost. "A" class items are those that represent a significant dollar value. They are counted frequently (at least quarterly), planned carefully, normally produced in small lot sizes (usually a lot size of one), and their level of inventory accuracy is held to $+/- 1$ percent margin of error or better. "B" class items are those of inter-mediate value. They are counted at least every six months, are held to an inventory accuracy level of $+/- 2$ percent or better, and are produced in small lot sizes (although not necessarily one). "C" class items are those of low dollar value. They are counted at least once a year, are held to an inventory accuracy of $+/- 5$ percent, and are produced in large lot sizes and planned as infrequently as possible.

To establish an ABC system for managing inventory, complete the following analysis for all your inventoried items:

1. List all inventoried items in descending order based on their total annual dollar value. Total annual dollar value is the total quantity used in one year times the unit price.

2. Look for a break point in the dollar values. Often there will be a gap between higher-value items and those of lesser value. If a gap exists, use it to separate classes.

3. If there is no break point, determine how you wish to separate the dollar values. Commonly used divisions are 80% A, 15% B, 5% C, or 75% A, 15% B, 10% C.

4. Multiply the total annual dollars for all items by the percentages you have chosen to use: .8 for A, .15 for B, and .05 for C. This is the total dollars for that class.

5. Starting at the top of the list, add the values of the items in descending sequence until the total reaches that calculated for "A" class. Those items are the "A" class items. Continue down the list until the dollar value for "B" class is reached. Those are the "B" class items. The remainder of the list represents the "C" class.

6. Review the items in each category. Consider any other factors that affect how inventory will be managed. For example, space occupancy may affect how an item will be managed, and you may want to make that item an "A" item because only a few can be stored at a time. Move individual items from class to class as you add other factors into the analysis.

7. When the lists for each class are complete, code the items in the master files and set up counting sequences, lot sizes, and ordering mechanisms for each.

"C" class items are ideal targets for the establishment of direct release mechanisms (see Chapter 6), as well as alternatives to inventory, which will be described later in this chapter.

Two measurements that are commonly used to quantify the level of inventory on hand and to establish target levels are *Inventory Turns* and *Weeks on Hand*. Inventory turns is the theoretical number of times the inventory that is on hand will be consumed and replaced (or "turned over") in the course of one year. Inventory turns (IT) is calculated by dividing the annual cost of sales by the value of the inventory:

$$IT = \frac{\text{Annual Cost of Sales}}{\text{Dollar Value of Inventory}}$$

The cost of sales is the total cost that is in a product when it is sold. In some companies it is also known as the standard cost. The standard cost of a single unit is multiplied by the forecast for annual sales volume to obtain the annual cost of sales. For example, if the standard cost of one widget is $9.00 and the forecast predicts that 10,000 units will be sold in the current year, the cost of sales for this year is $90,000. If there is currently $30,000 invested in total inventory for this product, the inventory turns is 3:

$$IT = \frac{\$90,000}{\$30,000} = 3$$

Inventory turns is frequently used to set goals for the total amount of inventory that a company wishes to keep on hand, and to determine whether the current level of inventory is competitive.

A variation on inventory turns is determination of the weeks on hand that the current level of inventory represents. Weeks on hand can be calculated from the inventory turns number or from original-cost data:

$$WOH = \frac{52 \text{ weeks/year}}{IT \text{ (Turns/year)}} = \frac{\text{Dollar Value of Inventory}}{\text{Annual Cost of Sales}} \times 52$$

The weeks on hand measurement says that if the inventory turns three times per year, there should be enough material on hand to last for 17 weeks (one-third of a year).

Although both inventory turns and weeks on hand provide relative information about the level of inventory versus the level of sales, both have a major weakness in actual use. They are aggregate averages. Seventeen weeks of material on hand in the above example does not mean that a company could actually build product for seventeen weeks. In reality, individual items will have more or less than seventeen weeks on hand.

Goals for inventory turns or weeks on hand must be translated to the line-item level to affect the actual management of material. One method of translation is to determine the turns that are competitive or that represent excellence for your industry and to translate those turns into a total dollars target for inventory. The total dollars target can be broken down into targets for A, B, and C items. The buyers and planners that manage the items can then determine how to manage the flow of material to the target.

ALTERNATIVES TO INVENTORY

A systems contract with a supplier for large groups of items, such as hardware, tools, or standard consumable supplies, accomplishes two objectives: it reduces inventory, since the materials are readily available from the supplier and do not have to be stocked; and it removes those items from the buyer's workload. Once a direct-release contract has been set up, the buyer is freed from having to process requisitions that the items generated.

When resupply lead time is less than the time for consumption, items can be ordered in response to actual need. In such an environment, a Kanban or the "breadman" resupply systems allow the resupply mechanism to function independentiy of purchasing and on an as-needed basis. Inventories become minimal under such an arrangement. (For more information on these systems, see Chapter 6.)

Consignment inventory is another option. In a consignment inventory arrangement, a supplier provides material to the customer and retains ownership of that material at the customer site until it is used. Consignment inventory arrangements are most commonly used for raw materials, such as steel, and for commodity consumables, such as hardware. For a consignment inventory system to function well, there must be a strong, relationship between supplier and customer, and sufficient security for the material at the customer site. Benefits to the supplier include regular business and minimal commitment of labor. Benefits to the customer include readily available material, no inventory, and minimal commitment of labor. Consignment inventory arrangement is a good way to reduce inventory for those items that are predictable and routinely used.

Some suppliers, at the customer's request, are willing to hold inventory at their own facilities. When a supplier holds inventory for a customer, the resupply lead time is reduced to transportation time. However, supplier-held inventory also carries a risk. If the material is no longer needed and the supplier cannot sell it elsewhere, the buyer may be held liable by the supplier for at least the costs that the supplier has incurred—usually materials and the supplier's labor. Inventory is inventory regardless of who owns it.

Inventory is expensive. If a supplier is providing the service and incurring the costs of holding the inventory, then those costs will be passed along to the buyer, either through the price charged for the service or in the price of the goods themselves. Supplier-held inventory represents a hidden liability for the buyer's organization which is not reflected in any of the normal measures for the business. It should be used cautiously. Consequently, supplier-held inventory should be an interim measure, viewed as one part of a larger plan to reduce inventory throughout the pipeline.

Distributors stock a wide variety of items and supply them to customers on short notice. Inventory is their business; their market advantage is service. They may be ideally positioned to help the buyer reduce inventory. They are good partners for some of the arrangements discussed above, such as consignment inventory, "breadman" resupply systems, and supplier-held inventory. Distributors cover their costs by marking up the prices of the items they stock and distribute. However, a buyer may find that the cost savings realized from using a distributor is well worth the higher prices.

CHAPTER PERSPECTIVE

Is inventory a necessary evil? Or is it an absolute evil? Your answers to these questions may have serious ramifications for reducing inventory. If inventory is a necessary evil, then it will be considered the answer to those problems that you believe are unsolvable. For example, if the forecast is not good, then inventory may be unfortunate but the better of the two alternatives. If you view inventory as an absolute evil, it is never the better alternative, and you will constantly seek methods to reduce or eliminate it. This is the more difficult path, but the more rewarding from a business standpoint.

The effect of inventory is narcotic. It provides immediate relief from the pain of the problem. Temptation to reach for it as the medicating solution is very strong. However, the immediate feeling of relief always wears off, and the real problem is still there. Since they are not addressed, these problems gradually grow. It takes more and more inventory to cover the pain. Sensitivity to problems (and the will to solve them) gradually deadens. Eventually, the inventory itself becomes the chief problem. Addiction to inventory is a very common disease in corporate America.

What is the proper amount of inventory to maintain? To find out, answer the following questions carefully and honestly:

- What function does this inventory serve?
- What if that need were not there?
- For what problem is the inventory compensating?
- How can the level of inventory be reduced?
- How can the reason for the inventory be eliminated?

Supply Sources

INTRODUCTION AND MAIN POINTS

How does a buyer find the right supplier? How can a buyer be sure that the supplier selected will fulfill expectations in delivery, price, and quality? Where are the good suppliers hiding?

Before any other purchasing factor can be considered, a buyer must know where to look for suppliers. This can be difficult when the item to be purchased is untested or is the product of new technology.

After studying the material in this chapter:

- You will know how to find suppliers.
- You will be better able to evaluate suppliers.
- You will understand how to develop a supplier base, both for the present and for the future.

WHERE TO START

New buyers can find potential suppliers by:

1. Examining prior purchases (purchase-order or supplier-history files).
2. Asking other company personnel, such as engineers, maintenance personnel, and users.
3. Looking in the Yellow Pages for local suppliers. This can be a valuable source of information for services, maintenance, and supplies.
4. Using library references such as the *Thomas Register* and *Moody's Industrials*. These books list information by commodity and company name. The *Thomas Register* (also known as the "Tom Cat") should be in every purchasing department.
5. Looking through trade and professional journals—a valuable source of information. These publications contain not only product advertising, but also articles concerning new product developments. Examples are *Purchasing* magazine, *Electronic Buyers' News, Purchasing And*

Materials Management, Insight, Purchasing World, Environmental News, and *The American Metals Market.*

6. Using the trade directories produced by various industries. These list manufacturers, distributors, and representatives for commodities such as electronic components, chemicals, electromechanical devices, health-care products, and materials-handling equipment.

7. Querying salespeople. These people can offer buyers information on the products they sell and perhaps even on products they do not sell.

8. Joining professional organizations, such as the local chapter of the National Association of Purchasing Management, offers buyers the opportunity to network with other buyers and with purchasing managers. These professional contacts can prove invaluable when a buyer has a sourcing problem.

9. Using foreign embassies that have trade organizations and business attachés that provide complete business profiles of manufacturers in their country. Major cities in the United States that have trade or business attachés include Boston, New York, Chicago, Washington, and Los Angeles. These attachés also have information on national trade organizations.

INITIAL EVALUATION

A buyer may start by placing a trial order with a new supplier. Placing a small, low-risk order may help the buyer determine if the supplier will be satisfactory for regular business orders.

If the prospective supplier is local, a buyer should make a point of visiting and touring its facilities. Such visits offer the buyer an opportunity to learn about the supplier's products, processes, technologies, and people. Most suppliers are proud of their facilities, products, and people, and a buyer's visit allows them to "show off" the plant and to make a more demonstrative and lasting sales pitch than could be made in the buyer's office.

The more suppliers a buyer visits, the better that buyer can make informed decisions about products, technologies, relative efficiencies of operations, and the suppliers' operating environments. The buyer may also be able to discern subtle differences between suppliers that will help in the selection process:

■ Supplier's degree of desire to sell to the buyer.
■ Condition of the plant and equipment.

- Supplier's general financial state of health.
- Relative activity level.
- Other customers of the supplier.
- Supplier's view and use of technology (state-of-the-art and developing new technologies, or merely producing to existing technologies?)

While learning about suppliers' capabilities, a buyer should also spend time within his or her own plant learning about how the products are used and about the technologies and products that will be required in the future.

EVALUATING SUPPLIERS

The easiest way to evaluate suppliers is to assess prior performance with existing suppliers. If the supplier to be evaluated is new, more investigation is required.

Many people begin with a Dun & Bradstreet (D & B) financial report on the supplier. However, only publicly available information and information a supplier voluntarily furnishes to D & B appears on the report. The report may also include interesting historical information and brief profiles on key owners and managers.

You can also conduct your own fact-finding survey of a supplier. You may find some of the following questions useful:

1. How long has the supplier been in business?
2. Who are the principal owners? If the company is privately held, are the owners also the current managers? If the supplier is a public corporation, obtain a copy of its current annual report.
3. Who are the supplier's major customers? May you contact some of them for references?
4. What have been the supplier's business trends over the past ten years?
5. What is its history in labor relations? Is there a union? When is the contract due for renegotiation?
6. What percent of sales is spent on research and development?
7. What quality-control systems do they use?
   - Reliance on inspection
   - Process controls (SQC)
   - Self-monitoring processes
   - None

8. What is its current backlog and delivery lead time?
9. What is its history of price changes?

MAKE OR BUY

Some manufacturers elect to produce a certain product, component, or material itself rather than purchase it. The following are some of the reasons a manufacturer may do this:

a) the item was not available in the marketplace
b) current sources of supply were unreliable
c) belief that the item could be produced at a lower cost or higher quality
d) need for greater workload

Another reason for producing an item internally is that it is critical to the manufacturer's principal product. The technology may be proprietary or so important to the principal product that the product's market position could be jeopardized if it were available to other manufacturers.

Sourcing strategies can be viewed on three levels (see Figure 8-1):

1. Critical Technology—Technology (component, material, or process) on which your company depends for survival of a major product. This technology must be controlled by the company either by producing the item internally or having it produced under an exclusive arrangement with an external manufacturer. The first option is preferable because you have control over the security of the technology, its future development, and its by-products, and you will not run a risk of restraint-of-trade accusations due to exclusive dealings.

2. Marginal Technologies—Technologies less critical to product survival may exist in the market prior to the buyer's first purchase. The buyer runs less risk of possible exposure to others having access to the purchased technology. Others may purchase the technology in different forms. For marginal technologies, be on close terms with your supplier and make sure that your supplier understands the impact on you should your specific use or application become public knowledge. This is a good area in which to develop strong supplier partnerships.

3. Commodities—Commonly available items usually bought based on price and availability. A buyer does not need to take precautions concerning other users. Supplier selection and partnerships may be established on commercial business criteria (such as just-in-time practices) rather than on technology.

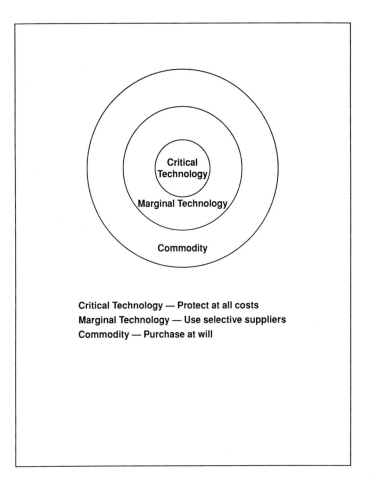

FIG 8-1. *Sourcing strategy.*

HOW MANY SUPPLIERS ARE ENOUGH?

A common purchasing question is "How many suppliers should we have?" There is an answer, but it is not easily derived.

Conventional wisdom says that a buyer should protect key items with multiple sources of supply. The reasoning is that should one supplier fail to deliver for any reason, there are other suppliers available. The more suppliers, the better. This strategy facilitates competitive bidding on existing items as well as new products. Commodities are often treated in a different manner. Since they are commonly available, there is little concern for the number of suppliers. Most items that fall within critical items and commodities should be multiple-sourced.

Another view gaining increasing acceptance is that the fewer sources, the better. The reasoning goes as follows:

1. If a buyer splits business between multiple sources, business volume with any one supplier may be small, and influence may be limited.

2. Since no two suppliers manufacture an item identically, the buyer introduces variation into the production process. The buyer may not know what the impact of this variation is on the manufacturing floor or on the end product.

3. If a buyer changes suppliers unpredictably, suppliers may be reluctant to invest in process or product improvements, or, not knowing if the buyer will purchase the item from them again, they may become unresponsive to special requests.

4. The buyer gives implicit license to all suppliers to delay shipments. If a supplier knows a buyer has other sources, the supplier may feel no urgency to resolve a problem or even to notify the buyer that there is a problem.

5. Many companies have found that they have so many suppliers that both the number and the relationships are beyond management.

For these reasons, there is a strong move within many companies to reduce the number of suppliers. Those suppliers that have an unsatisfactory quality history should be dropped first, followed by those unable to support the buyer's technological and product needs for the future, then by those with unreliable delivery records. The process of reducing suppliers may look like this:

Step 1. Reduce from multiple suppliers to two per item.

Step 2. Consolidate families of items with a few suppliers.

Step 3. Split the business for families of parts between two suppliers 40 percent and 40 percent, with the remaining 20 percent going to the better-performing supplier for the previous three months.

Start to single-source key parts, keeping in mind that there may be practical considerations that warrant multiple sources.

Single-source families of parts.

WHY SOURCE REDUCTION WORKS

An objective of reducing the number of suppliers is to form close working relationships with the suppliers that are retained. Mutually beneficial buyer-supplier relationships encourage both parties to search for ways in which they both can prosper. Many suppliers seek out long-term customers, because it assists them in their long-term survival and growth. Suppliers who think in terms of short-term gains and rely on opportunistic selling as their primary marketing strategy do not prosper in the long term.

A supplier that is dependent on its customers' success is more likely to share cost-saving ideas with customers, suggest product improvements, work closely with customers on technology developments, and make improvements that can lower costs and improve product quality.

If the supplier-buyer relationship is strong, the supplier is likely to inform the buyer of projected missed deliveries or production problems that may affect product quality. Similarly, the buyer may feel obligated to inform the seller of long-term requirements, business trends, and operational details that will assist the supplier in more closely matching the buyer's needs.

In addition to routine contact for discussion of matters such as order entry, quotations, and expediting, suppliers should be contacted at least once every other month for reviews of current order status, changes in processes, product quality status, and changes in the supplier's organization.

RATING SUPPLIERS

Many buyers monitor and rate supplier performance in the areas of delivery performance, product quality, and price changes. This information is usually generated through financial, receiving, and MRP (Material Requirements Planning) reports. What follows are some examples of these reports:

On-Time Delivery Report—June 1992

Supplier	Lots received	Lots received within +/− 1 day of request	% on-time
Able Mfg Co.	25	20	80%
Baker Supply	40	38	95%
Chandler Corp.	12	12	100%
Drury Stamping	15	10	67%

Supplier Quality Report—June 1992

Supplier	Lots received	Lots accepted at incoming insp.	% acceptance
Able Mfg. Co.	25	24	96%
Baker Supply	40	39	98%
Chandler Supply	12	9	75%
Drury Stamping	15	12	80%

Note: The buyer must be careful when using incoming inspection results as a measure of quality. Not all quality problems are detectable at incoming. Some problems appear in the conversion process, at final inspection, or when the product is in the customer's hands.

Standard Cost Variance Report—June 1992

Part No.	Supplier	Standard Cost	Price Paid	Variance
A12345	Chandler Supply	$ 4.69	$ 4.59	+ .10
A25367	Chandler Supply	$10.00	$9.50	+ .50
A39574	Baker Supply	$ 4.59	$ 4.59	0
A48530	Able Mfg. Co.	$12.43	$11.99	+ .44
A51094	Drury Stamping	$52.75	$53.50	− .75
A53173	Drury Stamping	$ 4.99	$ 5.07	− .08

In this case, all receipts would be counted by part number and supplier. A total percent variation (actual versus standard cost) would be assigned to each supplier for the measured time period. The monthly totals were:

		Factor
Able Manufacturing Company	− 2%	.98
Baker Supply	+ 3%	.97
Chandler Supply	0	1.00
Drury Stamping	− 5%	1.05

The information is summarized as follows:

Supplier	Delivery	× Quality	Cost × Factor	= Rating
Able Mfg. Co	.80	.96	.98	75.3
Baker Supply	.95	.98	.97	90.3
Chandler Corp.	1.00	.75	1.00	75.0
Drury Stamping	.67	1.00	1.05	70.4

In this example, the demarcation point between acceptable and unacceptable performance (as established by the purchasing department) is a rating of 75.0.

Armed with information, a buyer can perform objective analyses. One observation that can be made based on this data is that Drury Stamping must either improve delivery performance or be discontinued as a supplier. The data also show that Able is a marginal supplier because of its delivery performance, and that Chandler is marginal because of its poor quality record.

This type of information should be shared with suppliers on a regular basis, and an effort should be made to find and correct problems that affect supplier performance. It is a better use of the buyer's time and resources to assist suppliers to improve performance than to continually seek out new suppliers.

SUPPLIER DEVELOPMENT

A buyer's prime objective is to develop suppliers who meet the company's need for quality goods, delivered when required at an affordable total cost. To effectively manage suppliers toward this end, a buyer should:

1. Work closely with a small number of suppliers.
2. Understand and achieve the company's quality requirements.
3. Understand and achieve the company's affordable costs goals.
4. Assist suppliers in their efforts to achieve and exceed the company's business objectives.

Given these objectives, perhaps the term "supplier management" is a misnomer and the term "supplier leadership" is more accurate. As Rear Admiral Grace Hooper (U.S.N. Ret.), once said: "Things are managed, people are led." A buyer's real job is to provide the leadership suppliers require in order for both to prosper.

SUPPLIER QUALITY AUDITS

Many companies of all sizes are now performing quality audits or quality capability studies of their suppliers. In a quality audit, a buyer usually refers to evaluation sheets and is often accompanied by a member of his or her quality department. The evaluation sheets list items that are to be reviewed by the evaluation team.

The purpose of a quality audit is to evaluate a supplier's manufacturing, quality and management systems to determine if they are capable of producing the desired level of product quality. For example,

CERTIFICATION CHECKLIST

QUALITY	Yes	No	N/A	Rank
Cost of quality defined and measured	( )	( )	( )	( )
Total quality control program in place	( )	( )	( )	( )
Process controls in place (SPC)	( )	( )	( )	( )
Design requirements established	( )	( )	( )	( )
Design requirements in line with customer requirements	( )	( )	( )	( )
Design tied to process	( )	( )	( )	( )
Measurements of quality performance in parts per million	( )	( )	( )	( )
Calibration of measurement and test equipment per schedule	( )	( )	( )	( )
Receiving inspection records up to date	( )	( )	( )	( )
Quality procedures and policy current	( )	( )	( )	( )
Nonconformance procedures in place and followed	( )	( )	( )	( )
Material Review Board (MRB) guidelines in place and followed	( )	( )	( )	( )
Waiver/design compliance rules in place and followed	( )	( )	( )	( )
Corrective action system in place	( )	( )	( )	( )

MANUFACTURING				
Parts received with proper identification	( )	( )	( )	( )
Current drawing revision or supplier process sheets	( )	( )	( )	( )
Detailed instructions available	( )	( )	( )	( )

Operators follow instructions	( )	( )	( )	( )
Proper measuring equipment available	( )	( )	( )	( )
Measuring devices properly calibrated	( )	( )	( )	( )
Completed part corresponds to dimensions found on operating sheet/engineering drawings	( )	( )	( )	( )
Process capability established	( )	( )	( )	( )
First piece after setup approved by quality control	( )	( )	( )	( )
In-process inspections performed per supplier plan	( )	( )	( )	( )
Discrepant parts identified and segregated	( )	( )	( )	( )
Parts sent from area with proper identification	( )	( )	( )	( )
Proper marking and storage of tools	( )	( )	( )	( )

MANAGEMENT

Strategic plan in place	( )	( )	( )	( )
Structured for flexibility	( )	( )	( )	( )
Company issues and goals clearly communicated	( )	( )	( )	( )
Awareness of environment	( )	( )	( )	( )
Committed to improvement	( )	( )	( )	( )
Involved in the process	( )	( )	( )	( )
Open labor/management relationship	( )	( )	( )	( )
Overall positive atmosphere	( )	( )	( )	( )
Labor flexibility	( )	( )	( )	( )

Similar checklists are used for the supplier's planning process, training, purchasing, inventory management, warehousing, shipping, receiving, preventive maintenance, facilities management, finance, safety, and data processing areas.

These checklists can be quite useful, but they also present certain hazards, such as the following:

▬ They assume that an auditor can fairly evaluate all of the factors.

▬ There is an assumption that the auditing company can pass the same rigorous examination.

▬ An audit is time-consuming and requires full access to the supplier's facilities, people, and processes.

▬ Once a supplier is certified, will it allow its system to deteriorate, or will it continue to improve?

▬ The burden of proof is on the auditing company.

What will be a supplier's response should many of its customers wish to conduct surveys of its facilities with many different evaluation criteria?

AN ALTERNATIVE APPROACH

What if a buyer cannot accurately evaluate the supplier's processes and products? The supplier may have been in business for years and become proficient at hiding problems. Can an auditor find these problems in a few hours or days? Perhaps not. Isn't the burden of proof on the supplier, and not on the customer?

There is an alternative type of supplier evaluation, which is easier and faster than the audit method. It involves asking the following four basic questions:

1. The ratio between manufacturing cycle time and labor content, which is expressed as

$$Manufacturing\ Velocity = \frac{Manufacturing\ Cycle\ Time}{Work\ Content}$$

▬ In most U.S. manufacturing plants, the ratio is 80:1, which means that for every 80 hours goods spend in the manufacturing process, value is being added for only one hour.
▬ The initial objective is a ratio of 10:1. To achieve this velocity, a manufacturer must remove the time- and resource-consuming obstacles in the path of converting materials to finished goods. Examples of such obstacles are long setup times, unpredictable quality, unorganized processes, lack of worker involvement in process improvements, and ill-defined processes. Achieving a velocity of at least 10:1 yields shorter manufacturing cycle times, improved quality, quick response to changes in customer demand, lower inventory levels, and lower manufacturing costs.

2. Inventory Turns = 20 per year. The average American manufacturing plant turns over its inventory between three and six times a year. This greatly increases costs and slows the manufacturing process. Caution should be taken with this measurement; it is a by-product of the Manufacturing Velocity ratio and not solely a materials or supplier inventory control responsibility.

3. The Price of NonConformance (PONC). The cost of ensuring product quality may include the following factors:

- Incoming inspection.
- Work-in-process inspection.
- Product rework and repair.
- Warranty repairs.
- The cost of product change orders to correct design or quality errors.
- The activities of material review boards.
- The cost to return defective materials.
- Final product inspection.

In other words, the total cost of ensuring product quality encompasses the cost of error detection, error correction, and customer satisfaction. These costs, which can amount to 25 percent of the cost to manufacture, still may not assure customer satisfaction with the final product. (One computer manufacturer stated that the cost of warranty repairs to its equipment in the first ninety days of customer installation amounted to $500,000,000 during 1989.)

The supplier's objective should be to reduce PONC to less than two percent of the cost to manufacture. One way to accomplish this is to eliminate the need for incoming, in-process, and final inspection by developing predictable processes and robust product designs.

4. Profit After Tax (PAT) greater than 10 percent. A financially healthy supplier is one that will survive the rigors of time and economic cycles. A key factor a buyer looks for is that the supplier will exceed normal profitability. If a supplier is working toward the first three criteria, 10 percent PAT is within its grasp. What would be a supplier's response to a buyer who expects and will assist a supplier to exceed 10 percent profit after tax? Will the buyer have difficulty getting the supplier's cooperation? Not likely.

The objective is for the buyer and supplier to accept these four measurements and work towards improving them. A measure of goodness is that the supplier makes steady and continuous improvement towards the four goals. A supplier may never achieve them all but progress toward them will keep the supplier viable.

Because these four measurements are simple, anyone can monitor the progress and the current state of the supplier's manufacturing process. The measures allow the supplier to make improvements in its own fashion without being dictated to by a buyer who may or may not subscribe to the same manufacturing philosophies. These measures will certainly be compatible with those of the supplier. The measures also address the buyer's requirements for price, delivery, and quality.

CHAPTER PERSPECTIVE

A novice buyer or one working in a new company should be concerned with finding dependable supply sources. As the organization and the buyer achieve more experience, the focus should shift to purchasing strategies and developing a supply base that will meet long-term needs. Ultimately, the buyer should seek to form lasting, mutually beneficial relationships with only a few suppliers. It is this final objective and not necessarily the details of the process that is important. The smaller the supplier base, the more effective it is in furthering the immediate and long-range goals of the buyer's company.

The Quotation Process

INTRODUCTION AND MAIN POINTS

This chapter examines the process of requesting and evaluating bids for required goods and services. The request for quote (RFQ) is the buyer's first official contact with potential suppliers. The quality and content of the RFQ can determine the outcome of the bidding process, because it sets the stage for all subsequent discussions and negotiations.

Care and thoroughness are key in the preparation of an RFQ. Significant questions that must be addressed include:

- How much information should be included in the RFQ?
- What will be the measurements of quality?
- Other than the direct material or service, are there additional items or services that could be included?
- What are the time limitations?
- To whom should the RFQ be sent?
- What are the criteria for an acceptable response?

After studying the material in this chapter:

- You will know what should be included in an RFQ.
- You will understand the role the RFQ plays in setting expectations for subsequent negotiations.
- You will know how to plan for successful negotiations.

THE RFQ PROCESS

There are two occasions that call for a buyer to send out requests for quotations: 1) a requirement for a new item is received; and 2) an existing requirement is rebid.

New requirements require more care than a rebid. They often involve products that have untested specifications. The commodity or item may be totally new to the buyer or to the company. Searching for new suppliers and/or new technologies may be involved, and quality requirements may be ill-defined.

Existing requirements may be rebid to find a supplier that can surpass the quality or delivery performance from a current supplier, to locate a lower-cost producer, to add capacity beyond the existing sources of supply, or to test the market for current pricing. The rebid process entails gathering all current specifications, quality requirements, and projected usage volumes and forming them into an RFQ. After the information is gathered, decisions must be made regarding the selection of bidders and the appropriate information to be included in the RFQ.

An RFQ may use a standard form, which may be purchased at most stationery supply outlets, or be written as regular business correspondence. An RFQ states quantity and quality requirements, packaging, the required return date for the quotation, and other information to the buyer and seller. RFQs are usually sent to three or more potential suppliers. Bidders are selected based on a search (see Chapter 8), or on a list, developed by the purchaser, of qualified bidders. Potential bidders are usually allowed two weeks or more to respond to the request, depending on the complexity of the item to be quoted. After receiving quotes, the buyer evaluates them and selects a supplier.

NEW PRODUCTS

When suppliers are not involved in the creation of new product specifications, it becomes purchasing's job to find a supplier who can produce the item. The purchasing department and design personnel should jointly determine potential sources. This will assist a buyer in finding a source of supply appropriate for the specific product needed. A buyer should be part of the design process; this ensures that commercial interests are fully considered in the design of a new product.

In some cases, suppliers' salespeople meet with the purchasing company's design staff during product conception in order to influence the design of the product. If these meetings are unregulated, and purchasing is not involved, the outcome may include specifications that are so slanted in favor of one supplier that they effectively eliminate competition.

Product quality is seldom considered in the design stage. To correct this problem, the design community should state the quality requirements either on the documentation (blueprint, specification, etc.) or in a separate format so that these requirements can be included in the RFQ. Quality requirements are expressed as grades, parts-per-million, allowable variation based on process capability (Cp, Cpk), fit to mating components, or in any terms appropriate to the material being purchased. Quality requirements should be clearly understood before the quotation process begins.

EXISTING PRODUCTS

When a buyer is faced with a cost problem on an existing item, and the current supplier is unable or uninterested in reducing the selling price, then the buyer must seek a more effective supplier for the item. Not all suppliers have the same capabilities or costs. The more a buyer understands about the items, their processes, and their marketplace, the better he or she will be able to identify potential sources of supply. An RFQ may be exploratory—designed to find the suppliers who offer the most cost-effective processes and facilities. Advantages for a buyer requesting bids on existing items include the following:

1. Quantity needs are known.
2. Quality requirements are better defined.
3. Production and design problems have been experienced and identified.
4. Established selling prices exist.
5. The buyer knows the item.

Armed with this experience and information, a buyer can create an RFQ that assists both the supplier and buyer to create a better business arrangement while avoiding the mistakes of the past.

RFQ QUANTITIES

Many buyers understate quantities on the RFQ even when the anticipated quantity needed is known. This tends to encourage arbitrary price breaks from bidders. Sometimes buyers deliberately conceal the total quantity to be purchased over time in the belief that the supplier should know as little as possible and to avoid broadcasting future business trends to the buyer's competitors.

Consider this example. Tom has sent out an RFQ on a rectifier. The projected annual use for the next three years is 2,000 per year (a total of 6,000 units). Tom requests price quotes on quantities of 50, 100, 250, and 500 pieces, believing that monthly quantities will not exceed those numbers. Because the market is competitive and close-knit, there is the possibility that the quoting suppliers might discuss these requirements among themselves and possibly with Tom's competitors.

Now put yourself in the position of a rectifier manufacturer who has received a request for quote. How would you price the product? The quantities you see on the RFQ are 50, 100, 250, and 500. Perhaps your normal price breaks occur at unit quantities of 83, 202, and 627. Instead of three price breaks, you are asked to create four that do not coincide with your own manufacturing efficiencies or lot sizes. Further, if Tom needs 175 pieces in a particular month he may order 250 because of the price break and carry the additional inventory for a month. That pattern of behavior will create an erratic demand signal.

Both Tom and the supplier could make better business decisions if each knew more about the other's business. Tom could order in accordance with the supplier's price breaks or lot sizes, and the supplier could make better decisions about equipment investments and cost-improvement measures.

How can Tom state his requirements more clearly and still protect new-product information? He can meet with the supplier to discuss the need for confidentiality and for pricing based on a product-life agreement. He can also discuss the possibility of renegotiating each year. The quantity might be stated as 6,000 over three years, and the RFQ can stipulate "one price for the three years of business." If this is agreed to, release quantities will be insensitive to price breaks and monthly volume changes.

OTHER ITEMS ON THE RFQ
A buyer may wish to add other elements to an RFQ. For example, a buyer's RFQ may stipulate liberal payment terms, items packaged ten to the box in reusable containers, or delivery costs to be paid by the supplier and title transfer at the buyer's plant. If the buyer wishes to provide for ongoing technical support, the RFQ may contain a statement such as this: "The price of the goods is to include services of a design or applications engineer one day a month at the buyer's plant."

OPTIONS BIDDING
A buyer may consider including "adders" to the actual material needed and requesting that these options be priced separately. For example:

Price for the rectifier (6,000/3 years)	_____
Price if reusable containers (10 per)	_____
Price if F.O.B. Delivered	_____
Price of 1 day/month engineering service	_____
Total Selling Price	_____

One problem is that the sum of the options may exceed the total cost the buyer had in mind.

A different option-bidding method is one in which the buyer establishes the option and terms. For example: Betty requests bids for a new sheet metal press. There is a chance her company will need another press within twelve months. Currently the press is priced at $125,000, and the supplier has indicated that the price will rise 4 to 6 percent sometime in the next six months. Betty may request a bid with a provision that a second press may be purchased within twelve months at the same price as the first. This avoids both the price increase and the time and labor of a requote.

SELECTING POTENTIAL SUPPLIERS

There are those who believe that requests for quote should be sent only to those potential suppliers that the buyer knows to be qualified. One argument is that if the buyer sends an RFQ to suppliers who are not qualified, irresponsibly low quotes may be received. Others believe that it is unethical to ask a supplier to spend the labor to prepare a quotation unless the supplier is already qualified. One result of these views is that buyers are not encouraged to explore new sources of supply or new technologies. Perhaps the real question is, "What practices are in the best interest of the buyer's employer and of the product?"

A "qualified suppliers list" consists of suppliers who either have a history of satisfactory business experience with the buyer's firm or have been audited by engineering or quality staff. Some corporations use a qualified suppliers list to limit the addition of new suppliers by the purchasing department. It is also used as a safeguard against buyers' contracting with suppliers that are unqualified to provide the parts, services, or equipment. Such a list may be particularly useful where members of the purchasing function are poorly trained or new.

REQUESTS FOR PROPOSAL

Capital equipment purchases are more complicated than purchases of material or components. Bid requests for construction and capital equipment are termed "requests for proposal" (RFP). Equipment purchases occur less frequently than production purchases, and large amounts of money are involved in a one-time buy. Therefore, a buyer has only one opportunity to properly construct an RFP.

Quotes for equipment purchases may involve the following issues, which are not normally included in a quote for material or supplies:

━ Conformance to government regulations.

━ Rigging and installation.

━ Electrical and ventilation requirements.

━ Floor-load-bearing strengths.

━ Performance after installation.

━ Warranties.

━ Operator training.

━ Maintenance and spare parts.

━ Financing the purchase.

A buyer's company may know the function that it wants the equipment to perform but not how to specify the performance level expected or desired. A buyer may have incomplete specifications for an RFP. (This subject is discussed in detail in Chapter 14.)

There are two types of capital-equipment purchases:

1) commercially available or catalog equipment
2) equipment custom-designed to the user's application.

CATALOG EQUIPMENT

Purchase of catalog equipment holds less risk for the buyer, because specifications and capabilities of the equipment are known and the buyer is free to concentrate on commercial and installation issues. When there are suppliers of similar catalog equipment, competition may be stimulated with the bidding process. The RFP should include some or all of the following considerations, depending on the size, cost, and type of the equipment to be purchased:

━ F.O.B. (freight on board) point: Who will own the equipment in transit and pay for the cost of transportation? The risk of transportation is a real issue. If the equipment is damaged in transit, and the F.O.B. point is origin (the supplier), the carrier is acting as an agent for the buyer and any damage is the responsibility of the buyer. Whenever possible, a buyer should obtain "F.O.B. delivered" terms on capital-equipment purchases.

━ If the purchase is a large piece of machinery, special rigging equipment may be required to unload and position the machine. Who will pay for this service and who knows how to do it?

▬ Computer equipment is sometimes transported in a special cushioned trailer. A climate-controlled room (in which the floor is elevated to allow cables to pass between the floor and subfloor) is constructed to house the mainframe. Who will design the room, calculate the climate control and electrical requirements, connect the various pieces of equipment, and assure proper functioning. Who will maintain the system?

▬ What are the payment terms? Some equipment suppliers require an advance deposit at the time an order is entered. Some require payments at each stage of construction. However, a buyer may wish to withhold all or part of the payment until the equipment is operational.

CUSTOM EQUIPMENT

Equipment manufactured to a buyer's specifications may contain many uncertainties in the design, and should be purchased with great care. A buyer should invite several potential suppliers to work with engineering to develop specifications, since the buyer's engineers may be less familiar with the design criteria than the equipment manufacturers. With the supplier's design specifications in hand, the buyer can address the commercial issues discussed above.

QUOTE EVALUATION

As will be discussed in Chapter 10, a buyer should be concerned with total value, not with quoted prices alone. In evaluating quotes, a buyer should weigh the following factors:

▬ Supplier's past performance.
▬ Quality requirements.
▬ Terms (e.g., payment, F.O.B.)
▬ After-sale support and service.
▬ Delivery capabilities.
▬ Supplier's technology and product-development capabilities.
▬ Supplier's responsiveness to design or schedule changes.
▬ Price.

Different products require different emphasis. Commodities buyers may care little about after-sale support but place great emphasis on price. Buyers of edge-of-technology products may care little about price but place great value on a supplier's technology and product-development capability. For significant purchases, the buyer should construct a spreadsheet that compares quotes with respect to product requirements. Here is an example:

Rating: 3 = Critical
       2 = Important
       1 = Desirable

	Plastic molding compound	Sheet-metal parts	Semi-conductor	Capital equip.
Price	2	3	3	3
Delivery	2	2	2	3
Terms: cash	2	2	2	3
F.O.B.	3	2	1	3
Supplier technology	1	1	3	3
Product support	1	1	3	2
Quality	2	3	3	2
Supplier response	2	2	2	2
Past performance	2	2	2	1

For major purchases, a buyer should spread out the risks involved in supplier selection and seek outside input at the same time. Engineering, quality, and/or the user department supervisor should be included in decisions about suppliers.

STAGE-SETTING

A buyer may make a decision based solely on the RFQ and its responses. However, RFQs may be just the beginning of a negotiation process. Quotes may be counterproposals to the original RFQ. Suppliers may take exception to specifications or terms and conditions in the RFQ. A buyer can meet with the supplier's representatives to refine the quotations or resolve misunderstandings. For example, the suppliers and the buyer's engineering department may have to meet to clarify specifications.

The quotation process can be a means of refining product designs, inviting counter-proposals, establishing expectations for subsequent negotiations, and syndicating the source-selection process within the company. While the primary objective of the bidding process is to locate an acceptable supplier at an acceptable price, it can also assist a buyer in resolving any conflicts between company specifications and supplier capability. It can also create a foundation for subsequent negotiations when the buyer expresses terms and conditions to which the seller may take exception.

Not all RFQs lead to agreement and immediate purchase orders. The RFQ process has many uses for a buyer, including refinements to the item to be purchased and to the buyer/seller relationship. To paraphrase Winston Churchill: "This may not be the end, it may not be the beginning of the end, but it is the end of the beginning."

THE REQUEST FOR QUOTATION PROCESS

The following is a recap of the RFQ process:

1. Obtain specifications for the item to be purchased.
2. Determine the likely quantity to be used in the short term (3–12 months) and long term (1–3 years or the life of the product).
3. Agree on the quality requirements, packaging, desired F.O.B. point, desired payment terms, frequency of delivery, etc.
4. Locate three or more suppliers who have the potential to supply the required item.

    use known or qualified suppliers where possible.

    if there are no known suppliers, check reference materials (*Thomas Register, Moody's Industrials,* trade journals, etc.).
5. Determine what information is to go on the request for quotation. The buyer may want to save some issues for subsequent negotiation, especially if it is a unique or large purchase.
6. Allow sufficient time for potential suppliers to analyze the RFQ and create a quote. Two to three weeks is common. Grant suppliers additional time to discuss or clarify the RFQ, particularly if the purchase is major.
7. Analyze the quotations. Determine if suppliers understood the request and replied uniformly.
    a. Were exceptions taken? Were there alternative proposals made?
    b. Are quoted delivery times acceptable?
    c. Are quality requirements understood and agreed to?
    d. Are there misunderstandings that warrant a telephone call to the bidder(s)?
    e. Is there a need to visit one or more of the bidders? This may be required only in the case of large or critical

purchases or when the buyer has had no prior business with the supplier(s).

   f. If the bidders are known to the buyer, the buyer should balance quoted prices with past performance in quality, delivery, and dependability.

   g. Supplier' sales representative may visit the buyer to discuss the quote prior to the buyer making a final source selection.

8. Negotiations may follow the initial analysis of the bids. These negotiations may be formal or informal.

9. Select a supplier and place a purchase order.

CHAPTER PERSPECTIVE

The RFQ is the formal beginning of the supplier-selection process. The outcome of the RFQ process depends on the amount of information the suppliers are given, the involvement of others within the buyer's organization, the nature of the purchase, and certain issues of importance to the buyer. The RFQ may result in an immediate purchase, a round of negotiations, or a series of meetings inside the buyer's organization and with prospective suppliers to refine quotations and resolve misunderstandings.

Price

INTRODUCTION AND MAIN POINTS

The price paid for purchased materials is a major ingredient in the cost of doing business. On average, 60 percent of the cost to manufacture is attributable to purchased materials. In high-technology manufacturing, purchased materials may represent 90 percent of the cost to manufacture, while in service industries purchased materials may represent 20 percent of the cost of providing services.

A buyer must balance purchase price with other factors, such as product quality and delivery scheduling. The problem is determining the proper balance among all purchasing considerations.

After studying the material in this chapter:

■ You will understand the difference between price and cost.

■ You will understand the market forces that shape pricing.

■ You will be able to better determine an appropriate price to pay for materials.

DETERMINING PRICE

Product prices are determined in three ways:

1. Competitive bidding.
2. Price based on cost (material, labor, overhead, and profit.
3. Supply and demand.

Competitive Bidding

Competitive bidding works well under the following conditions: 1) a sufficient number of suppliers in the market, 2) product specifications are common, 3) no unique technologies or capabilities are required, and 4) the request for quote contains all information and the buyer need only choose the lowest quote.

Competitive bidding does not accommodate the need for

products more complicated than the request for quote can properly describe. It does not consider the price requirements of the buyer or what the buyer can afford. If the buyer receives quotes from untried suppliers, there is no measure of quality or past delivery performance to evaluate. The only variable in the quote is price, and the buyer merely selects the lowest.

A supplier prices its products based on the information in the request for quote, its own costs, competitors' past pricing of similar items, and input from its sales organization regarding the immediate competitive environment and the prospective buyer. A buyer considers not only quoted prices but suppliers' past performance and input from the buyer's organization.

Competitive bidding is used for existing as well as new products. A buyer may be unsatisfied with a supplier's current prices or delivery performance. Or the buyer may be presented with new opportunities from new suppliers, and may want these suppliers to bid on a current requirement to make comparisons.

Prices Based on Cost

A supplier's costs can be divided into three groups:

1. Fixed—Costs that remain constant regardless of the plant's activity level. These costs include mortgage, loan payments, and cost of materials.
2. Variable—Costs that vary with the plant's activity level such as direct wages, FICA/retirement contributions.
3. Semivariable—Costs that vary, but not in direct proportion to the activity level in a plant. These include the utilities, heating fuel, and indirect labor. These costs are allocated to individual products, and profit margin is added, yielding a selling price.

Since estimated manufacturing costs are based on an individual supplier's internal costs, there may be no opportunity or need for them to compare their manufacturing efficiencies with others in similar business. How does the supplier or the buyer know if the supplier is an effective producer? There are differences between suppliers and processes which yield the same product. If a supplier is not an effective producer yet shows the cost figures to produce the product in order to justify their selling price, what meaning do the figures have to the buyer? Price based on cost is a reasonable means for a supplier to establish selling prices but may be irrelevant to the buyer if those prices are not competitive or do not meet the buyer's needs.

Supply and Demand

Prices are also determined by the market place—by the supply and demand for products. For example, when AIDS became a widespread health problem, hospitals and health-care offices increased their demand for disposable rubber gloves tenfold. Manufacturers of these gloves could not keep pace with the initial demand and prices soared to whatever levels the health institutions would pay.

STANDARD COST

Often the finance and purchasing departments will establish a standard cost—the cost of component items based on past purchases. These prices are then used by the company to establish the selling price of the finished product. The standard cost becomes the target purchase price for the coming year.

The problems with standard costs include the following

1. They are usually established by purchasing, which is then measured against them. What other function in business is allowed to set the standards by which they are measured? Purchasing tends to set standard costs it is comfortable with.

2. Standard costs may not take into account future needs and market conditions. Can we afford to pay the same or higher prices in the future? Will the product price decrease dramatically in the future, as is the case with so many semiconductor products? Over the past twenty years, the retail prices of televisions and clothes washers have remained constant while the cost of everything else has increased dramatically. If the cost of material had been allowed to increase with inflation, these consumer items would be unaffordable to most households. The manufacturers of a number of consumer goods recognized that it was imperative that new designs, technologies, and material costs be blended to assure that the function and cost be competitive and acceptable to consumers.

3. Standards are usually set annually. Can a buyer whose business is high-tech or volatile afford an unchanging standard cost for twelve months?

Standard costs should be used to value inventories. But the needs of the business should determine the prices sought by the purchasing department.

INSTALLED VALUE

The only true measure of price is the value of the purchased item when it is performing successfully in the buyer's finished product. The price on the purchase order may give no indication of the actual value of the purchased item. Dr. W. Edwards Deming, the noted quality expert, has stated that "Price has no meaning without a measure of quality."

Quality requirements must be clearly stated in the request for quote and on the face of the purchase order. They can be stated in parts per million, process control requirements, or other defined quality requirements. (These are described in detail in Chapter 12.) Basically, a buyer is looking for items that have minimum variation and whose critical qualities are centered on a target value. When items with broad tolerances are assembled or brought together for use, the variations in tolerance may combine in unpredictable ways. This is known as "stack-up of tolerances." Buyers may not comprehend the effect this has on process yields, rework and scrap costs, inspection costs, returns to suppliers, and warranty repairs and replacements. In most companies, these unseen costs average 20 to 25 percent of the cost to manufacture.

ON-TIME DELIVERIES
Will the supplier ship goods when needed, even if this need changes? Many buyers maintain safety stock to compensate for suppliers who do not meet delivery needs.

As delivery requirements change, buyers find themselves performing more expediting duties. These activities are costly and are only marginally productive and cost effective. To reduce late deliveries and expediting effort, buyers should work closely with production planning and suppliers to 1) identify and correct problems, 2) reduce suppliers' manufacturing or response times, and 3) improve supplier quality, a cause of parts shortages.

TECHNICAL SUPPORT
Suppliers can be a good source of technical information for new products, processes, and technologies. They can also assist customers in design processes and in the use and application of products. It may be difficult to assign a dollar value to these services, but they do increase the buyer's resource base in areas such as engineering and product development.

EASE OF DOING BUSINESS
A supplier who is responsive to a buyer's requests and needs, offers extra services, works overtime in response to an emergency, delivers goods in its own vehicles, offers design assistance,

and lowers administration costs may be seen by a buyer as a desirable business partner. For example, a buyer may be able to lower levels of safety stock and thus lower the cost of doing business.

TRANSPORTATION

Transport costs, from raw material to finished product to the buyer, represent the largest portion of the selling price of goods. Furthermore, most goods are shipped F.O.B., point of origin. The buyer owns the goods in transit but does not have access to them. Consequently, the longer the transit time, the higher the cost of the goods to the buyer. A buyer receives greater value if the terms of the purchase are F.O.B. delivered.

TERMS OF PAYMENT

A common term of payment is "2%—10, Net 30 days," meaning that the invoice amount will be discounted by 2 percent if it is paid within 10 days of the date of the invoice, but is due in total within 30 days of the invoice date. To a buyer with a tight cash flow, a payment term of net 60 is of real value. However, a buyer with available cash may benefit from higher cash discounting (e.g., "5%-10, Net 30 days").

TIME

It is often said that time is money. For example:
▬ The less time it takes a supplier to produce goods, the lower the cost of these goods. On average, only one percent of the time that an item spends in the production process is value added. Imagine the reduction in the supplier's cost of production if the item is worked on even 10 percent of the time.
▬ Faulty product quality adds production time. Inspection, rework, repair, scrap, and return procedures are needed.
▬ If time were a measurable factor in price, goods would be delivered more frequently and with higher degree of predictability, and there would be less need to maintain high inventories.

COST OF OWNERSHIP

Assume that a buyer is to purchase 20,000 injection-molded parts at a price of $6.25 each and that the conditions of the purchase are as folows:
▬ The standard cost is $6.65 each.
▬ The supplier is located 600 miles from the supplier's plant.

■ The buyer's plant uses 1,000 parts per week (assume four weeks to the month).

■ Existing inventory at the buyer's plant is 12,000 pieces, plus 4,000 in safety stock (to cover for unplanned events such as late deliveries, quality problems, and unexpected demand).

■ The supplier's lead time is eight weeks. The supplier's actual manufacturing time is two days. The buyer requires one week to process the purchase order, one week transit time, and one week to receive, inspect, count, store, and issue the product to the manufacturing floor. The real lead time to replenish manufacturing is 11 weeks. The cost to carry inventory is 50 percent of the purchase price per year (see Chapter 7 for the explanation of this figure).

■ The supplier quotes the part as follows:

5,000 pieces $7.05
10,000 pieces $6.65
20,000 pieces $6.25
50,000 pieces $5.95

The buyer decides to order 20,000 pieces (20 weeks' supply) to achieve a unit price that is better than the standard cost of $6.65 (actual price is $6.25—a savings of $8,000 on the order). The value of the inventory already on hand is $106,400 (bought at the $6.65 price). When the new order is received in 9 weeks (8-week lead time plus 1-week transportation time), the inventory will be 3,000 pieces plus the 4,000-piece safety stock, or a total value of $46,550. The costs for an 18-week period look like this:

Week	Inventory on hand	Inventory value	Cost to carry/wk*
1	16,000	$106,400	$1023
2	15,000	$ 99,750	$ 959
3	14,000	$ 93,100	$ 895
4	13,000	$ 86,450	$ 831
5	12,000	$ 79,800	$ 767
6	11,000	$ 73,150	$ 703
7	10,000	$ 66,500	$ 639
8	9,000	$ 59,850	$ 575
9	8,000	$ 53,200	$ 512
10	7,000	$ 46,500	$ 448
11	26,000	$164,900	$1586
12	25,000	$158,250	$1522
13	24,000	$151,600	$1458

14	23,000	$144,950	$1394
15	22,000	$138,300	$1330
16	21,000	$131,650	$1266
17	20,000	$125,000	$1202
18	19,000	$118,750	$1142

Total carrying costs for this part/period $18,252

*Weekly inventory value divided by 50% cost to carry, divided by 52 weeks.

By increasing the purchase volume from 10,000 to 20,000 pieces, the buyer increases the average on-hand inventory for the year by 10,000 units and the carrying costs by $601 per week ($6.25 × 10,000 × .50 / 52 weeks). If demand and price remain constant, the lower ($6.25) price will yield $20,800 ($.40 per unit savings × 52,000 units) savings for the year, but the inventory carrying costs will increase by $31,252 ($601 × 52 weeks). The company will suffer a net loss of $10,452.

This example is for only one part number. Its impact can be multiplied by all the dollars spent or all the part numbers on the company's bill of material. The buyer could benefit more from reducing on-hand inventory by scheduling weekly deliveries and negotiating a price based on 52,000 units per year instead of conforming to arbitrary quantity price breaks.

HOW TO OBTAIN BETTER VALUE

Competitive bidding is the best and most widely used means of obtaining quoted prices. The secret to success is the information and requests the buyer includes in the request for quote.

Quantity

Buyers often request prices for arbitrary quantities. These quantities may accurately reflect monthly usage, but they may not reflect either the total projected usage or the supplier's quantity price breaks. For example, the buyer may request quotes for 250, 500, and 1,000 pieces, and the seller's price breaks may be at 197, 316, and 602 pieces. A seller who knows that the buyer intends to use 5,000 over one year or 17,000 over three years may throw away the standard price and create a price based on the long term.

Instead, the buyer should state the full projected quantity needed, and request a single price for a single quantity. A buyer who offers arbitrary quantities for quotations creates an opportunity for the supplier to fabricate price differences. This approach works best when there is an ongoing need for the product.

Quality
A quality expectation and its measurement should be stated on the RFQ. However, merely stating that all material must comply with the specifications is not sufficient. For commodities, the buyer can state the required grade (e.g., reagent or electronic grade of chemicals). For goods made to the buyer's specification, the supplier should be required to furnish evidence with the shipment that the goods were produced under process controls. This evidence can take the form of quality-control data or error-frequency measures such as parts per million.

Deliveries
A buyer's RFQ should also stipulate delivery flexibility. This may involve a required cycle time, a required time in response to change in demand, supplier-held inventories, or some combination of these factors.

F.O.B.
Free on board encompasses both the responsibility for the cost of transportation and the point of title transfer. It should be stated on the request for quote. If the buyer obtains goods F.O.B., the supplier pays the freight costs and assumes the risk of transporting the goods to the buyer's place of business. The supplier is responsible for settling any damaged-goods claims with the freight carrier.

COSTING ASSUMPTIONS
Most manufacturers use an accumulation cost accounting system. This distorts the real cost of manufacturing and may lead a company to make decisions against its own interests.

Generally speaking, 60 percent of manufacturing cost is for material, 10 percent is for labor, and 30 percent is for overhead and profit. Overhead costs have increased more than any other cost element in the past thirty years. These costs are often arbitrarily allocated to products based on plant square footage, total direct labor, and other factors not related to the product. Also, overhead charges are period specific; that is, they are allocated based on the accounting cycle and not on the production period of the product. The overhead charges for the buyer's product may bear no resemblance to the actual indirect costs to produce the item.

A buyer should question a prospective supplier's overhead allocation practices. Some questions to ask are the following:

▬ Does the product use all of the overhead for which it is charged?

▬ Engineering

▬ Supervision

▬ Distribution

▬ Sales

▬ Product support

▬ Quality

▬ Are the overhead costs current? Was the product built in the accounting period in which the overhead costs were allocated?

▬ Is the product burdened with costs from other products? For example, does the product's price reflect costs of other manufacturing lines or research-and-development costs of new products?

Given present cost accounting systems, most manufacturers have a distorted view of manufacturing costs, and therefore, their selling prices are equally distorted.

OTHER FORMS OF PRICING

Price Lists

Many suppliers of catalog and MRO (maintenance, repair and operating) items publish price lists. These lists reflect the highest prices the supplier charges for its products. It is common practice for suppliers to offer discount prices to large-volume users. For example, suppose the price for a voltmeter is $47.00. Certain buyers may enjoy discounts as follows:

▬ electricians: list less 35%, or $30.55

▬ electrical contractors: list less 35%, less 15%, or $25.97

▬ a contractor purchasing 10 or more at one time: list less 35%, less 15%, less 8%, or $23.89

▬ add a 4% discount for cash, list less 35%, less 15%, less 8%, less 4%, or $22.93

Thus, the voltmeter may be bought for $47.00, $30.55, $25.97, $23.89, or $22.93. A buyer should immediately ask for discount prices. The buyer may have to increase purchase quantities to receive the best discounting.

NEGOTIATED PRICES

After the quoting process is complete and price lists have been submitted, a buyer may not be satisfied with the price or the terms of the offers. Or a supplier may realize that to acquire the business, the original quoted price should be lowered. A negotiation may be called for. This discussion can refine the pricing, resolve issues, or better define the product or the terms. A price quote is a general price to a general user of the item or commodity. Negotiation moves a general relationship to a specific one—specific quantities, at specific times, in a specific market, in specific packaging, to a specific user. Purchases that involve significant amounts of money or that will be repeated should be negotiated.

AFFORDABILITY

A buyer may be given a budget for purchased materials from engineering, marketing, management, or finance. The buyer knows that component costs must be at or below a certain level before beginning a search for suppliers. The buyer may share this information with suppliers who will be submitting quotes, or may elect to save this information for subsequent negotiation.

CHAPTER PERSPECTIVE

The buyer's job is to find the lowest price consistent with quality and delivery objectives. The lowest price usually comes from the most efficient producer—the one that uses state-of-the-art technology, has a high regard for quality, and uses time as a measure of cost and customer satisfaction.

Simply comparing prices and choosing the lowest bid is a dangerous practice. A buyer's objective should be to achieve the greatest installed value for the funds spent.

Negotiation

INTRODUCTION AND MAIN POINTS

Negotiation is the resolution of differences through discussion so that both parties benefit. Negotiating skill often determines which party benefits more.

Often, what a buyer needs cannot be gotten through normal business dealings. Hence, there are times when it is in a buyer's interest to influence the seller to come up with a better deal.

After studying the material in this chapter:
- You will understand the various modes of negotiation.
- You will be able to determine when you should negotiate.
- You will understand key negotiating strategies and tactics.

GENERAL VIEWS CONCERNING NEGOTIATION

Most Western societies, the United States in particular, consider negotiation in everyday business as a form of haggling. "Don't waste everyone's time. Pick the lowest bid and go with it!" is often the response by management and some purchasing personnel to a proposed negotiation.

Other cultures view negotiation as a necessary part of the pricing process. For example, many Eastern cultures negotiate even for items of little value. A buyer involved in international purchasing should consider how cultural factors affect the expectations of the other party. Electing not to negotiate may send an undesirable signal.

Many negotiations can be uncomfortable or even threatening to those unaccustomed to the process. There are also risks for the negotiating buyer. What if the buyer should lose the negotiation or fail to achieve management's objectives? Will management feel that the buyer should have gotten a better deal or more concessions?

STRATEGIES

All purchasing strategies should address three basic questions:
- What is wanted?
- What is needed?
- What is achievable?

Questions a buyer should ask and answer before negotiation include the following:
- Is this the proper item to be negotiated?
- What is the current situation and what are my objectives?
- Do I have sufficient information concerning the seller, the product or service that is the subject of the negotiation, the marketplace, and management's expectations?
- What does the seller expect to obtain from the negotiation?
- Do I have the time and resources to negotiate well?
- Does management support my objectives and the use of company resources? Will management become involved?
- What have been the seller's practices in past negotiations?
- Who will do the negotiating for each side?
- What do both parties want to achieve in the session?
- Will there be future dealings with this seller? How much and for how long?

WHEN TO NEGOTIATE

Negotiation requires considerable expenditure of time and resources. Further, there is an element of risk involved: The other party may fare better than the buyer. Not every purchase warrants a negotiated settlement. Generally, the following situations warrant negotiation:
- The purchase involves a significant amount of money (e.g., a capital-equipment purchase).
- The buyer has searched the market and has found no acceptable offer.
- Competition in the marketplace is insufficient to determine a fair price.
- The potential gain is greater than the risk of loss.
- Management attention of either or both the buyer and seller needs to be drawn to an important issue.
- The buyer wishes to involve his or her management because they have been skeptical of prior efforts.
- There are new technologies or processes involved, and the selling price cannot be readily determined at the outset.
- The buyer wants to make a general offering price specific to his or her needs.

▬ There is large seller investment in capital equipment or other resources.

▬ Technical and/or commercial issues must be resolved.

▬ There is insufficient time to explore other options.

▬ There is a need to bring about a cooperative effort between the two companies.

▬ There are risks to continued seller support.

PREPARING TO NEGOTIATE—ENVIRONMENTAL ANALYSIS

About 300 B.C., the Chinese strategist Sun Tzu wrote of the ability to foretell triumph[1]:

> Those who triumph,
> compute at their headquarters
> A great number of factors
> prior to a challenge.

> Those who are defeated,
> Compute at their headquarters
> A small number of factors
> prior to a challenge.

> Much computation brings triumph
> Little computation brings defeat.
> How much more so with no computation at all!

> By observing only this,
> I can see triumph or defeat.

The first step in preparing for a negotiation is assessing the environment in which the negotiation will take place. Does the economic environment favor the buyer or the seller? Is there an immediate need or a vague need in the future? Does it involve new or existing technology? How important is this product to the business?

PREPARING TO NEGOTIATE—DETERMINING OBJECTIVES

A buyer must have clearly stated goals. Simply asking for, say, a lower price or early delivery is not sufficient. Goals may be stated as follows:

▬ a unit price of $1,387.00

▬ delivery on the 15th of September

▬ a product-development contract valued at no more than $50,000 for a design that is acceptable to marketing and will be completed by May 1 installation of a plant air-conditioning system by June 1 that will maintain an ambient temperature of 68 degrees Fahrenheit

PREPARING TO NEGOTIATE—ANALYZING THE OTHER SIDE

Knowing the seller's expectations and tactics can assist a buyer in setting tactics and expectations. By the same token, a buyer should try to prevent information about the negotiation from leaking to the seller. This can be difficult, particularly in large organizations where many employees are possible sources of information to the seller.

The more the buyer knows about the seller, the better the outcome for the buyer. The less the seller knows about the buyer, the better the outcome for the buyer. In the weeks preceding the negotiation time spent in gathering information and controlling the outflow of information (counterintelligence) will serve the buyer well and help to assure a favorable outcome.

MANAGEMENT EXPECTATIONS

A buyer should completely understand what management expects to accomplish during the negotiation process. If management has a high interest in the negotiation, the buyer is well advised to include them on the negotiation team. Then management will "co-own" the result and is not likely to second-guess the outcome or to insist that a better result should have been produced. Also, if management is involved, the buyer is more likely to receive the resources needed to conduct a thorough negotiation.

SELLER EXPECTATIONS

A buyer who can ascertain the seller's objectives prior to the negotiation is at an advantage. The seller's real objectives may not always be apparent. A buyer would be wrong to assume that a seller merely wants to sell more. What is really being sold may not be the product itself but other, more intangible, items. Companies sell their products at varying prices for many reasons:
- The desire to penetrate a new market.
- Surplus inventory or capacity.
- Competitive pressures.
- Immediate financial needs.
- The desire to work with a particular customer.
- The possibility of acquiring or developing new technology.
- The promise of future business.

The desired outcome for the seller may not be in conflict with the objectives of the buyer. Knowing the seller's position would allow the buyer to capitalize on the seller's interest—satisfying the seller without a cost to the buyer.

RESOURCES FOR THE NEGOTIATION

Successful negotiations require time, skill, resources, and practice. A buyer may be able to call upon experts within the company to assist in the preparation for negotiation or to participate in the negotiation itself—people from finance, engineering, legal, marketing, top management, quality, production scheduling, maintenance, or production, for example. Other people can contribute valuable expertise. For example:

- Lawyers can assist in drawing up a final agreement and see to it that no antitrust laws are violated.
- Engineers can ensure that there are clear specifications and can offer interpretations and clarifications.
- Quality-control personnel can explain the need for quality, how the firm measures quality, and assist the seller in achieving required quality levels.
- Finance personnel can offer the buyer assistance in evaluating the seller's financial position, analyze the seller's cost-breakdown information, and assist with negotiated payment terms.

MANAGEMENT SUPPORT

Again, management must be willing to understand and support the objectives of the negotiation or the time and effort spent may be to no avail. The buyer may do well to brief management on large, upcoming negotiations so there will be no surprises. If the negotiation between the buyer and seller is escalated to the buyer's management, management will not be caught unaware and can support the buyer's position.

SELLER'S PAST PRACTICES

The buyer may have access to information about the seller's past practices in negotiating sessions. Is the seller unyielding, vindictive, flexible, or cooperative? Is the seller willing to negotiate differences and interested in long-term customer satisfaction, or interested only in the short-term benefit of a single negotiation?

THE NEGOTIATORS

The authority and personalities of the people involved in the negotiation can have a direct bearing on the outcome. In large negotiations, the buyer must anticipate that the seller will bring in its "top guns"—and be prepared to counter with equal resources. For example, if the seller will have its chief executive officer as the primary negotiator, the buyer must be prepared to counter with a similar show of strength.

If the seller's negotiator has a rough personality or a special skill such as an extensive legal background, the buyer will want equal resources to counter a bluff, an aggressive approach or a specialized (intimidating) skill. The buyer must make every effort to anticipate the seller's strategy so as not to be surprised or intimidated during the negotiation. The buyer can thus remain focused on his or her goals for the session.

WHAT IS SATISFACTION TO BOTH PARTIES?

Since a negotiation is a one-time event and the buyer and seller must live with the outcome, the buyer must know the areas of common interest and what would be a reasonable settlement for *both* parties. If the outcome is unreasonably disproportionate in favor of one party over the other, the "loser" will make up the difference at some point in time.

For example, one seller was under great pressure to obtain the business at any price. His plant was nearly idle and employee layoffs were eminent. The buyer drove a hard bargain and the seller accepted the business at cost. Then the seller's business picked up, and the buyer's order was pushed back in the manufacturing queue. The benefit to the buyer of lower price was more than offset by late delivery.

Normally, the buyer has more control and more perceived power before the negotiation since he or she controls the cash and the possibility of future business. These are things of value to the seller who is willing to concede something to get them.

However, as soon as the contract is signed, the focus of power shifts 180 degrees. Now it is the seller who is in control and the buyer who is vulnerable since the seller must perform to the agreement.

If the negotiated agreement is unlivable, even though it is concluded, performance may be at risk and the buyer may ultimately lose more.

If at all possible, the buyer should determine what the seller considers to be success. Success is unique to each party and each negotiation. The seller must walk out of the room convinced that the agreement will be workable.

The possibility of future dealings should also be considered.

Even if this is a one-time buy, the buyer should be concerned about the seller's feelings or position at the end of the negotiation. If there are to be subsequent dealings over a long period of time, the buyer has a stronger motive to be sure that the seller is well satisfied with the outcome of the initial session.

PREPARATIONS—THE SETTING

The setting for a negotiation can play an important part in the outcome. At the start of peace talks that would ultimately end the Korean War, discussions centered on the shape of the room and the conference table. A buyer who wishes to project the image of a cooperative, nonconfrontational environment may choose a round table for the session. A rectangular table tends to place each team of negotiators in a "face-off."

Whenever possible, the buyer should conduct the negotiation on his or her own "turf." This allows the buyer ready access to additional resources, such as finance, engineering, manufacturing, and top management, should the need arise. It also forces the other party to bring to the session all available resources.

Time of day is also important. If the seller must travel a great distance, the buyer may want to schedule the session to allow for minimum seller preparation immediately preceding the session. A buyer who wants a relatively short negotiation should schedule the session for the afternoon. Discussions beyond the end of the business day entail an overnight stay and an additional day for the seller, which will encourage the reaching of an agreement during the afternoon session.

The buyer should also be certain that any required resources are available on the day of the session. For example, the schedules of participating financial and engineering personnel should be open for that day.

PREPARATION—ATTITUDES

The object of the negotiation is the other side's position. The buyer's goal is to move the other side to a different position. The object of the negotiation should never be people. If a negotiation is focused on individuals or personalities, it will fail. Personal attacks or ego battles will overshadow any change in position or desired business result. *Move the position, not the person.*

Conduct practice sessions prior to the actual negotiation. After choosing the negotiators, have them rehearse the various possible scenarios. This increases skill level, hones tactics, and reduces the possibility of being caught unprepared for any development during the actual session.

POWER

Perhaps the prime determinant of the outcome of a negotiation is which side has or appears to have power over the other. Many buyers for small companies complain, "How can I possibly win in a negotiation with a large seller? I have no leverage, no power." However, every buyer has a measure of power, regardless of the size of the purchase. The power is represented by the money to be spent.

"Power, like beauty, is to a large degree a state of mind."[2] The buyer has power if he or she believes they have it, and it is accepted by the other side. Without belief, regardless of whether it actually exists in money or position, power does not exist.

Power or the illusion of power is not always necessary. No matter how small the purchase, it is important to someone. A car buyer entering a large dealership may feel intimidated by the salesman's knowledge and array of offerings. But car dealers make their living by selling one car at a time to one customer at a time.

Power is not always an asset in a negotiation. The mantle of power assumes that one has the authority to conclude a negotiation. In fact, the buyer may not want that power. He or she may want the ability to defer the decision. This is especially true where very large amounts of money are involved, company policy may be affected or licensing agreements are established or altered.

TACTICS

Tactics are the maneuvers that take place during the actual negotiation. These tactics have been developed over thousands of years of history. Many are based on military tactics such as the Trojan Horse, while others come from social practices and folklore. One thing they have in common is that they all work and are used in many forms today.

A caveat to the negotiator is that not all tactics are appropriate in all cases. Do not fall in love with one particular tactic or style. The following are some common negotiation tactics. One or a combination of them may be appropriate in any given negotiation. However, what works in one negotiation may not work in another.

The Hidden Agenda

Pursue one item (eg. price) while holding back the real item of interest (eg. delivery). It may be in the buyer's interest not to reveal the real objective of the session until late in the negotiations. This tactic may be appropriate in a situation where the buyer has an advantage in price but a disadvantage in delivery. A pricing concession granted to the buyer may be later exchanged for the required delivery. Sun Tzu states[3]:

> The Ultimate Positioned Strategy
> Is to be without an apparent Position
> Without Position even the deepest Intelligence is
> unable to spy;
> And those who are clever are unable to plan.

Good Guy/Bad Guy

In many old police movies, a suspect is brought in for interrogation and badgered by one officer. Then another officer, a mild-mannered and reasonable fellow, takes over the interrogation. The Good Guy seems to the suspect more reasonable and non-threatening, so he is able to elicit the information that is being sought.

Likewise, in a purchasing negotiation there may be a person on the buyer's team who is unreasonable and demanding. After a convincing act, he or she leaves the room. Another member of the team continues, in a more reasonable tone, to request the same concession. Usually, the other party is more likely to grant the concession.

The Sleeping Giant

The Sleeping Giant is simliar to the Good Guy/Bad Guy tactic, except that the Bad Guy is invisible. For example, "My boss has a very nasty disposition—not the sort of temperament either of us would care to deal with during this negotiation. So I suggest we reach an 'equitable' settlement without having to bring him in." The implied threat of introducing an irrational personality into the discussion may assist the buyer to achieve a desired end.

Limited Authority

Using this tactic, a buyer may claim, for instance, that he or she does not have the authority to accept a unit price above $2.31. So try as they may, the seller will be unsuccessful in achieving their goal of $2.55 each. This puts the seller on notice that the buyer's negotiator has no power to negotiate after this limit.

No Authority

The negotiator who uses this tactic claims a lack of authority to reach an agreement. The negotiator is present only to gather information for those who will ultimately do the actual negotiating. A buyer should ascertain at the beginning of a negotiating session whether the other parties present have the authority to negotiate and conclude an agreement.

Many retail automobile dealerships work this way. For example, a customer and a salesperson settle on the price of a new car. The salesperson then informs the customer that the price must be approved by the sales manager or owner. At this point, the customer has no deal. Often, the seller then informs the customer that the deal was not approved and that the price must be renegotiated. The salesperson is gathering information, while the customer is getting anxious to acquire the new car. The customer is then more likely to agree to pay a higher price for the car.

The Standard Cost

This tactic is also known as a "boggie." The buyer claims that the purchase price cannot exceed the standard cost for the item— say, $2.31. The standard may be an engineering or finance estimate of cost or affordability. The standard cost is the "bad guy," not the buyer. Both parties now cooperate in arriving at the standard cost.

Facts and Data

A buyer should always insist that the seller provide facts and data to support claims made during a negotiation session. For example, if the seller claims that the requested price is below cost or that the price quoted is the lowest offered, the buyer should ask to see data that support the claim. This practice serves to deflate sales hype and increase credibility on both sides.

Fair and Reasonable

A seller may claim that the price or position offered is "fair and reasonable." The first problem in dealing with this tactic is that everyone believes themselves to be fair and reasonable. Second, the tactic implies that a buyer who does not accept the position is by definition unfair and unreasonable. Third, "fair" and "reasonable" are purely subjective assessments. What appears to be fair and reasonable to one party may be unacceptable or even unconscionable to another party. A buyer should insist on seeing evidence that the offer would be fair and reasonable to a third party.

False Menu

A false menu involves presenting something as being important when, in fact, it is not. This ploy diverts the attention of the seller from the buyer's real objective. The seller may expend his or her energy to gain concessions for items on the false menu so that when the buyer's real issue comes up for discussion the seller has few items in reserve to use as barter. A buyer will develop a list of items which will be used in negotiation. Some items are important while others are of little interest to the buyer. These unimportant items will be used to obtain concessions the buyer wants or can be used to match the seller's concessions while relinquishing nothing of value to the buyer.

"I Don't Understand"

A very powerful tool and an excellent means of obtaining added information is to merely state "I don't understand." At that point, the seller has a vested interest in the buyer's understanding the issue and is obligated to provide more complete information. This tactic can also provide a respite for the buyer. However, many people are reluctant to admit that they do not know or understand something, and so do not use this tactic.

"I Can't Make Up My Mind"

This is much like "I Don't Understand." The buyer is looking for a concession that will sway the final decision. This puts the seller in the position of having to assist the buyer in making a choice.

For example, one buyer received two quotations for an item. Company A quoted $23.47 each for 1,000 units and company B quoted $23.42. The sellers were in all other respects equal in the buyer's mind. The buyer told a salesperson from Company B: "You are both so close in price that I just can't make up my mind." The salesperson asked: "What can we offer that would make your decision easier?" They talked of shipping costs, payment terms, and, of course, price. Ultimately, the salesperson made the decision very easy for the buyer.

"What If?"

"What If" is a great tool for exploring alternatives without making a commitment or changing position. A buyer might suggest,

"What if I allow a price increase of two cents a pound? Would you guarantee that there would be no more increases for a year?" A seller might say, "We seem to have an impasse. What if we contributed fifty percent of the installation costs?" This tactic allows attention to be directed to new possibilities while not relinquishing prior positions.

The Caucus
A buyer who sees that a negotiation is not going well or has stalled may call for a caucus. The caucus allows both sides to discuss the negotiation among themselves, clear the air, or restart in a new direction. A buyer can bring in other people to discuss an issue with the negotiating team. If the negotiation has become heated, tempers have a chance to quell and composure is regained.

Switch of Players
If a buyer finds that the seller is not responding as expected, he or she may wish to bring in a new negotiator. This tactic can be an excellent opportunity for the buyer to involve top management in the negotiation so that they can see firsthand the problems in resolving disputes or in achieving the desired objectives. It also permits the buyer to take a rest and plan new strategies. The substitution may also disorient the seller.

Nibbling
A buyer who is unsuccessful in obtaining an objective may ask for small concessions: extend the payment terms from net 30 to net 40 days, extend the warranty by 30 days, 3 percent cash discount, added packaging, etc. These little extras can have a significant impact over the term of the agreement.

"You Can Do a Little Better"
Near the end of the negotiation, the buyer may challenge the seller by saying, "We are very close, but I know that your company can do just a little bit better." Many sellers accept the challenge and offer a little extra.

"Take It or Leave It"
This tactic occurs when the seller or buyer signals that they have gone as far as they can and, for them, the negotiation is over. They may declare that the buyer must "take it or leave it!" This

is an ultimatum. But once stated, there is no opportunity to back down.

Walk Out

A buyer must be prepared to walk away from the negotiation—if, for example, it is obvious that the seller is not bargaining in good faith, or the two sides are so far apart that reconciliation is extremely unlikely. This tactic also demonstrates resolve.

Split the Difference

When a small difference separates the buyer and the seller, one of the parties may suggest "splitting the difference." For example: "You're at $2.00 and we are at $2.10. Let's settle at $2.05." This compromise may be satisfactory to both parties, unless five cents is a lot of money over the total volume, or may move one party more than they had planned. The buyer may not want or may not be able to afford to split the difference.

OTHER POINTS

These are a few of the more common tactics used in business negotiations. They can be used by either side. In addition to selecting the proper tactic(s), a negotiator should also know how to counter when the other party presents an identifiable tactic. As a negotiator gains experience in the use of tactics, he or she can more readily identify a tactic when it is being used.

When a negotiation is producing the desired result for you as a buyer, leave room for the seller to retreat gracefully and intact. Some of the best advice comes again from Sun Tzu[4]:

When the opposition withdraws, never interfere;
When surrounding the opponent, leave an opening;
When the opponent is desperate, never press.

Such is the execution of an Artful Strategy.

DEMANDS AND CONCESSIONS

Dr. Chester L. Karras has done much research on the patterns of concessions and their effects. What follows are his six findings:

1. Large initial demands improve the probability of success.
2. Losers make the largest concessions in a negotiation.
3. People who only make small concessions during a negotiation fail less.
4. Losers tend to make the first compromise.

5. Skilled negotiators make smaller concessions as a deadline approaches.
6. An unexpectedly high initial demand tends to lead to success rather than failure or deadlock.

THE QUICK NEGOTIATION

Not all negotiations are lengthy or major. Most negotiations begin and end within a period of fifteen minutes. Many of these are in the form of telephone negotiations. A seller may call a buyer and ask if they were successful on a quotation submitted last week. Most of the time, the buyer is not prepared for these unexpected calls. The seller may ask, "What do I have to do to get the business?" or "What if I lower the price by four cents each?" There are several tactics a buyer can use when put in this position:

■ If caught off guard, a buyer can tell the seller that he or she will call back within a specified time. This allows the buyer time to get a copy of the quote, review the process, and prepare a response (or request).

■ A buyer should always be ready for this type of call and have a pad of paper and pencil close by the telephone to take notes.

■ Don't make a snap decision based on recall. No decision is better than a bad decision. It is quite acceptable to postpone a response until the buyer has reviewed the situation and goals.

LEGITIMACY

Legitimacy is akin to power and often adds to a negotiator's ability to exert power. Virtually anything that is in print carries a measure of legitimacy. For example, suppose a seller wants certain items or terms accepted at face value. Because the seller does not want prices questioned, he or she may use a price list. The assumption is that the prices are not negotiable and offered to all buyers. Yet price lists are often discounted and separate deals negotiated.

Company policies are always in writing and often quoted:
"Our terms are net 30."
"Company policy is that all returns must be authorized."
"This quotation is good for 15 days."

A negotiator may seek to establish legitimacy through the use of leases, bank loan forms, acknowledgments, quotations, and other forms. These forms, however, are created by people for general consumption. They can be and should be challenged by buyers. Even the Internal Revenue Service provides for renegotiation of deadlines and policies. Bank loan interest rates can be negotiated, leases can be changed, deadlines extended, prices improved, and policies modified or totally discarded. The buyer's first instinct should be to reject any preprinted form or quoted policies.

Legitimacy can also be conveyed in the form of titles, letterheads, business cards, and any other form of impression or image conveyance. Be certain that the person with whom you are dealing is equal to the image that is being conveyed.

SUCCESS

Success is unique to each individual and is often based upon an individual's expectations. Low expectations of the outcome of a negotiation lead to satisfaction with modest results. Conversely, high expectations create a different definition of success. Further, success feeds success. Someone who has been successful at negotiations in the past will likely have high expectations during any negotiation. A basketball team that has a record of 23 wins and no losses may expect to win the balance of the season's games and are likely to play well. If a team has not won a game all season, they may expect to lose the balance of their contests and play accordingly.

Building a pattern of success in negotiations is important. Therefore, novice negotiators should begin with small, "easy-win" situations. A learning process can take place with minimum risk, and the negotiator therefore has an opportunity to develop high expectations of success.

COOPERATIVE NEGOTIATION

Cooperative negotiation has its roots in a recognition that the world has become more competitive. Many North American companies, all of which are buyers and sellers, are not faring well in the world market. There is a growing sense of mutual survival and interdependency—if a seller's customers are not competitive, for example, there will be fewer customers and the seller will not fare well.

In a high-technology environment, these issues may not be clear-cut. Often, there is a need to jointly develop products, technology, and processes between buyer and seller. The adversarial nature of competitive negotiations does not lend itself to joint development undertakings.

In practice, there is an interdependence between buyer and seller, and their futures are dependent upon mutual prosperity.

If this is recognized by both sides, a sense of mutual trust may develop. The product, its market acceptance, and success become the goals of the parties. The buyer develops a product that prospers, and the seller has a prospering customer that needs the product and the support of a viable seller. Both parties win. Negotiations in this environment are often called "Win-Win."

SITUATIONS THAT LEND THEMSELVES TO WIN-WIN NEGOTIATIONS

Although nearly all items and situations can benefit from Win-Win negotiations, those that best lend themselves to this type of negotiation include the following:

■ Noncompetitive environment. There are items and technologies for which there is but one possible seller or one possible customer. This situation may encourage a cooperative type of negotiation.

■ Both parties have more to lose than to gain from negotiation.

■ Mutual trust between the buyer and seller already exists.

■ There is not enough basis for competitive negotiations. For example, an agreement for a seller to develop a technology for a buyer may draw the two parties closer together in order to mutually develop an agreement that benefits both. There is likely to be more openness on issues such as cost and potential markets.

■ The survival of one or both parties is at stake. Some industries are faltering and threatening to take their sellers with them. The automotive, steel, and electronics industries are examples.

■ Business start-ups. Fledgling businesses often depend upon close working arrangements with their sellers. These arrangements may include special financing and technical and product support. A seller may see a new venture as a potentially large future customer and therefore have a vested interest in supporting the new business.

■ Intangibles are more important than tangibles. A buyer of advertising services promoting the introduction of a new product may be more interested in the quality of market research and advertising than in the price of those services. The advertising agent may be more interested in acquiring a new account for the long term than in the cost of this introduction campaign. The buyer and seller are drawn into new and different roles. The question changes from "What advantage can I gain?" to "How can we both guarantee the success of this product and the futures of our two companies?"

A buyer stands to benefit from developing a close relationship with a seller. For example, if a seller is involved in the design stage of a customer's new product, the seller's engineers can make suggestions for increasing functionality and quality, lowering costs, and ensuring that the design is produceable.

CHAPTER PERSPECTIVE

Negotiation is about moving people's positions or beliefs. People are not changed in the process. A buyer should focus on the seller's position and not on attempting to change the seller.

At the start of a negotiation, the buyer has the advantage. The buyer has the business and the money that is sought by the seller. At the conclusion of a successful negotiation, the seller has the advantage, for the buyer is now dependent on the seller to deliver what has been negotiated. If the negotiation produces terms and conditions that strongly favor the buyer, the seller may falter on the commitment. Sooner or later, an inequitable agreement is neutralized by the party that is injured by the agreement.

REFERENCES:

[1]R.L. Wing. *The Art of Strategy*. (New York: Doubleday, 1988), p. 27

[2]Chester L. Karrass. *The Negotiating Game*. (New York: Thomas Y. Crowell, 1970), p. 56.

[3]R.L. Wing, p. 87.

[4]Ibid., p. 99

[5]Chester L. Karrass, pp. 18–19.

Quality

INTRODUCTION AND MAIN POINTS

Every buyer, every maker, every user wants quality products, components, material, and services. Therein lies part of the problem. We expect quality in the goods we buy. Why would sellers ship anything but quality goods? Poor-quality goods cause economic loss for all who come in contact with them.

What is quality? Is it goods that pass as merchantable in trade as suggested by the Uniform Commercial Code? Goods that pass inspection? Goods that meet buyers' expectations? Goods that meet specifications? The answer is all of the above and none of the above.

After studying the material in this chapter:
- You will know how to define quality.
- You will be able to identify the quality you need.
- You will have the tools to ask for the quality you need.
- You will know how to assist suppliers to attain the quality levels you require.

DEFINING QUALITY

If a buyer were to purchase a barge load of caustic soda, the definition of product quality would be different from that for a purchase of twelve pacemakers for heart implants, or 40,000 8-36 hex nuts, or two motor vehicles, or a one-year contract for office cleaning services, one mainframe computer, or 200 chickens for a restaurant.

Some definitions of quality involve commercial grade and trade custom, while others adhere to federal standards or blueprint specifications of either the buyer or the supplier. A common thread is that the goods must have minimum variation item to item (uniformity) and they must meet or exceed the buyers' expectations. The problem, then, is "what are the buyers' expectations?"

MIL STD 105

During the Korean War era, the federal government established an inspection standard called MIL STD (Military Standard) 105. The government, like many in industry, was searching for a method to standardize quality requirements from its suppliers. The product of their efforts took the form of a sampling plan. Many products were purchased in volume by the branches of the armed services; this plan offered a means to inspect for quality in these products. Simply, it was a chart that listed qualities down the left side and required quality levels across the top. An inspector need merely match the quantity received in a single lot with the acceptable error level allowed or assured quality level (AQL) across the top.

For example, a lot of 50,000 parts is received and a quality level of 4.0 AQL—normal is desired (the sample size and quality are determined by the categories of normal, tightened, or reduced). The chart would tell the inspector to take a sample of 80 pieces (since inspecting all 50,000 would be impractical), accept the lot if only 2 bad or nonconforming parts were found, and reject the lot if 9 bad parts were found. If the quantity found bad was between 2 and 9, another larger sample would be taken.

The problems with MIL STD 105 are: 1) it presumes that, in any population of parts, there is bound to be some level of unacceptable parts and that errors are unavoidable; 2) the process focuses on error detection and not on error correction; and 3) it is the "grandfather" of all sampling plans and has been used, in various forms, for the past forty years. Better sampling plans are now available.

The problems with inspection are that it is not accurate and that it does not remove the causes of nonconforming parts. Further, if some level of nonconforming parts is unavoidable and acceptable, a product that uses these nonconforming parts will also be unacceptable. If the finished product contains many parts, there is the likelihood that there will be a number of nonconforming parts in the product.

Inspection should be used only in cases where there is a critical use and human intervention is of value and is necessary. The production of life-supporting devices such as pacemakers is an example of required inspection. As Dr. W. Edwards Deming, the noted quality expert, says about *routine* inspection: "Inspection does not improve quality, nor guarantee quality. Inspection is too late. The quality, good or bad, is already in the product."[1]

TO SPECIFICATION

Many buyers purchase goods to a specification or blueprint. This, too, presents possible problems in quality. Design engineers often create a specification for a part. The print may contain dimensions and tolerances. The dimensions are created in response to a need to fit or mate with another part. The tolerances are an engineer's best guess (often with the assistance of a textbook or design guide) as to what is reasonable or obtainable from possible suppliers.

Tolerances allow for variation. When many parts are assembled, the phenomenon known as a "stack-up of tolerances" occurs. Each part has its own allowable variation and, when the parts are assembled, the end product may contain many unique variations. The result is that each end product can operate differently from the others; their operation becomes unpredictable.

VARIATION

Eli Whitney had a unique and powerful idea: rifles with interchangeable components. Prior to this creation, each rifle that was issued to military personnel was unique and if a component required replacement, it had to be custom made and fitted to that particular rifle. Interchangeability fostered the Industrial Revolution in America. It required machines that made component parts one like the other—consistency part to part and interchangeability.

The new definition of quality in production is "minimum variation part to part from a target value." To accomplish this requires that processes capabilities are known, variation in the process is minimized, that processes are controlled to operate within their capabilities, and that goods are designed within the capabilities of the processes that produce them.

PROCESS CAPABILITY

The first step in determining the capability of a process is to observe the output of the process and collect and display the data. This effort tells the users where they are and characterizes the process as it exists today. Data collection may be in the form of measuring temperature or dimension variations, fluctuations in time (variable data) or pass-fail, or go/no-go measurements (attribute data).

Sample Number	Dimension (target 1.000)	Variation (from target)
1	1.002	+ .002
2	1.004	+ .004
3	.998	− .002
4	1.001	+ .001
5	.999	− .001
6	.998	− .002
7	.996	− .004
8	.995	− .005
9	.994	− .006
10*	.993	− .007

(* Normally, many samples, sometimes hundreds of observations, must be taken for the data to be statistically meaningful. In this example, we use only ten observations.)

The specification calls for 1.000 +/− .010. Therefore, all of the parts sampled are within the specification (.990 to 1.010), but there is a variation of .011 (1.004 to .993). A frequency distribution chart may be used to gather and display the information. For example:

```
1.010
1.009
1.008
1.007
1.006
1.005
1.004    /
1.003
1.002    /
1.001    /
1.000    /
 .999    /
 .998    /
 .997
 .996    /
 .995    /
 .994    /
 .993    /
 .992
 .991
 .990
```

Calculation of the central value can be done by adding all the values and dividing by the number of values. Mathematically, this is shown as:

$$\overline{X} = (EX)/n$$

Or in our example:

$$\overline{X} = (9.982)/10, \text{ or } .9982$$

Dispersion is a measure of how far the data spreads from the central value. The further we get from the central value, the fewer occurrences of that value there are. A common measure of dispersion is the range:

$$\text{Range } (R) = \text{Max.} - \text{Min.}$$
$$\text{or}$$
$$R = 1.002 - .993 = .011$$

```
F                    X
R                  XXXXX
E                 XXXXXXX
Q               XXXXXXXXX
U               XXXXXXXXX
E             XXXXXXXXXXX
N             XXXXXXXXXXX
C           XXXXXXXXXXXXX
Y        XXXXXXXXXXXXXXXXX
      XXXXXXXXXXXXXXXXXXXXX
```

$$>>VALUE>>$$

By defining the measures of central tendency and dispersion, we know where the process is located and how much variation to routinely expect. Figure 12-1 illustrates the results of our sampling in the form of a histogram.

CAUSES OF VARIATION

Once the process has been characterized, we can start to identify the causes of the variation. The people closest to the product and the process—the production workers—are the ones best able to identify and test possible causes for the variation. The cause-and-effect of Ishakawa diagram is a helpful tool (see Figure 12-2).

The problem of nonlinearity is stated in Figure 12-2. "Ribs" are drawn; each represents a major area of possible contribution to the problem. The workers on the floor place observations, those that could contribute to the problem, on the side of the

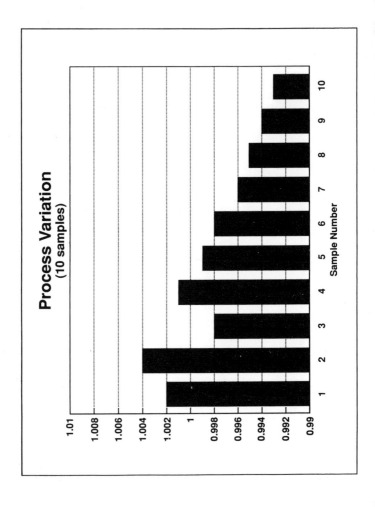

FIG 12-1. *Process variation.*

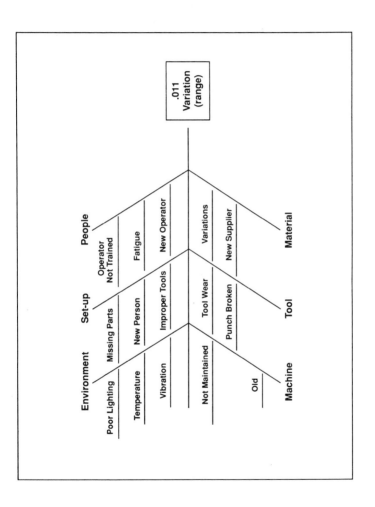

FIG 12-2. *Cause-and-effect diagram.*

ribs. Each possible cause is then tested to determine the impact, if any, on the problem. Trial and error is used to reduce the possible causes.

A Pareto chart (Figure 12-3) assists the user to prioritize the problems so that the user focuses on the right problem and working the right solutions. Pareto charting requires a discipline that forces users to qualify and quantify problems and their causes. This removes guessing and assumptions and introduces objectivity and analysis into the evaluation process. Removing subjectivity from the problem-solving process allows a focus on facts.

Once the prime causes are identified, the corrections are made and tried. The process is continually refined until all controllable causes are identified and corrections are implemented. Standard operating procedures are changed to reflect these improvements.

In every process (manufacturing or administrative), there is natural and uncontrollable variation; this is known as signal-to-noise ratio. The signal is refined and the noise is recognized as uncontrollable.

A new characterization is performed and the new capability is established. To visualize this new capability, a process control chart is drawn (see Figure 12-4) and is used in the process by the operators so that they may control the process to the new capability or process width. The process width should be narrower than the specification (spec) width. The relationship between the width of the specification and that of the process is expressed as:

$$Cp = \frac{\text{Spec. Width}}{\text{Process Width}}$$

The narrower the process width, the closer the process is to being under control. However, the possibility of an item in the process exceeding the process width or the specification width is not eliminated. This is where statistics and reality depart. Statistics is the estimation of probability through the use of mathematics. It tells us that, while the process is under control, there is still the possibility or probability that an item can and will exceed the control limits. For instance, statistics tell us that if the process width and the specification width equals one (Cp = 1), there is the probability that for every one million parts processed, 2,700 will exceed the limits or fail. If the Cp is 2, the

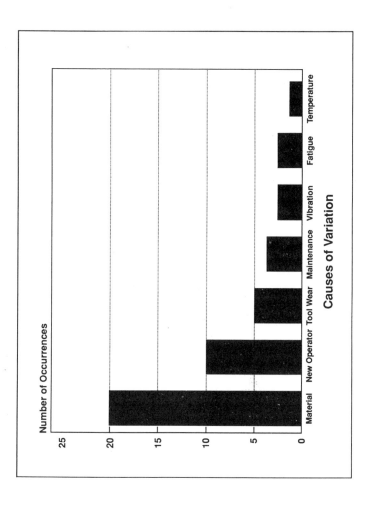

FIG 12-3. *Pareto chart.*

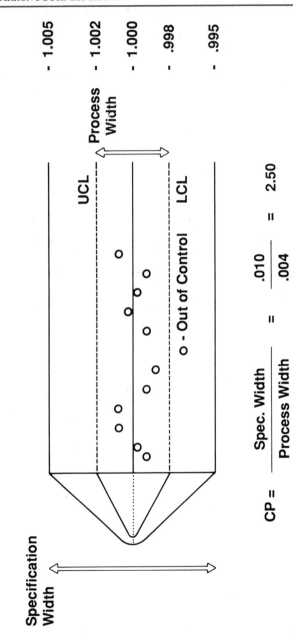

FIG 12-4. *Run chart with Cp.*

probability of failure is 2 parts for every billion processed as shown in the following table:

STATISTICAL CONVERSIONS

Cp	PPM* Defect	Quality Yield
0.67	22750	97.725%
0.83	6210	99.379%
1.00	2700	99.730%
1.17	233	99.865%
1.33	63	99.9936627%
1.50	3	99.9997%
1.67	574 PPM**	99.9999426%
2.00	2 PPB	99.9999998%

* is parts per million.
** is parts per billion.

In statistics, as the process improves, the probability of the process producing unacceptable parts is greatly reduced but is never zero.

This, then, is the manner in which variation is measured and reduced to achieve the definition of quality that is "minimum variation part to part." But this is also a continuous process. Therefore, it is necessary to have a means of continually monitoring the process and adjusting it as required, finding the problems that cause the undesirable variation, and solving those problems at the source.

AN ARMY OF INSPECTORS

A company never has enough inspectors everywhere in the process unless every operator is trained in and responsible for product and process quality. Even the term "inspector" is misleading in this context. Every operator would have to be a trained quality specialist whose duties include finding problems that cause undesirable variation, correcting those problems, and maintaining process stability.

When you enter a supplier's plant and production area, look for the army of quality specialists. Evidence of the army's existence may be found on the walls where process control charts are displayed, in the training record of all employees that have operator training and retraining in quality, and in the regular process improvement meetings held in the production and office areas of the plant.

OTHER DEFINITIONS OF QUALITY

It was discussed earlier that there are different definitions of quality for varying products and customer expectations. Capital-equipment manufacturers often use the term "mean time between failure" (MTBF) to describe the nominal operating or "up" time of their equipment. The longer the operating time, the better for the user. For example, the MTBF on the central processing unit of a computer may be 10,000 hours. This means that history has shown that a computer sold or leased by its manufacturer will operate without failure for 10,000 hours after its installation, on average. This MTBF can be compared to other manufacturers of a similar product to determine the relative quality or reliability of competing equipment.

Suppose a buyer were to purchase a commodity such as wheat. There are commercial standards to measure the wheat's quality that include contaminants and grade of the wheat. Cp, PPM, or MTBF would not be applicable measures of quality. There are no means of applying these measures to wheat.

Industrial and government quality standards are applied to meat (grade A), chemicals (reagent grade), and drugs (FDA approved), to mention a few. The goods are measured against the standards and definitions to determine the quality of the goods. In some cases, visual inspection is sufficient; in others, there may be requirements for chemical analysis, prolonged testing, and the like.

Some items do not warrant extensive testing or inspection. An example is 8-penny common nails to be used in construction. In a lot of fifty pounds of nails, there may be ten nails unfit for use and the carpenter may just discard them with no measurable economic loss. Because the bad nails are easily detected at the point of use, it is better to discard them than for the producer of the nails to implement extensive and expensive quality processes at the point of manufacture.

The buying company must determine the appropriate level of quality for each item or commodity to be purchased. Figure 12-5 is a matrix that may be used by a company to classify each commodity by the type of quality process to be used.

SUPPLIER-TO-CUSTOMER QUALITY

The quality process starts with the customer defining quality needs. The design and engineering of the product and its components is critical. The designs must ensure that not only will

	Metal Parts	Plating Chemicals	Packaging	Printed Circuit Boards	Machinery	Electronic Components
Cp<1	X					
Cp 1-2						X
Cp>2				X		
MTBF					X	
Inspection			X			
Certification		X				

FIG 12-5. *Quality matrix.*

the product perform as expected but that there exists suppliers who can make the product, that the design is sufficiently robust that the product can survive the rigors of the manufacturing or conversion process, that the end product is serviceable, that the product has an acceptable market price, and that the product is appealing to the end consumer or user. To the old definition of quality and value of "form, fit and function" (the "three Fs"), we must now add "features and feel."

These conditions of quality require that the customer, supplier, and the suppliers' suppliers are involved in the quality process. If any one of these elements fails to produce quality in its processes, the end-user will not receive quality.

THE CUSTOMER

The customer must enlist its suppliers in the design process. This has several beneficial effects: 1) the supplier brings added resources to the design effort, 2) at the end of the design effort, the customer knows that it has a supplier who can produce the item, and 3) costs and product quality can be considered at the design stage.

The customer must have a clear idea of the end-user's definition of quality. From this definition, design can define the product elements that are important to the end-user and interpret them into specifications and quality parameters.

By linking the customer, manufacturer (provider), and supplier at the design or product conception stage, all of the parties can assure that the item is appropriately designed, quality and its measurement are incorporated in the process, and that value is received by all parties.

BUYING QUALITY

Purchasing must understand the quality requirements of the items to be purchased and place those requirements on the face of the purchase order. It is surprising how few purchase orders that are sent to suppliers contain quality requirements. It is as if there is an understanding that the buyer wants only good parts, whatever "good" means. Often the definition of quality is left to a separate document, one negotiated between the buyer's and seller's quality departments or simply imposed on the supplier by the buyer's quality department. When the quality requirement is left to an understanding or is relegated to a separate, noncommercial document, the relative unimportance of quality is communicated to the supplier. Quality and its measure must be part of the commercial purchase order.

If a supplier is not knowledgeable in the quality measure techniques the buyer requires, the buyer may have to offer assistance to the supplier, including training of the supplier's personnel. In fact, the best way for the buyer to obtain the required quality and of communicating its importance to the supplier is for the buyer to provide necessary training. Perhaps the buyer personally can conduct the initial training sessions at no cost to the supplier and then arrange for further training to be provided for by a third party and at the supplier's expense.

This approach accomplishes three objectives:

1. The buyer must be sufficiently knowledgeable in quality requirements and measures to be able to pass it on to the supplier.

2. The supplier and its employees understand that quality is important to the buyer.

3. Both the buyer and seller must make substantial investments in time, people, and training. There is established between the buyer, seller, and seller's employees a commitment to quality practices and continuous improvement. Such mutual investments tend to create long-term relationships between buyer and seller. Each has a vested interest in the success of the other party.

BENEFITS

If you were to add up all of the costs associated with the lack of assured quality, you would find that they total 15 percent of the cost to manufacture or provide a service. These costs include the following:

- inspection (incoming, in process, final)
- rework, repair, replacement and scrap
- product testing
- warranty repairs
- service calls
- retrofits
- replacement orders
- extra inventories
- dissatisfied customers

Clearly, high-quality products cost less than those of lower quality. Further, there is the possibility that, if customers do not return, the future of the business is at peril. This is as true for your suppliers as it is for you.

SUPPLIER QUALITY AUDITS

It is of little use for a buyer to enter a supplier's facility and attempt to determine if that supplier is capable of and, in fact, delivers quality products. Process capability cannot be seen by peering into the operations or checking records. Buyers must shift the responsibility to the supplier to prove that their processes are under control through the use of capability studies and process control charts, through the efforts of their quality-control personnel to find and correct problems, and through their contribution to their customers' design and quality efforts.

CHAPTER PERSPECTIVE

Buyers cannot judge the value quoted by a supplier or the value of goods received unless there is a measure of quality. Quality, therefore, is an integral part of the buyer's function—the definition, conveyance, and receipt of quality from suppliers.

Quality is not a matter of a product passing or failing inspection. Rather, it is a robust design, consistently executed with minimum variation item to item, that meets or exceeds customer expectation at a price that the customer deems to be of value.

There are many tools that can be used to assure this level of quality, but predictable processes with improving results carried out by well-trained personnel familiar with the item are common to all quality-assurance methods.

REFERENCES

[1]W. Edwards Deming. *Quality, Productivity and Competitive Position*. (Cambridge, MA: MIT Press, 1982), p. 69.

International Purchasing

INTRODUCTION AND MAIN POINTS

During the 1960s and 1970s, many companies sought foreign sources of supply to lower their purchase prices and, ultimately, the selling prices of their finished goods. They were in search of lower labor costs, and they found them. The trend continues today. The real question is, Did they achieve lower manufacturing costs, and were they more competitive as a result of foreign sourcing? Cost accounting analyses indicate they saved money. Oddly enough, the same analyses indicate they lost money in their total operations.

In this chapter we will discuss the discrepancy of these two findings and the real costs of buying internationally. Some companies were quite justified in buying abroad, while others lost money and market share in the process of seeking lower costs.

After studying the material in this chapter:

■ you will understand the costs of buying foreign goods.
■ you will be able to evaluate the advantages and disadvantages of buying internationally.
■ you will understand why so many companies purchase goods from foreign sources.

HISTORICAL PERSPECTIVE

Historically, foreign sourcing has been driven by cost accounting in most manufacturing industries and not by purchasing departments. As the cost to manufacture domestically increased in the 1960s and 1970s, producers went looking for lower costs. Interest in foreign goods was first aroused by high-labor, low-material content items: textiles, labor-intensive assemblies, and finished goods, including everything from toys to wire bonding of lead-frame semiconductors, cameras, and sports equipment. The labor-cost differences were 10:1, 20:1, and more. The low labor cost areas were Japan, Hong Kong, Taiwan, and Korea.

In the early years the quality of these products was not very good, but these countries have a legacy of individual craftsmanship and a long commercial history. Labor and overhead costs were low. Quality improved over time through the efforts of individuals such as Drs. Deming and Ishakawa and agencies like Japan's Ministry of International Trade and Industry (MITI).

Manufacturers thought that if these countries could produce components with lower costs and improving quality, why not have them produce the finished goods and save even more money? Domestic manufacturers exported their technology for ever-increasingly complex goods. The cost accountants told American managers that their costs were decreasing. But were they?

Goods produced in the United States carried the full burden of the overhead functions of research and development (R & D), manufacturing engineering, equipment design, distribution, sales, and customer service. Efficiencies of mechanization and automation reduced the need for direct labor workers; therefore, there were fewer laborers to share the overhead burden. A laborer who made $9.00 per hour with benefits was burdened with 300 percent overhead, making the labor rate in the area of $36.00. And the fewer the laborers, the higher the rate. Foreign producers were charging $2.00 per hour, $1.00 per hour, or even $.50 per hour. The cry became "Send more of the work to Hong Kong" (which only increased the burden on the remaining U.S. laborers).

Soon U.S. manufacturers were importing more than they manufactured, and there was a growing dependency on foreign-made goods. Quality increased. U.S. manufacturing and product technology was not only exported but improved upon, and ultimately we became addicted to foreign-made products. Many products created and formerly made in the United States were no longer available domestically.

OTHER COSTS

Businesses did not account for the "other" costs of buying foreign goods. Most did not account for a host of hidden costs. They only compared their manufactured costs with the price on the purchase order. Hidden costs of international purchasing include the following:
- risk of currency fluctuations
- difficulty in communications
- added costs of communication
- problems in returning rejected materials

- customs brokerage fees
- import duties
- higher transportation costs
- longer lead times, which increase buyer's inventories
- interruptions in supply due to political or economic unrest in the producing country
- the possibility of U.S.-imposed trade embargoes, which can interrupt or limit supply
- slower response times to buyer's change in demand
- the cost of sending a buyer or an engineer to the producing country in case of difficulties
- decreased cash flow (most foreign shippers require that goods be paid for at time of shipment; they do not ordinarily offer payment terms)
- the risks and costs of owning the goods in transit

If all these costs were included in the price of goods bought abroad and were a part of the original sourcing strategy, it is unlikely that manufacturers would have been so eager to move manufacturing and sourcing abroad.

The added length of the supply line is of concern to buyers. Goods shipped by vessel from the Far East are in transit for three to five weeks. If the buyer is located a great distance from the port of arrival, the goods are transferred to a common carrier for delivery to the buyer. During that time the goods are out of the control of the buyer and the supplier, and can be difficult to trace. Further, if the intended port of arrival is closed due to a labor dispute and the vessel is diverted to another, it is even more difficult to know the location of the goods or the date of their arrival at the buyer's company.

THE ULTIMATE HIDDEN COSTS

It may be of only academic interest, but the ultimate cost of moving manufacturing and product technology abroad may well be the economic undoing of this country.

A country has two ways of creating wealth: selling value-added manufactured goods and selling its natural resources. The five biggest exports of the United States are wheat, corn, soy beans, cotton, and coal. U.S. export wealth comes primarily from agriculture and mining, not from manufacturing.

Further, as we lose the ability to compete internationally and produce less at home, we lose the ability to create the technology and products for future business and exports. Research and development (R & D) are funded by the profit from products they create. No R & D means no products; no products means no R & D. Fewer and fewer products are being invented or developed in the United States. The Japanese and others are now creating, manufacturing, and exporting new products to the United States. They are also building plants in the United States and employing American workers to manufacture goods destined for the American consumer. One might ask, "Are they using cheap American labor to lower their costs?" If they are, they are not using the same accounting practices or the same management philosophy we have used.

In the last decade, an entirely new list of up-and-coming countries that manufacture for the world market has developed. They include the Philippines, Malaysia, Thailand, India, and China. And we have just begun to understand the impact of the inclusion of the Soviet Union and the Eastern Bloc countries in the Western economy.

The problem lies not with those countries that look to serve the world with exports while acquiring national wealth, but with those who abdicate their position as world producers and allow others to capture their markets.

THE BUYER'S CHOICE
There are many valid reasons for buyers to explore and buy in the world marketplace. Some of these reasons are: 1) the goods are not available domestically, 2) after adding all of the hidden costs to the quoted price, there is still a clear advantage in buying foreign goods, and 3) there may be a requirement for "domestic content" in order to sell in a particular country's market.

AVAILABILITY
Goods not available in domestic markets include items that were exported for manufacturing and are no longer manufactured in the United States, items where the quality or grade of domestically produced goods is not sufficient, and items for which process or product technology does not exist in this country.

Items no longer manufactured in the United States include many electronic components, machine tools, capital equipment, specialty metals and alloys, and electromechanical products. Examples include the razor manufacturer who imports stainless steel from Japan because domestic manufacturers are unable or unwilling to meet the required quality standards, and the large computer manufacturer that purchases 40-layer circuit boards from a division of a Japanese computer manufacturer because no domestic supplier has developed the technological capability to produce them. In the latter case, the domestic computer manufacturer may feel that buying a key component from a potential competitor is not a threat because the Japanese will not master the difficulties of software languages and it will keep them from entering the world market. But manufacturers must look at all possibilties. One Japanese supplier bought an English computer manufacturer and not only entered the market but established itself firmly in the European Economic Community. It now competes directly with U.S. manufacturers in Europe.

COST COMPETITIVENESS

There are many opportunities for U.S. buyers to take advantage of the world's dispersion of raw materials, talents, and technologies in order to find goods of superior quality at affordable prices. Some items that are especially labor intensive are widely imported due to lower delivered or installed costs. Examples are textiles, apparel, shoes, molds and dies, hand-wired assemblies, and some capital equipment.

Buyers should review those items that benefit from the lower labor costs, specialized skills, patent rights, or accessibility to raw materials which give foreign producers a distinct advantage. Buyers should be international in their thinking and their sourcing when it benefits their employers, and exercise prudence when sourcing "core" items—those items crucial to the survival and growth of the buyer's firm. (See Chapter 8.)

Raw materials are often less expensive when converted to finished or semifinished goods by the producing country. Many are not available or not available in abundance in this country—tin, mercury, chromium, gold, vanadium, and industrial diamonds, for example. These raw materials must be imported, and it may make sense to import them as finished products.

Certain skills and technology, such as those specialty glass products, rubber, and synthetics, are naturals for certain foreign producers. It is surprising that the Republic of Ireland is not a major producer of television tubes, cathode ray tubes, and related products. The glass technology is in place (Waterford, Galway Glass, etc.), there is a skilled and educated work force, labor rates are relatively low, there are export incentives in place, and the country is close to many consuming nations. Instead, many tubes are produced by Taiwan and Singapore for the world market. Recently, when the People's Republic of China was searching to buy a television-tube manufacturing plant, it turned to Japan for the plant and the technology. It was becoming too costly for the Chinese to import finished television sets from Japan. The plant is now producing 1.5 million tubes a year in Beijing. This might have been Ireland's business.

One capital-equipment manufacturer in the United States purchases machined castings from Shenyang Heavy Machining Plant #1 in Shanyang, China. The cost of labor is U.S. $30 per month. Even with relative labor inefficiencies, the castings are delivered at prices considerably below those available domestically.

Likewise many manufacturers establish assembly plants across the Mexican border. Wire harness assemblies for Ford Motor Company are produced in Mexico at considerably less cost than those produced domestically. The labor rate is $1.50 per hour, and there are preferential duty considerations. The materials are shipped to the Mexican facility, assembled, and returned, often duty free or with duty on only the value-added portion of the product.

DOMESTIC CONTENT

Some foreign governments require that those goods sold to their country contain a certain percentage produced in that country. This is especially common in the purchase of military hardware. Suppose that the government of Portugal wishes to purchase ten F-14 "Tomcat" fighter aircraft and that the aircraft sells for $10 million dollars each. One hundred million dollars is a lot of money for a small country, and Portugal may wish to get more out of the purchase than mere hardware. Their country may also need industry and jobs. So the Portuguese government may require of the seller that they or their subcontractors purchase the equivalent of $2 million in components or support equipment in Portugal as a condition of the sale.

Similar arrangements are made for commercial goods. A buyer must have knowledge of manufacturing sources and capabilities throughout the world in order to effectively support the organization's sales plan.

COUNTER TRADE

Many countries of the world do not have hard currencies. Hard currencies are those that are recognized and accepted in trade by other countries. Other countries do not have the immediate wealth to purchase the items they need to import. These countries must resort to barter, or trading goods for goods. These situations offer buyers opportunities to strike mutually beneficial deals. Further, they offer companies entry into otherwise neglected markets through their domestic purchasing departments. If a buyer has need for materials from a region with a soft currency, the company may be able to "sell" finished goods in return for raw material. Often, a company will trade finished goods for finished goods, enter the domestic resale market, and produce profit from the sale of a new product. For example, Pepsico wanted to bottle and sell Pepsi Cola in the Soviet Union. Because the ruble has no value outside that country, Pepsico negotiated a deal in which, in return for their product, Pepsico obtained vodka for resale and leased vessels for shipping.

GETTING STARTED

In Chapter 8, a number of channels of information and contacts for foreign sourcing were outlined. There are many foreign companies doing business in the United States. The yellow pages of any large city lists the sales agents for foreign producers and their associated trading companies.

One of the best methods, if you have a little money, is to fly to Taiwan and, when registering with their customs agents, state that you are a buyer for a certain item or items. Within forty-eight hours you will receive a host of telephone calls at your hotel from local producers offering to pick you up in their company limousine and take you to their plant. The Taiwanese are superb marketeers.

PRODUCT DEFINITION

Prior to sending a request for quote to a foreign supplier, agent, or trading company, consider how the request will be phrased. Specifications must be clearly stated in terms familiar to the seller. The metric measurement system is used more commonly throughout the world than the Imperial system, so you may want to have blueprint dimensions stated in metric terms. Units of volume, such as tons or gallons, should also be in metric terms.

Quality requirements must be clearly stated in the request for quote, because different countries have varying quality standards. Many European countries are in the process of adopting quality standard ISO 9000, while other countries use the AQL (assured quality level), and others use Cpk (specification width vs. process capability). Many electronics firms use PPM (parts per million) or PPB (parts per billion) standards, while others rely on the inspection process or industry-standard specifications.

LETTERS OF CREDIT

Many foreign countries require a letter of credit as payment for goods. The letter of credit is also a means for a company new to the international buying scene to receive credit acceptance by suppliers. The following steps outline the procurement cycle using a letter of credit[1]:

Step 1: The buyer and seller agree upon the terms of sale. The sales contract dictates that a letter of credit is to be used to finance the transaction.

Step 2: The buyer completes an application for a letter of credit and forwards it to the buyer's bank, which will issue the letter of credit.

Step 3: The buyer's bank then forwards the letter of credit to a correspondent bank in the seller's country.

Step 4: The correspondent bank relays the letter of credit to the seller.

Step 5: Having received assurance of payment, the seller makes the necessary shipping arrangement.

Step 6: The seller prepares the documents required under the letter and delivers them to the correspondent bank.

Step 7: The correspondent bank negotiates the documents. If it finds them in order, it sends them to the issuing bank, and pays the seller in accordance with the terms of the letter of credit.

Step 8: The issuing bank, having received the documents, examines them. If they are in order, the issuing bank charges the buyer's account and sends the documents to the buyer or the buyer's customs broker. The issuing bank also reimburses the correspondent bank.

Step 9: The buyer or broker receives the documentation. Picks up the merchandise from the shipper (carrier).[1]

SHIPPING TERMS

It is helpful to the buyer to be familiar with shipping terms to determine the point of ownership and shipping-cost responsibilities. Here are some of the most common:

EX WORKS—The title to the goods and responsibility for

transport move to the buyer at the seller's place of business.

F.A.S. (Free Along Side)—The seller is responsible for transporting the goods to a pier and within the reach of a named vessel's loading tackle. Ownership and responsibility pass to the buyer at this point.

F.O.B. Vessel—The seller's price includes loading the goods on a named vessel.

F.O.B. Airport—The seller will move the goods to a named airport.

C.I.F. (Cost, Insurance, and Freight)—The seller assumes the cost and responsibility of insurance and freight charges for the goods, but the title passes to the buyer when the carrier accepts the goods.

C & F (Cost and Freight)—C & F is the same as C.I.F., except that the buyer is responsible for insuring the goods.

DDP (Delivered Duty Paid)—The seller assumes all responsibilities incurred in delivering the goods to the buyer's place of business.

In most cases, the point of title transfer is the country of the supplier. This means that that country's courts will have jurisdiction in case of a dispute over the contract or purchase order. The buyer is at a distinct disadvantage if a legal dispute arises.

CHAPTER PERSPECTIVE

There are many opportunities for buyers in the international purchasing arena. As a profit-producing agent for an organization, a buyer has a responsibility to understand the benefits and risks of such activities.

First, the buyer should be completely aware of the cost-comparison basis on which decisions are made to purchase goods from foreign sources, making sure all appropriate costs have been included. Second, the buyer should be prepared to deal with cultural differences and communications problems that are likely to arise. Third, the buyer should understand the implications of greater supply-line distances. Fourth, the buyer should recognize that international purchasing may open opportunities to sell finished products in the supplier's country.

REFERENCES

[1]N.A. DiOrio. *International Procurement.* National Association of Purchasing Management (Oradell, NJ: 1987), p. 13.

Capital-Equipment Purchases

INTRODUCTION AND MAIN POINTS

Capital-equipment purchases occur in all businesses, regardless of the type of goods produced or services rendered. These are purchases of equipment such as production machinery, computers, laboratory equipment, vehicles, and construction. Capital-equipment purchases involve large amounts of money, and there is usually only one opportunity to do it right. In this chapter, we address this critical area of purchasing.

After studying the material in this chapter:

■ You will be able to assess and syndicate the risks involved in the purchase of capital equipment.

■ You will know how to execute a purchase order that considers the unique variables of capital equipment.

■ You will understand the various types of orders that can be used in these purchases

■ You will be able to protect your interests in capital-equipment purchases.

PRODUCTION VS. CAPITAL-EQUIPMENT PURCHASES

What makes capital-equipment purchases different from production or normal service purchases are the following factors:

1. They occur infrequently, and there may be no repeat buys.

2. There are large amounts of money involved. Some purchases may involve a special effort to raise funds for the acquisition (e.g., a stock issue, the use of special reserves, pledging the equipment as collateral for a loan, a mortgage).

3. There may be no specifications at the outset of the project. An individual, often the buying firm's president, facilities manager, or information systems manager, may be the only person who knows what is required. These people tend not to consult purchasing during the specification-development process and initial supplier conversations.

4. The large dollar value and the uniqueness of the requirements increase a buyer's perceived risk of error and likelihood of failure to satisfy the end-user.

5. There are more variables involved in a capital equipment purchase, such as rigging and installation, operator training, warranties, financing the purchase, service and spare parts, government regulations, options, and acceptance criteria.

TYPE OF CAPITAL EXPENDITURES
There are three categories of capital-equipment purchases:

1. Equipment that is standardized without major modifications and that is often bought through catalogues or advertisement brochures. Examples are fork-lift trucks, automobiles, shipping/receiving doors and docks, standard presses and computers, earth moving-equipment, auto-insertion machinery, and laboratory equipment.

2. Equipment that is significantly modified to the buyer's needs or produced wholly to a buyer's specifications. Examples are robots, specialized packaging machinery or product assembly equipment, and machines that perform a unique operation or process. In industries such as papermaking, textiles, and chemical industries, even standard equipment designs may have to be adapted to a buyer's particular needs.

3. Construction or renovation of a facility involves the creation of a product that is completely unique. This uniqueness includes architectural design, state and local statutes, the lay of the land, and the impact on the community and environment.

Each type of purchase and each industry has its own variations on the three categories. The greater the dollar value involved, the greater the need for the purchasing department's participation in the specification and acquisition process.

INITIAL STEPS
There should be a company policy and process that involves purchasing at the conceptual stages of all capital-equipment purchases or leasing. Purchasing must be in on the "ground floor."

For the purchasing department, the issue is not limited to the contributions it can make at the formative stages of the buying process. If the process is not conducted properly in the early stages, the purchasing department will be called in at a later stage to correct the problem.

If organizational support and company policy do not already exist, the purchasing manager will have to ask end-users and decision makers for whatever input they can offer in the supplier selection and purchase processes.

Step One

Once a decision has been made to investigate a major purchase, a "buy team" should be assembled. This team includes the using organization and finance, engineering, facilities, and purchasing departments. The composition of the team may vary somewhat, depending on the nature of the intended purchase.

The function of the team is to define the nature of the purchase, define approximate specifications, estimate cost and payback (expenditure justification), investigate possible sources of supply, assess the purchase's impact on other functions, and identify any government regulations that may be involved. Each member of the team has specific responsibilties. Purchasing's responsibility at this stage is to be a resource to the rest of the team. A buyer investigates potential sources of supply, provides source and technical data to the team, and is the commercial contact with potential suppliers. Purchasing's goals are to provide the team with outside resources, keep all options open, and ensure that no representations or commitments are made that will limit future choices.

Step Two

Once the project has been defined, justified, and approved, the purchasing department requests suppliers to meet with the team and refine the design to final specifications. The final specifications should be sufficiently broad that several potential suppliers have the ability to bid on and furnish the product.

If a specialized piece of equipment is to be purchased, the team must decide whether to develop detailed specifications or a work statement. If the buying company is absolutely confident of the detailed design of the unit, it may elect to provide all the detailed specifications to a supplier. If so, the supplier is responsible for conformance to the design and the buyer is responsible for the functionality of design and the product. However, if the buying company lacks the technical or design skills to design the unit, it may elect to produce a work statement. This is a specification that defines what outcome a machine is to produce, not the details of how it is to perform the specific function. Most companies are interested in having a function performed by a piece of equipment for a certain price; the detail of the machine's design may be inconsequential.

An example of a work statement is the following:

"The supplier will design, build and install a machine which will produce 1,000 gallons per hour of 2-percent-fat yogurt. The unit will permit the addition of solid or liquid flavorings prior to the production of finished yogurt. The unit will yield yogurt to the packaging line at a temperature of 2 degrees Centigrade. The unit will interface with XYZ company's Alpha packaging machine. The unit and its installation will comply with all federal, state, and local regulations concerning the treatment of effluence, food handling and processing, purity, safety, and licensing requirements."

Many design engineers pride themselves on their knowledge of the workings of machinery and assume an excessive amount of risk in the expression of their knowledge. Sometimes it is better not to have or express this knowledge but rather to focus on the function of the equipment.

The work statement shifts the responsibility for the design and function of equipment to the supplier. In the above example, it puts the burden of installation and regulatory compliance on the manufacturer of the equipment. The manufacturer is usually in a better position to know and conform to applicable regulations.

Step Three

Next, a request for proposal is prepared, including all specifications, architect's drawings, and work statements. This request should state all commercial factors to be included in the quote, such as terms of payment, F.O.B. point, rigging and installation, required delivery, performance guarantees, and preinstallation site assessment.

All questions and responses concerning the request for quote should be directed to purchasing. This will avoid any "back door" selling to the user community.

Step Four

Next, the team evaluates all of the quotations, visits potential suppliers to review their capability and capacity, selects a supplier, and makes a recommendation to the plant management staff. If approval is received to proceed, purchasing arranges for final negotiations to commence.

Step Five

In the negotiation session, the key members of the team are present, and the purchasing representative is the spokesperson for the team. Besides the price of the equipment, items the team should consider for negotiation include the following:

1. Terms of payment. Some suppliers will press for progress payments—paying sums of money at various stages of project completion. One of the buyer's objectives is to hold on to payment money for as long as possible. The buyer should also provide for the withholding of a significant amount of money (at least 10 to 15 percent) until the unit is installed and functioning properly. This will provide leverage for resolution of any problems after delivery.

2. Transportation, rigging, and installation. Who will bear the costs and risks of transporting the unit from the supplier's to the buyer's plant, moving the unit from the truck or flat-car and placing it on the buyer's floor, and ensuring that the unit is properly situated with adequate load-bearing capacity in the flooring, ventilation, plumbing, compressed air, and proximity to interfacing equipment?

3. Product acceptance. How will both the buyer and supplier determine that the supplier has performed all of the duties of the contract and should be paid in full? Using the example of the yogurt-producing equipment above, the buyer might require that the machine comply with the work statement and that it "produce the specified yogurt for 72 consecutive hours with three product change-overs (changing flavors three times) without machine failure or need for attendance." In minor or standard purchases, delivery may be all that is required for acceptance.

4. Warranties. For how long should the buyer expect the equipment to operate without intrinsic failure? Should there be a 30-day, 90-day, or 2-year warranty, or more? In the event of equipment failure within the warranty period, what are the obligations of the supplier in parts, service, and the timing of rendering those services? For building renovation or plant construction, certain portions of the product may be warranted for a long time. For example: "The roof is warranted not to leak for 25 years. If a water leak occurs due to natural wind and rain causes, the contractor will repair the leak and resultant damage within 48 hours of receipt of notice."

5. Spare parts. The aftermarket for spare parts and repairs is an area where high mark-ups in price are commonplace. The best time to negotiate the price and availability of spare parts is when the contract for the equipment is being negotiated. For example, a buyer may request that a complete set of replacement bearings be supplied with the machine at no added cost, or negotiate a 50 percent discount off list price for all machine maintenance, repair, and replacement parts for the next 10 years.

6. *Service contracts.* Computers, specialized equipment, ultrasonic diagnostic equipment, and sophisticated test equipment are examples of items requiring ongoing periodic maintenance that the buyer's company may not be able to render. Address the inclusion of a service contract during equipment-purchase negotiations.

7. *Licenses and permits.* Who will be responsible for obtaining building permits, waste-disposal permits, and licenses? Now is the time to determine these responsibilities. A buyer should try to have the supplier provide the required licenses and permits.

8. *Compliance with other laws.* The Occupational Safety and Health Act (OSHA) places many restrictions on the manufacturers and users of various types of equipment. Who will ensure that the equipment meets OSHA regulations? Areas of concern are "pinch points" (exposed moving parts that put clothing or body parts at risk), emission of harmful fumes or waste, radiation leaks, insulation and grounding, electrical parts, compliance of radio frequencies with Federal Communications Commission (FCC) regulations, and so forth. If the design of the equipment is the sole creation of the buying company, then the buyer's firm must ensure that their design complies with all applicable laws.

9. *Service manuals and diagrams.* The buyer may wish to negotiate for multiple sets of schematic electrical diagrams, blueprints, and service manuals instead of the number of copies that normally accompany the unit. This will save the buyer from having to purchase these documents at a later point. Replacement and additional documents can be expensive.

10. *Training.* Who will train the operators and maintenance personnel in the proper operation and maintenance of the equipment, and how will that training be conducted? Merely reading a training manual may not be sufficient preparation for the buyer's operating personnel. A specific number of supplier-provided, "in-house" training hours can be provided for in the purchase contract.

11. *Follow-on buys and options.* A buyer may want to use the negotiation session to specify purchase options for additional

or similar pieces of equipment. For example, after agreeing on a price for a current item of $100,000, the buyer may want the option to buy another unit within twelve months for $95,000. Using the yogurt-equipment example above, the buyer may wish to have the option to add a chiller (a $25,000 option) to the yogurt equipment within two years, and request that the quoted price remain in effect for the two-year period. Similarly, a hospital purchasing manager may want to guarantee the purchase of a second X-ray machine at the current fixed price.

12. Time and penalties. The installation date may be critical. If so, the buyer may wish to consider the inclusion of financial penalties in the event the supplier fails to deliver the unit on time. This is a common practice in negotiations of construction contracts.

13. Insurance. If the supplier is to perform any of the work on the buyer's premises, the buyer should insist on proof of insurance (e.g. workman's compensation, business-interruption insurance) to protect the buyer's employer in case of an accident. The buyer may also want to consider a "hold harmless" agreement, which protects the buying firm from liability associated with unlawful or careless actions of the supplier's employees.

Step Six

Next, the results of the negotiation session are reviewed with management and approval to place the purchase order is granted. A face-to-face meeting between the management staff and the buy team should precede major purchases. All of the negotiated agreements should be incorporated into the order, including the completion date, product acceptance, progress payments, and options.

Step Seven

The buy team is responsible for monitoring the supplier's progress, approving any progress payments, alerting management to problems, and determining the acceptability of the delivered unit. It may also provide for permits and licenses and for subcontract labor. The buy team should not disband until the unit is accepted, all operators and maintenance personnel have been adequately trained, and the supplier's invoice has been paid.

This team approach ensures that there is adequate communication between all concerned parties, and that all commercial and technical considerations have been addressed. Further, with input from all sources, there is likely to be greater use of standardization in equipment design. This helps to minimize spare-parts inventories and simplifies maintenance. Since there is always an element of risk involved in large purchases, the team approach ensures that the risks and rewards are spread out.

CHAPTER PERSPECTIVE

Capital-equipment purchases cannot be done effectively by one person or a small group. Rather, a team approach should be used. The team size and the degree of cooperation should be determined in light of the size of the purchase. In most cases, purchase of a large or sophisticated piece of equipment is best handled using formal, standardized work statements and acceptance criteria.

Purchasing Law

INTRODUCTION AND MAIN POINTS

Buyers must have an understanding of the laws that govern business relationships, especially those concerning contracts. The major areas covered in this chapter are contract law, the Uniform Commercial Code (the UCC), and agency law.

Buyers are reasonably well protected in normal business dealings, especially in the purchase of goods, but there are a host of legal issues of which the buyer should be aware. The intent of this chapter is not to eliminate the need for legal advice but to create an understanding of legal obligations and when to seek competent legal counsel.

After studying the material in this chapter:
- You will understand the basic rights and obligations of buyers and sellers.
- You will know the elements of a contract.
- You will have a fundamental command of contract law.
- You will have an understanding of antitrust laws.

INITIAL CONSIDERATIONS

All business dealings require that the element of "good faith" be present. This is the foundation of commercial law. Good faith may be defined as the honest application of earnest effort. Good faith is substantiated when an agreement is converted to a written form clearly stating the agreement between the parties to a commercial agreement or contract. Such an agreement must be sufficiently clear that a disinterested third party can read it and understand the nature of the agreement and the specific duties of the parties.

Contract Elements

There are five basic elements required for a contract to be legal:
1. An offer
2. An acceptance

3. Consideration
4. Legal purpose
5. Competent parties

There must be a valid offer to sell an item. The offer can take the form of a response to a request for quote, an unsolicited offer, or an advertisement for a product. There must be a clear intent to offer an item for sale. The offer must be more than a preliminary negotiation; it must be definite and complete and communicated by the offeror (seller) to the offeree (buyer).

Unless otherwise stated, an offer remains valid until it is accepted or terminated by one of the following conditions:
- revocation of the offer by the seller
- the terms of the offer
- lapse of a reasonable time
- rejection of the offer by the buyer or a counteroffer
- destruction of the goods offered
- subsequent illegality of the offer or the goods
- death or insanity of either party
- bankruptcy

Acceptance of the offer must be clear. The offer must be accepted by the party to whom the offer is made and with a clear intent to accept. The form of acceptance may vary depending on trade practices, the provisions of the Statute of Frauds, and the UCC. In some cases, written acceptance is unnecessary (e.g., an auction or an agreement to purchase items of low dollar value).

Silence, however, is not acceptance. Suppose, for example, the seller states, "If I don't hear from you within fifteen days, I will assume that you accept this offer and ship the goods." This statement and lack of response on the part of the buyer do not constitute acceptance or the existence of a contract.

An acceptance must reach the seller within a reasonable time and in a reasonable manner. If the offer contains the terms by which the buyer must accept, then the buyer must conform to these terms. For example, if the offer states "this offer is good for 30 days," and the buyer communicates the acceptance in 45 days, the offer has terminated and the acceptance is not valid.

Consideration is the requirement that something of value be tendered in exchange for the goods. In business, this is usually money, and this discussion is limited to the use of money. The law requires that value be exchanged, but the courts will not pass judgment on the adequacy of the price unless the amount is unconscionable and the court has reason to suspect fraud or deceit. There may be valid reasons for a seller to offer goods below market value, just as there are reasons why a buyer may be willing to pay a price higher than the value of the goods. Once a contract has been executed, neither of the parties can claim that the contract is invalid because the price was not adequate (unless fraud or misrepresentation is present).

The objective of the transaction must be legal. Illegal agreements include the following:

- contracts to commit crimes
- usury (illegal interest rates)
- contracts involving usury
- contracts against public policy (i.e., those that would jeopardize public safety, health, and general welfare)
- contracts in restraint of trade
- contracts that violate licensing requirements

A contract must be between competent parties. The law identifies those who are incompetent as:

- legal minors (the age of legality varies between states)
- insane persons
- intoxicated persons

Seldom is a buyer confronted with a legally incompetent party in the normal course of business.

STATUTE OF FRAUDS

The Statute of Frauds originated in a 1677 English statute called "A Statute for the Prevention of Frauds and Perjuries." Both the English and American versions require that certain contracts be in writing to be legally enforceable. These statutes were enacted to prevent people from claiming that a contract existed when it did not.

The Statute of Frauds requires that the following types of contracts be in writing to be enforceable:

1. Contracts for goods in excess of $500.00
2. Contracts for the purchase and sale of real estate
3. Contracts that have a duration greater than one year

The writing need not be elaborate. It must contain a description of the item being purchased, including the quantity, and be signed by the party to be charged. This is evidence that a contract exists. A familiar example is a credit-card purchase.

PAROLE EVIDENCE

The term "parole evidence" refers to verbal commitments. Such verbal evidence may not be used to modify or contradict a written contract. For example, if Bob has a contract with Able Company for the purchase of 100 wrenches at $7.00 each, Able Company cannot later claim in court that there was a verbal agreement to change the price from $7.00 each to $7.50 each. Verbal evidence, however, may be used to clarify an issue. In the above example, the court would entertain a verbal description of the wrenches if that was an issue.

UNIFORM COMMERCIAL CODE (UCC)

During the nineteenth century, each U.S. state and the federal government had its own set of laws regulating commerce. As transportation and communication improved, and interstate commerce increased during the twentieth century, this lack of uniformity created problems for buyers and sellers.

Suppose that you are a buyer in Massachusetts and place an order at a supplier in Ohio. Your order form contains terms and conditions on the back side. The supplier has different terms and conditions on the acknowledgment it sends to you in response to your order. In a dispute, the courts would have ruled that since the terms and conditions of the order and of the acknowledgment were not identical, there was not a meeting of the minds, and hence no contract. In order to conduct normal business, buyers would have had to be familiar with the laws of all the states in which they had suppliers.

In 1952, the Commissioners of Uniform State Laws produced a single body of interstate law, called the Uniform Commercial Code. This code has now been adopted by all fifty states. The UCC consists of ten articles: 1) General Provisions, 2) Sales, 3) Commercial Paper, 4) Bank Deposits, 5) Letters of Credit, 6) Bulk Transfers, 7) Document of Title, 8) Investment Securities, 9) Secured Transactions, and 10) Effective Date and Repealer. The majority of the laws affecting purchasing are in Article 2, Sales. This chapter will examine the most significant parts of Article 2.

The UCC makes a distinction between a merchant and a nonmerchant. A merchant is a party who normally engages in the business of buying and selling. A nonmerchant is one who buys infrequently, such as a consumer. A merchant is held to a standard of conduct and conformance to the law higher than that to which a consumer is held.

The UCC deals primarily with the purchase and sale of goods. Intangibles and services are not addressed.

Section 2-305: Open Price Terms

(1) The parties if they so intend can conclude a contract for sale even though the price is not settled. In such a case the price is a reasonable price at the time for delivery if

    (a) nothing is said about the price; or

    (b) the price is left to be agreed by the parties and they fail to agree; or

    (c) the price is to be fixed in terms of some agreed market or other standard as set or recorded by a third person or agency and it is not so set or recorded.

The Code does allow for the lack of immediate consideration (value not stated on the order) and imposes the "reasonable price" rule. Buyers must state the price on the purchase order or specify a means of establishing the price without resorting to someone else's interpretation of what is reasonable. For example: The manufacture of electrical contacts often utilizes precious metals. It is common practice for buyers and sellers to agree on a base price plus an adder for silver or gold. The price may be stated as "$234.00 per thousand, to be altered $1.56 per thousand for every $1.00 change in the price of gold above or below the Handy & Harmon posted gold price of $400.00 per ounce on date of shipment."

The application of "reasonableness" appears throughout the UCC. If the buyer does not state specific requirements on the purchase order and a dispute results, the court will attempt to discern what would have been reasonable under the circumstances in order to find an equitable remedy for the parties. For example, when buyers are in a hurry for an item, they may state the delivery requirement as "A.S.A.P." or "As Soon As Possible" rather than using a required date.

Suppose, for example, John needed delivery within a week of an item that has a lead time of eight weeks. The supplier promised to do its best to ship within three weeks. After two weeks, the supplier was struck by the local labor union. In the tenth week of the strike, with no resolution in sight, John canceled the order for nonperformance. Fourteen weeks after the order was entered, the supplier shipped the goods. John refused delivery because he had canceled the order. The supplier responded, "But I delivered the goods as soon as I possibly could. I could not have shipped them any sooner." The court ruled that under the circumstances the supplier shipped as soon as possible, and John was bound to accept the goods. John learned that buyers must place a specific date on a purchase order, even if it is an unreasonable request.

Section 2-312: Warranty of Title and Against Infringement; Buyer's Obligation Against Infringement

(1) Subject to subsection (2) there is in a contract for sale a warranty by the seller that

(a) *the title conveyed shall be good and its transfer rightful; and*

(b) *the goods shall be delivered free from any security interest or lien or encumbrance of which the buyer at the time of contracting has no knowledge.*

Section 2-314: Implied Warranty: Merchantability; Usage of Trade

(1) Unless excluded or modified (Section 2-316), a warranty that the goods shall be merchantable is implied in a contract for their sale if the seller is a merchant with respect to the goods of that kind.

(2) Goods to be merchantable must be at least as such as

(a) *pass without objection in the trade under the contract description; and*

(b) *in the case of fungible goods, are of fair average quality within the description; and*

(c) *are fit for the ordinary purposes for which the goods are used; and*

(d) *run, within the variations permitted by agreement, of even kind, quality and quantity within each unit and among all units involved; and*

(e) *are adequately contained, packaged, and labeled as the agreement may require; and*

(f) *Conform to the promises or affirmations of fact made on the container or label if any.*

(3) Unless excluded or modified (Section 2-316) other implied warranties may arise from the course of dealing or usage of trade.

Sections 2-312 and 2-314 of the UCC are the only warranties or requirements for quality imposed on the seller by the UCC. If the buyer wants a particular grade or quality of goods, there must be a statement to that effect on the face of the purchase order. The statement of quality may include parts per million, minimum variation, the use of process controls, Cpk, conformance to specification, or some other standard. A buyer should not assume that the seller is required to meet unstated quality requirements.

The two sections quoted above apply only to merchants in the trade. No warranty is involved or implied for purchase of goods or equipment from a merchant who is not normally in the business of selling those items.

Section 2-601: Buyer's Rights on Improper Delivery

Subject to the provisions of this Article on breach of installment contracts (Section 2-612) and unless otherwise agreed under the sections on contractual limitations of remedy (section 2-718 and 2-719), if the goods or the tender of delivery fail in any respect to conform to the contract, the buyer may

(a) reject the whole; or

(b) accept the whole; or

(c) accept any commercial unit or units and reject the rest.

If the goods do not meet the quality requirements of the contract or the definitions stated in Section 2-314, a buyer has the three above alternatives. The best course of action is for the buyer to work with the supplier prior to fulfillment of the contract or shipment to ensure that the goods conform to the stated quality requirements. Remedy after receipt of the goods and detection of a problem is too late and costly to both the buyer and seller.

Section 2-319: F.O.B. and F.A.S. Terms

(1) Unless otherwise agreed, the term F.O.B. (which means "free on board") at a named place, even though used only in connection with the stated price, is a delivery term under which

(a) when the term is F.O.B. the place of shipment, the seller must at that place ship the goods in the manner provided in this Article (Section 2-504) and bear the expense of putting them into the possession of the carrier; or

(b) when the term is F.O.B. the place of destination, the seller must at his own expense and risk transport the goods to that place and there tender delivery of them in the manner provided in this Article (Section 2-503).

This section of the UCC clearly defines the responsibility for the cost of transport and the point of title transfer. It is in the buyer's interest to obtain terms of F.O.B. delivered or buyer's place of business. In these two cases, the seller bears the responsibility for the security of the goods during transit.

ANTITRUST LAWS

The Sherman Antitrust Act of 1890 states, "Every contract, combination in the form of trust or otherwise, or conspiracy in restraint of trade or commerce among the several states or with foreign nations is declared to be illegal." In the American economic system, one belief is that the public is best served by free and complete competition in the marketplace, which ensures fair and equitable prices. To a buyer, however, four areas of antitrust behavior are of concern: 1) price fixing, 2) boycotts, 3) reciprocity and 4) The Robinson-Patman Act.

Price Fixing

Price fixing is normally confined to sellers. However, there are buyers who may occasionally band together to control the price they are willing to pay for certain commodities. This practice has not been uncommon in the purchase of foodstuffs and certain commodities where buyers had a command of the market by virtue of their combined strength of purchase and, therefore, strongly influenced or controlled selling prices. Such control of pricing leads to violation of the antitrust laws.

Boycotts

Similarly, boycotts have historically involved sellers. Buyers, however, are subject to violations under the law. For example, agreements between a seller and a buyer that the seller will not sell to the buyer's competitor is a per se violation of the antitrust laws. As a rule, any agreement between two companies to refrain from purchasing from (or selling to) a third company is a violation of the antitrust laws.

Reciprocity

Reciprocity is conditioning a purchase on a sale—if you buy from me, I will buy from you. On the face of it, this practice is a form of restraint of trade. There are three types of reciprocity, and they have differing degrees of legal implications. The three types are: 1) coercive, 2) mutual agreement, and 3) passive participation.

Coercive reciprocity occurs when there is an absolute precondition of purchase based on a sale. There may be the use of threat or coercion in the position. This is an unfair method of competition, is in violation of Section 5 of the Federal Trade Commission Act, and is therefore illegal. A buyer faced with such coercive pressure should seek the assistance of management or the legal staff.

Mutual agreement involves the acceptance by a buyer and a seller that both companies are served if they buy and sell to each other. There is no threat, no coercion, and no intent to monopolize a market. Legally, this is a gray area, because appearances may indicate a breach of the law where none was intended. It is best to avoid any implication of violation of the Act or attempt to injure the competitive environment. A buyer dealing with a supplier who is also a customer should exercise caution.

Passive participation is also known as mutual patronage. Incidental purchase and sale between buyers and sellers is common and harmless. For example, General Motors buys steel from USX, and USX may buy or lease company cars from GM. The transactions are independent and unrelated. There is no intent to monopolize; nor is there a conditioning of the purchase upon sales of one to the other. This type of reciprocal purchase is both legal and common.

Robinson-Patman Act

Of all antitrust laws, this 1936 amendment to the Clayton Act has created the most difficulty for buyers and sellers. Originally, R-P was intended to eliminate discriminatory and predatory pricing practices to customers who are competitors in the same market. For example, if USX were to sell a certain type of sheet steel at $.25 per pound to General Motors and $.45 to Ford Motors for the production of cars, Ford would be placed at a competitive disadvantage in the market. The Act reads as follows:

2. (a) That it shall be unlawful for any person engaged in commerce, in the course of such commerce, either directly or indirectly, to discriminate in price between different purchasers of commodities of like grade and quantity, . . . and where the effect of such discrimination may be substantially to lessen competition or to create a monopoly in the line of commerce, or to injure, destroy, or prevent competition with any person who grants or knowingly receives the benefits from such discrimination, or with customers of either of them: Provided that nothing herein contained shall prevent differentials

BARRON'S BUSINESS LIBRARY

which make only due allowances for differences in the cost of manufacture, sale, or delivery resulting from the differing methods or quantities in which commodities are to such purchasers sold or delivered; . . .

> *(f) That it shall be unlawful for any person engaged in commerce, knowingly to induce or receive a discrimination in price which is prohibited by this section.*

The key points of the Act are the following:

1. Discrimination must occur between purchasers who are buying a similar grade or quality. Usually this applies to commodities.

2. The transactions must have the effect of lessening competition or creating a monopoly within an industry. Small producers and consumers are not affected by the Act.

3. Differences in price are allowed where those differences can be substantiated by extenuating circumstances.

A seller may offer differing prices under two conditions: 1) the price is cost-justified, or 2) to meet competition. Using the previous example, USX could justify a lower price to GM if it sells GM 200 tons of sheet steel and only 10 tons to Ford. Further, if USX were to sell steel at different prices to Ford for cars and to Carrier for air conditioners, Robinson-Patman is not violated, because Ford and Carrier are in different industries with different customers and competition is not an issue between them.

The "meet competition" condition presents a problem to buyers. Many companies have a policy that buyers not reveal competitive prices to the bidders. How, then, can a seller claim that the price is lowered to meet competition? Unfortunately, many buyers try to provide price guidance to sellers without revealing the actual quoted price. For example: "You're ten percent high" or "You're not even close." These statements may become intentionally misleading in order for the buyer to obtain better pricing, which is a violation of Section 2(f). The seller cannot be certain without access to the competitive information.

In the case of *Great Atlantic & Pacific Tea Co. (A & P) vs. The Federal Trade Commission (FTC)*, the A & P buyer told Borden that its bid to supply milk was not competitive. The buyer said: "You are not even in the ball park." Borden requoted with a second price which they thought met competition but which was, in fact, substantially below competition. The buyer accepted the second price without comment and bought the milk from Borden. The buyer was ruled to be in violation of Section 2(f) of the Robinson-Patman Act and faced a stiff legal judgment against him personally.

In another case, a buyer for Kroger foods lied to Beatrice Food company concerning competitive pricing, and Beatrice Foods lowered its price to "meet competition." This buyer was also convicted after the issue came to court.

In the first case, the buyer said nothing. He was doing what he thought a good buyer should do—get lower prices. Is silence the same as lying to a supplier? According to the law, if it has the effect of misleading a supplier, yes.

AGENCY

The law of agency provides that when a principal (the company) appoints an agent to act on its behalf, and the agent performs the action, the principal (the company) is bound by those actions—not the agent. In purchasing, this means that when a buyer signs his or her name to a purchase order, the company is obligated for the order—not the buyer who signed it.

Before the twentieth century, the original owners of a company usually did not need to delegate many functions in order to conduct business. As owners or officers, they had the power to commit the organization to binding contracts. However, as businesses grew, owners did not have the time or the resources to conduct all of the company's business personally. Purchasing and sales became two of the agents empowered to make commitments on behalf of the company.

Purchasing and Sales Agencies

There are many different kinds of agency and varying levels of authority delegated to agents. A buyer, purchasing agent, or purchasing manager has the authority to bind the company in contracts for goods and services to be used by the company. A buyer's agency extends to the limit of his or her signature authority. Salespeople, on the other hand, have the authority only to solicit business. Salespeople are known as "special" agents. Unless there is a separate agreement between a salesperson and his or her principal, salespeople cannot bind their companies to contracts. They also cannot change or alter existing agreements or quotations.

An illustration of the importance of the distinction is one in which a zealous salesperson is sitting with a buyer inquiring about the status of a quote. The buyer notices that the quote is valid for 30 days and informs the seller that the purchase will not be made for 45 days. The seller, wanting to close the deal, says: "That's no problem, I'll just change it to 45 days and initial it." Such a change by the salesperson is not binding on his or her company. The quote may or may not be honored by the parent company when the order is actually placed. In order to be sure of its validity, the buyer should request that the quote be re-submitted by an authorized agent of the company.

"Unofficial" Buyers

In many companies, people outside the purchasing organization commit the company to purchases. For example, engineers or maintenance people call suppliers and request that parts be delivered or services rendered. If this is a recurring practice, and the company has not objected in the past, then the company is prevented from claiming that these people did not have the authority to bind them to a purchase. This legal principle is known as "apparent authority." If it appears to people outside the company that the person placing an order has the authority to do so, the company cannot later claim that person did not have such authority.

In order to effectively combat such unauthorized transactions, the buying company should take action each time a violation occurs. The most effective course of action is to take corrective action with the employee who made the purchase, then notify the supplier that only purchases made by specifically authorized people will be binding, and that anything else should not be accepted.

Ultra Vires Acts

Ultra vires is a Latin term that means "beyond the powers." It is applied to any action that is beyond the scope of a buyer's agency. If a buyer acts beyond the scope of his or her authority, that buyer is responsible to the company for exceeding the bounds of the agency agreement. For example, if a buyer purchases a new car for personal use and uses his or her position with the company to make such a purchase, the buyer is liable to the company for payment.

CHAPTER PERSPECTIVE

Legal issues in business are primarily a matter of common sense and integrity. Laws exist to facilitate commerce and encourage competition and free enterprise. This brief summary is intended to provide a glimpse of some of the key factors in the UCC and contract law that may be experienced in purchasing activities. There are volumes written on each of the subject headings addressed in this chapter. The reader is referred to the many texts on the subject and encouraged to seek competent legal advice when a major issue arises.

Contracts

INTRODUCTION AND MAIN POINTS

A contract is an expression of a need and an agreement to fulfill it. It includes the commercial terms of purchase, legal considerations, and specifications for the purchased goods. Today, the conduct of business is increasingly complex, and contracts may reflect that complexity. Writing a contract that accurately reflects the company's needs requires that buyers fully understand the long-term requirements for the material, equipment, or services and that they develop the ability to accurately express those needs.

After studying the material in this chapter, you will:

■ Understand what elements should appear in a contract.
■ Be able to create the types of contracts required for different types of purchases.
■ Be able to clearly state your needs, protect your company's interests, and avoid unpleasant contractual difficulties.

TYPES OF CONTRACTS

There are many different type of contracts. Which contract type may be useful for a given purchase depends on the item to be purchased.

After the legal content of the agreement has been satisfied, buyers are free to include in a contract anything on which the two parties agree. Therefore, contract writing is one of the most creative forms of business and business relationships. Contracts need not merely state what is to be purchased but can and should include the nature of the relationship between buyer and seller, product or service quality, and current and future pricing.

This chapter addresses discrete purchase orders, blanket orders, systems contracts, requirements contracts, service contracts, and letters of intent.

Discrete Purchase Orders

A purchase order is a contract. The most common form of purchase order is the single-item order with one or more deliveries (see Figure 16-1). These orders are appropriate for limited needs such as maintenance, repair and operating supplies, production goods of a limited quantity (job shop environment), and projects of limited duration. They are not appropriate for long-term, high-volume materials, service contracts, or purchases of capital equipment.

In this chapter we will consider what information should appear on the face of the purchase order and assume that the back of the order contain the usual and attorney-approved fine print or "boiler plate."

Blanket Orders

A blanket order is a purchase order that covers a large quantity over a period of time. It is very much like a parking meter—the order contains a fixed quantity and this quantity is released over time. When the quantity on the order has been consumed, the order expires.

Blanket orders are useful when the quantity of the purchase is reasonably assured; the buyer's commitment yields lower prices than if a series of discrete orders were used. The longer time frame, however, creates the risk of possible future alteration in the part or the volume. If the order is canceled, or the purchased part is significantly altered, there may be a "charge-back" for the difference in quantity or design change actually shipped and received. This may come as an unpleasant surprise to the buyer's employer. The buyer must weigh the benefits of lower cost against the risks of the costs of changes to a blanket order.

A typical blanket order is shown in Figure 16-2. This order is for a quantity of parts to be taken over time. The quantity is firm at 10,000, while the time period is not defined.

1. The buyer will send individual written releases as parts are required and will allow four (4) weeks for delivery from the date of each release.

2. The supplier will maintain sufficient inventories of components and material to assure a four (4)-week delivery on any release.

3. The buyer will send forecasts of demand each month. Shipments, however, will be made only upon the receipt of a "release" form.

| PURCHASE ORDER | | | | # PO 7832 **IMPORTANT!** This PO # to be shown on all invoicing and shipping documents. | |

To: Page Hill Corporation
21 Uphill Road
Anytown, PA 00000

Ship:

date 3/4/92	reg # A1234	delivery see below	ship via Best Way	**F.O.B.** Destination Prepaid	terms Net 30
item #	**quantity**	**unit**	**description**	**unit price**	**amount**
1	10	ea	Part number BR 12345 spiral bearing (specification attached) Delivery: 5 to arrive on April 1, 1992 5 to arrive on July 1, 1992	$63.10	$631.00
			Purchasing Manager		

| **Mail invoices in triplicate to:** Our Company 123 45th Street Anycity, AZ 12345-6789 | This order subject to conditions on face and reverse thereof. No changes may be made without written permission of purchasing manager. |

FIG 16-1. *A purchase order.*

PURCHASE ORDER	**# B 1324** **Blanket Order** **IMPORTANT!** This PO # to be shown on all invoicing and shipping documents.

To: Page Hill Corporation
21 Uphill Road
Anytown, PA 00000

Ship:

date 3/4/92	reg # B44325	delivery see below	ship via Best Way	F.O.B. Destination Prepaid	terms Net 30

item #	quantity	unit	description	unit price	amount
1	10,000	ea	Part number P42367-3 sheet metal part (specification attached) print rev. 4 This is a blanket order. See the attached for a continuation of this order.	$2.15	$21,500

Purchasing Manager

Mail invoices in triplicate to: Our Company 123 45th Street Anycity, AZ 12345-6789	This order subject to conditions on face and reverse thereof. No changes may be made without written permission of purchasing manager.

FIG 16-2. *A blanket order.*

4. The buyer has flexibility of releases as follows:

4 weeks—+/− 30% change in forecast demand

8 weeks—+/− 60% change in forecast demand

10 weeks—+/− 100% change in forecast demand.

5. Should the buyer no longer require parts (cancel order), the buyer will assume responsibility for the raw material and work in process at the supplier:

a. Actual raw material not to exceed 1,000 pieces.

b. Actual work in process not to exceed 500 pieces.

6. Should the buyer cancel this order prior to the shipment and the receipt of 10,000 pieces, the price for those parts shipped and received will be adjusted as follows:

parts shipped	price
1000	$3.05
2500	$2.76
5000	$2.60
7500	$2.37

After notification of the buyer's intent to cancel the order, the supplier will submit an invoice for the price difference between $2.15 each and the price which corresponds to the actual quantity shipped.

7. Should the buyer's engineering department or customer change the part specification during the term of this order and such change has the same impact as an order cancellation (eg. change of material), the supplier will be compensated in the same manner as item #6 of this order.

8. This order may be extended beyond the quantity of 10,000 pieces upon mutual agreement of the parties and an amendment to this order.

9. Quality—Supplier will provide proof with each shipment that the parts are all uniform and specification compliant. The supplier will ship copies of the process control charts used during the manufacturing process. If this order exceeds one year in duration, the supplier will furnish evidence that all parts meet Cp2 (the manufacturing process uses only one half of the specification tolerance on each of nine critical dimensions) during the second year of this order.

10. This order will expire upon the shipment of 10,000 pieces unless extended as provided for in paragraph 8.

Requirements Contracts

A requirements contract is one in which the buyer commits to purchase material requirements, or some fixed portion thereof, from one supplier. The order quantity is based on an estimate of use.

Requirements contracts have been around since the late 1800s and were written into the Uniform Commercial Code (Section 2-306) in the 1930s. This form of contract was not popular in the first half of the twentieth century, due to the wording of the relevant UCC section. It required that "no quantity unreasonably disproportionate to any stated estimate or otherwise comparable prior output or requirements may be tendered or demanded." This was interpreted to mean that estimates of future product use had to be accurate or at least in line with past consumption. Given this requirement of the UCC, buyers tended not to use this type of contract, favoring the blanket purchase order in its place.

During the early 1960s, an Ohio court considered a case in which the amount of goods (natural gas) shipped was far less than the estimates in the requirements contract. The buyer had modified the facility that consumed the gas and no longer required the large amount of gas estimated in the contract. The court ruled that as long as the buyer used "good faith" (a requirement in 2-306), the buyer was free to use business judgment and discretion in the conduct of his business or improving his plant.

This ruling changed the use of requirements contracts in business. Buyers were free to use the contract as it was originally intended. Future product requirements cannot be accurately forecasted. There is no such thing as an accurate forecast. If a forecast were accurate, it would not be a forecast.

This type of contract assists in forging new supplier partnerships, because it assures the supplier of the business so long as the buyer has the business, or at least to the terms stated in the contract. The supplier, then, has a vested interest in the success of the buyer's product and benefits in direct proportion to the buyer's success.

One requirement of the contract under UCC 2-306 that gives large purchasing organizations a problem is that which states that the buyer must exercise "good faith." Good faith is not a problem in normal business dealings, but good faith with regard to administering the contract can create a problem. For example, if a purchasing organization places a requirements contract with supplier X for 100 percent of its requirements, and a buyer places an order with another supplier, the buying organization has not exercised "good faith." During the oil embargo of the 1970s, one buyer placed several 100 percent requirements contracts with several fuel suppliers to assure that the firm would not run out of fuel. The firm did not run out, but the suppliers became aware that they were not receiving 100 percent of the business based on estimated consumption. Several suppliers sued the buyer, because the buyer had not exercised good faith.

A requirements contract need not be for the full amount of goods or services. A buyer may split the business among any number of suppliers so long as this split is clearly indicated in the contract and the total does not exceed 100 percent of the total requirement. A buyer may place 10 percent the total use with supplier A, 30 percent with supplier B, and 60 percent with supplier C. Those estimates of use are just that, estimates. So long as the buyer is faithful to the contract, the contract works. Here is an example of a requirements contract:

REQUIREMENTS CONTRACT
This is a requirements contract for 100 percent of our estimated needs for the following:

Part No.	1992	1993	1994	1995	1992 price
A 3759	5000	6000	7000	7500	$4.26 ea
A 5839	2000	1500	3500	4000	$3.12 ea
B 9645	2000	4000	2500	1500	$7.50 ea
C 7463	9000	10000	11000	12000	$4.75 ea

Quantity. The quantities are estimates and will vary as the demand for our product varies. Buyer will provide supplier with a monthly forecast of projected demand.

Prices. Prices stated are fixed for the year 1992. Should supplier's costs exceed those originally quoted in subsequent years, supplier will furnish buyer with documentation of cost increases. The 1992 prices shall remain in effect until such time as supplier's costs increase or decrease and evidence of cost changes have been furnished to the buyer.

Quality. a. As a requirement of this contract, supplier is required to institute statistical process controls by July 1, 1992 on those processes which provide the parts ordered. Control charts are to be shipped with each lot of goods for the first six shipments after the July 1, 1992 date. It is agreed between buyer and seller that the quality requirements for the subsequent years of this agreement are:

1993	1994	1995
200 PPM	75 PPM	15 PPM

The buyer will furnish assistance to the supplier in the form of three four-hour courses in statistical process control at the supplier's place of business to start the quality training process. Further training will be at the supplier's expense.

Forecasts and Releases. Buyer will furnish the supplier with a monthly forecast of demand by part number. Each monthly forecast will contain four weeks of firm scheduled deliveries plus eleven months of forecast.

Example: June 1 forecast—A3759

Firm releases:

June 7	June 14	June 21	June 28
100	125	250	110

Forecast:

July	Aug.	Sept.	Oct.	Nov.	Dec.	Jan.	Feb.	Mar.	Apr.	May
200	400	520	375	310	300	430	450	400	500	600

Receipt of the monthly forecast is the supplier's authorization to ship the four weeks quantities of firm shipments on the dates indicated.

Packaging. Supplier will ship in standardized containers, each container holding 25 pieces.

Shipping. (If the supplier is located within a 50-mile radius of the buyer's plant.) Supplier will deliver in their own vehicles to the buyer's receiving dock. The buyer may change delivery instructions to "deliver to the point of use on the manufacturing floor" during the term of this contract without incurring added part or transportation costs.

TERMS

F.O.B. Delivered   2%-10 days/net 30 days Signed:

_____   _____   _____

Buyer   Seller   Date

CREATIVE TERMS

Since a contract can include any legal point that two parties agree on, the buyer may want to consider such items as:

1. Delivery methods and F.O.B. point.
2. Cash discounting of invoices for prompt payment.
3. Quality requirements such as parts per million (PPM), parts per billion (PPB), Cp, Cpk, or other measures appropriate for the purchased item.
4. Supplier-held inventories of raw material and/or finished goods.

5. Firm prices for extended periods of time or price increases linked to actual increases in costs. Using the example above, the supplier would have to document its original costs in its quotation and provide evidence that costs have risen over the intervening time.
6. Regular joint product specification reviews between the buyer's and supplier's engineering personnel to reduce costs and price.
7. The use of recyclable shipping containers.
8. Prices that reduce over time due to learning or experience curves.
9. Service levels such as technical product support and lead time reductions.

These are just a few of the possible terms to consider. Individual circumstances offer numerous ways of increasing value for both parties.

SYSTEMS CONTRACTING

Systems contracting was first developed and published by Ernest L. Anderson, Jr., in 1957. His intent was to reduce the paperwork and administrative labor involved in the purchase of maintenance, repair, and operating supplies (MRO). These orders are usually small in dollar value and large in number. Normally, they require the same amount of administrative time and attention as the large material purchases. In a manufacturing environment, MRO orders can account for 80 percent of the volume of paperwork and administrative time but only 20 percent of the dollars of expenditure. In service industries such as insurance, banking, and health care, MRO purchases may be 100 percent of purchasing's activity.

These low-value orders should not consume the same amount of time and attention as major purchases. Systems contracting is a means of automating these low-value, repetitive purchases. "In simplest terms the systems contract is a highly refined arrangement or agreement between the purchaser and the supplier. The objective of this agreement is fourfold: (a) elimination of paperwork, (b) reduction or elimination of inventory, (c) improved flow of material, and (d) the realization of the best possible price for the goods involved.[1]

The process begins with an examination of all MRO items: their use, family grouping, location of users or requisitioners, the amount of thought or intelligence required for their purchase, and their specifications. Next, these repetitive buys are grouped by families (e.g., office, mill, electrical, and pipe-fitting supplies are common groupings).

1. Suppliers are requested to quote on families of parts or commodities.

2. A supplier is selected for each family.

3. Purchasing creates an agreement that encompasses all of the family items.

4. The user is tied closely to the suppliers, and the release system involves only the user and the supplier. The user calls or sends a release to the supplier, and the supplier delivers the goods to the user. The user sends a copy of the receipt to the company's accounts payable department for payment.

5. Purchasing monitors the process but does not participate in the daily administrative activities.

The advantages of this approach are the following:

1. Parts are grouped and placed with a single source for the best pricing.

Purchasing performs the decision-making processes, including pricing and source selection, at the initial stage and the user performs the release process with minimum paperwork.

3. The user knows the purchased parts better than anyone else, and this process puts the user and the supplier in direct contact. This direct contact greatly reduces the time required to perform the administrative functions, allowing lower inventories and safety stocks. Issues are resolved directly between the user and the supplier without the intervention of non–value-added intermediates.

Here is an example of a systems contract:

This is a systems contract between Buyer and Seller for 810 office supply items as listed on the attached pages (Attachment 1). Provisions:

1. Prices will remain in effect until such time as they may be re-negotiated between the supplier and the buyer.

2. This contract will remain in effect until such time as it is terminated by either party on 60 days notice to the other party.

3. Consolidated billing—The supplier will submit invoices once a month for all goods delivered during that month. All invoiced prices must agree with the requisition prices.

4. Release and delivery process:

   a. The office supplies clerk will notify the supplier by telephone that a three-part requisition form which contains this systems contract number, the release number, item and price (from supplier's quote).

b. The supplier will deliver the goods to the supplies clerk. The clerk receives a copy of the packing slip, attaches it to a copy of the requistion, and forwards them to accounts payable. The delivery person is given a copy of the release for their records and as proof of delivery.

c. Any differences in type, quantity, brand, or quality are to be resolved on the spot between the clerk and the delivery person.

d. There shall be no partial shipments or back orders.

Systems contracts are much like requirements contracts in that no quantities are specified. Since the primary force behind a systems contract is the reduction of effort and paper, it tends to draw the user and the supplier closer together. Interests merge and mutual dependencies develop, to the benefit of both user and supplier.

Systems contracts were designed for and have been used in the MRO or indirect materials area. They are equally applicable for direct material. If requirements and systems contracts were merged for direct material needs, there would be significant savings in the price of goods, fewer suppliers, delivery to point of use, consolidated billing, lower inventories, direct user/producer contacts, and far less time spent in administering orders.

SERVICE CONTRACTS

Service contracts are different from contracts for the purchase of goods. Individual talents may be involved, and the services or the result of services may be evaluated in subjective terms. The buyer of services must consider the following elements when constructing a contract:

1. Are the skills of a particular individual required to perform this service? These individuals include consulting services, an architect, advertising personnel, legal services, and mediation services, to mention a few. If a particular skill is required, the contract should depend on the services of that individual.

2. The results of the service should be quantifiable. The completion date should be clearly defined, and the definition of the "finished product" should be stated in the contract. It may take the form of a blueprint, a specific remedy for a current situation, a new product, or an advertising campaign containing certain elements.

3. If work is to be performed on the buyer's premises, provisions should be made for adequate insurance coverage. There should be a requirement for workman's compensation, personal

injury liability, and business-interruption insurance, as appropriate to the task. The type of insurance required will vary depending on the type of risk involved. If the work involves exposure to confidential information, contractors should be required to sign a "nondisclosure agreement" binding them not to disclose the nature or content of the work they are performing or the information they have access to.

4. If some of the work is to be performed off site, the buyer may require periodic progress reports in order to monitor the progress toward completion and to ensure that the contractor is progressing in the desired direction.

5. The buyer may wish to limit the amount of work the contractor may subcontract to others. If the objective is to utilize the skills of a specific individual or organization, the buyer may not want that individual to accept the contract only to have the work performed by others.

6. The buyer should receive from the contractor a clear definition of the work to be performed and the resulting product prior to awarding the contract. This will reduce the possiblity of contracting for a service that will not satisfy the end need. If, for example, the company wants an advertising campaign designed to sell a new line of footwear, it will not serve the buyer or the company if the contract merely states that a campaign is to be developed that is acceptable to the company's sales manager or president. In this case the ad agency may develop a campaign only to find that it is not acceptable to the company. The complete proposal should be submitted with the quotation, and the resulting contract is merely a refinement and implementation of the proposed concept.

In a service contract, the people's efforts are the product, and defining the product can be extremely difficult. The service contract should put as much in writing as possible at the outset of the effort in order to avoid misunderstanding and an unsatisfactory product.

LETTERS OF INTENT

Letters of intent are used to reserve a supplier's capacity and to establish a position in a supplier's queue when long lead-time purchases are anticipated. The lead time for capital-equipment purchases can be from several months to several years. While the buyer's company is contemplating the placement of an order, it may wish to minimize the delivery time. Therefore, the buyer may express an intent to purchase without committing to an actual purchase order.

A problem arises in differentiating between intent and commitment. If intent is improperly worded, it can be interpreted in fact and in law as a binding contract to purchase. Further, if the letter of intent contains too much information, it may preclude subsequent negotiation for price, accessories, installation, transportation, training, delivery, or other collateral items. A salesperson in receipt of a letter of intent may consider the order as good as closed and see no reason to negotiate collateral items in the future. A carefully worded letter of intent can avoid these problems.

For example: It is the intent of the ABC Company (buyer) to enter into negotiations with the XYZ Company (seller) for the future possible purchase of one model 4A Packaging Machine. The seller will reserve a machine in its production schedule in the event a purchase results. The seller agrees that a Model 4A will be shipped during the month of April 1993, provided an order is placed on or before September 1, 1992. Collateral issues, including machine configuration, price, and terms, will be resolved prior to the placing of any order should an order result.

CHAPTER PERSPECTIVE

A contract can be simple or complex, but it should contain all of the understandings between the two parties. Long-term contracts exist not only to purchase goods and services, but also to forge a relationship between the buyer and the seller. Value can be created by the terms of the contract and the manner of performance. Price and delivery will be greatly improved by the business relationship the contract cements. The economic interests of the parties will drive the relationship.

REFERENCES

[1]Ernest L. Anderson, Jr., and James P. Morgan. *The Systems Purchasing Handbook.* (Boston: Systems Purchasing, 1985), p. 13.

Financial Analysis

INTRODUCTION AND MAIN POINTS

The concepts and skills of financial analysis are critical to the purchasing function. Purchasing is responsible for obtaining goods and services as required and at the lowest total cost. What is the "lowest total cost"? This chapter will explore several key concepts of financial analysis in purchasing, including total cost, analysis of quoted prices, the time value of money, the cost of administration, the cost of quality, and the financial strength of suppliers.

After studying the material in this chapter, you will be able to:

■ calculate the total cost of purchases.

■ analyze and compare quotations.

■ understand the time value of money and know when it is in your interest to negotiate cash discounts.

■ calculate the cost of administrative practices.

■ calculate the cost of quality.

■ assess the financial strength of suppliers.

TOTAL COST

The total cost of a purchase is the price paid plus all other costs associated with the purchase. Identification of "all other costs" is often not easy or obvious. The associated costs also change from purchase to purchase, so there is no simple formula that will fit all cases. The starting point is the analysis of what factors (including price) are significant to each purchase. Once these have been identified, they can be costed to arrive at a total cost. Associated costs include transportation, administrative costs, the costs associated with nonquality goods, inventory, and time.

THE COST OF ADMINISTRATION

Calculation of the cost of administration can benefit the purchasing function in two ways: it can provide a basis for comparison of one business process to another, and it can be used to compare ease of doing business among suppliers.

Within the purchasing function, calculating the cost of administrative functions can be a primary leverage point for justifying process simplification. The costs of purchase orders, changes to purchase orders, return of defective materials, administration of systems contracts, and other processes can all be calculated and compared. This cost comparison can be used to justify changes to the processes.

Historically, however, there has been a glaring misuse of this information. When the costs of administrative transactions are used to justify the number of people, damage to the business may result. The purpose of costing transactions is to compare them and move toward the most cost-effective way to perform a certain task. The more cost-effective methods of doing business are also the quickest, because there is a dollar value to people's time. When simplification of the process is used to eliminate people, the benefits from what those people should have been doing instead are lost. For example, many buyers say that they do not have time to do the analysis and negotiations required to establish better business arrangements with suppliers because they are buried in paperwork. If new methods of doing the paperwork cut the time in half, buyers will have the time to do this other work, and the rate of business improvement will accelerate. If cutting the transaction times in half is viewed as an opportunity to cut the staff in half, then no further business improvements will be possible.

The real benefit of costing transactions is to compare them and look for simpler ways. For example, if a purchase order costs $250.00, and a systems-contract release costs $85.00, then there is justification for using more systems contracts.

To calculate the cost of administration, two steps are necessary: the first is to define the process in exact detail, including the time required to perform each step and the person who does that step; the second is to attach a dollar value to each step and then calculate a total. Definition of the process and who is involved varies with each company's particular methods. The process of defining the steps in the transaction is often enlightening. Steps that are unnecessary will begin to become visible.

Assignment of costs to each step is next. The cost of tangible goods (such as forms) can be determined from their purchase price. The cost of people's time can be determined as follows:

1. Determine who does the step (by position title).
2. Determine the average salary for that position.
3. Translate the average salary into cost per minute:

$$\frac{\text{Annual salary } \$}{\text{Standard work hours per year}} = \frac{\text{Cost}}{\text{Hour}}$$

$$\frac{\text{Cost / Hour}}{60 \text{ minutes/hour}} = \frac{\text{Cost}}{\text{Minute}}$$

For example, the cost per minute of a buyer's time whose average salary is $35,000 is $0.38. The cost per minute of a data-entry clerk whose average salary is $25,000 is $0.20.

4. Multiply the cost per minute of an individual's time by the time (in minutes) that each transaction step consumes.
5. Add the salary costs for each of the steps; this gives the total labor cost of the transaction.

Calculation of intangible costs, such as computer time and memory storage space, can be more difficult. Asking the information systems management function may yield the information required. If this function is unable to provide the information, suppliers of computer systems or businesses that provide time-sharing computer services can be asked.

Be certain to include *all* costs involved with the process under study. Although costing the transaction may require some time and effort to obtain accurate numbers, it need only be done once. The data remains valid until either the process changes or costs change significantly.

As a case study, review the following data for the cost of a simple purchase order that requires no formal request for quote process in a system with an average amount of bureaucracy:

Process	Cost
1. Requisitioner fills out form.	6 min @ .40 = 2.40
Obtains approval signature.	15 min @ .40 = 4.00
Delivers requisition to purch.	3 min @ .40 = 1.20
2. Punch clerk logs/date stamps and reviews requisition for completeness.	4 min @ .20 = 0.80
Gives requisition to appropriate buyer.	
3. Buyer chooses suppliers, checks Approved Supplier list, adds new supplier if necessary. Checks all appropriate computer system files (supplier codes, inventory locations, item data, specs, etc.)	15 min @ .38 = 5.70 computer system time @ 7.32 / min = 36.60

4. Buyer calls suppliers for price and delivery information. Waits for a callback from some suppliers, places order, explains terms and conditions to supplier, selects transportation method, adds P.O. to P.O. log book,

15 min @ .38 = 5.70
telephone calls = 2.30

5. Data entry clerk enters P.O. into computer system. Picks up printed P.O.'s, sorts by buyer, delivers to buyers to check over and sign.

10 min @ .20 = 2.00
system time = 73.20
(10 min @ 7.32)
P.O. form = .24
5 min @ .20 = 1.00

6. Buyer proofreads P.O. and signs.

3 min @ .38 = 1.14

7. Buyer takes P.O. to higher signature authority, gets approval cosignature.

15 min @ .38 = 5.70

8. Purchasing clerk splits P.O. form, mails copy to supplier, attaches requisition, and files copy in P.O. files, delivers copy to requisitioner and accounts payable department.

15 min @ .20 = 3.00
envelope + stamp = .30

9. Buyer receives acknowledgment, reviews for signature and changes

1 min @ .38 = .38

10. Clerk attaches acknowledgment to P.O. in files and refiles.

3 min © .20 = .60

11. Cost of file space/storage for 7 years

@ .08/pg = .24

Subtotal of costs to the purchasing function = $146.50. If straight salary is burdened with overhead costs, as it is in many companies, then the cost will increase by 50%–100%. A mean burden rate of 75 percent increases purchasing function costs to $171.74.

12. Receive material at docks, unload, sign manifest. Open box and check contents, log receipt into dock log, sort containers for delivery.

10 min @ .18 = 1.80

10 min @ .18 = 1.80

13. Enter receipt into computer. Print receiver form.

5 min @ .18 = .90
receiver form = .12
computer system time
5 min @ 7.32 = 36.60

Split form, attach one to packing slip, and send to accounts payable, staple one to carton.

2 min @ .18 = .36

14. Deliver material to requisitioner. Log delivery into docklog

10 min @ .18 = 1.80

Subtotal of costs to the receiving function = $43.38. The same overhead burden applies to receiving labor costs. Burdened cost of the transaction to receiving is $48.38.

15. Accounts payable clerk receives, date-stamps, and files P.O. copy and receiver copy.	8 min @ .22 = 1.76
16. Accounts payable clerk receives mail, opens it, sorts invoices in mail, and pulls P.O. to match invoice.	20 min @ .22 = 4.40
17. Clerk cross-checks data between P.O., receiver, and invoice. If all three agree, invoice is batched for data entry.	5 min @ .22 = 1.10
18. Accounting data entry	3 min @ .22 = 0.66
computer system time =	3 min @ 7.32 = 21.96
19. Validate printout (address, etc.), consolidate multiple P.O.'s into one check.	2 min @ .22 = .44
20. Computer check-run process.	5 min @ 7.32 = 36.60
21. Separate checks, stamp signature on checks, attach check to copy of invoice, stuff in envelope, and mail.	15 min @ .22 = 3.30
	envelope + stamp = .30
22. File completed documents and reports in "Closed" file. Store for 7 years.	10 min @ .22 = 2.20
	8 pages @ .08/page = .64

Subtotal of costs to the accounting function = $73.36. The same overhead burden applies to accounting labor costs. Burdened transaction costs to finance total $83.77.

Total Process Costs:	Unburdened	Burdened @ 75%
Purchasing	$146.50	$171.74
Receiving	43.38	48.38
Accounting	73.36	83.77
TOTAL	$263.24	$303.89

If the process above looks familiar, it may be a valuable exercise to cost your own process. Once this is done, areas of opportunity become clearer, and efforts to simplify the process can be easily cost-justified.

Many buyers have done business with suppliers who are very easy to deal with and suppliers who require significantly higher levels of their time and attention. Experienced buyers can put an emotional and stress "cost" on suppliers who are more difficult, but rarely is this factor expressed in terms of dollars. Yet a buyer's time has value. The time required to manage a supplier is not only a direct cost, but also the cost of lost opportunity—work that did not get done because this extra effort was required.

This time factor can be costed in the same way that transactions are. Compare the amounts of time that different suppliers require. Multiply that time difference by the value of your time. This is the incremental cost that a difficult supplier adds to your operations. This incremental cost can be factored into the comparison of quoted prices as one of the elements of total cost.

THE COST OF INVENTORY

Inventory is expensive. Many companies attach a cost of 25 percent to 30 percent per year to the carrying of inventory. This percentage covers only a few of the factors that are easy to calculate, such as the cost of money. Inclusion of the more intangible costs pushes the true cost of carrying inventory closer to 75 percent. Figure 17-1 lists the factors associated with carrying inventory and approximate annual percentage costs.

An understanding of the true cost of inventory and the calculation of the costs specific to your business may make you reconsider the business practices that drive inventory. (For a fuller discussion of these practices, see Chapter 7.)

In addition to calculating the cost to carry inventory, it is important to ask, "If the money that is tied up in inventory were available to the business, what else could be done?" The impact of this money can be substantial: development of new products that would expand the business, retirement of corporate debt, and increases in staff salaries, for example.

COST OF NONQUALITY

The true cost of material or services rejected for insufficient quality can be substantial. The time, labor, and direct expenses have to be considered.

When delivered goods are defective, time must be spent inspecting the goods, verifying the problem, and working with the supplier to resolve the problem. If the material must be replaced, the supplier packs and ships replacement stock, which must be received and inspected at your facility prior to use. This can lengthen the lead time by weeks. If inventory is being carried to cover for the problem, the cost of carrying that inventory should be considered. If inventory is not on hand to cover the delayed delivery, a shortage may result. The costs associated with a shortage include the cost of lost production, the labor cost of the fire-fighting activities, and additional direct costs for premium freight shipment and possibly premium purchase prices.

The Cost of Carrying Inventory

Visible costs	Approximate % per year
Interest rate of money	10%
Taxes (vary state to state)	5%
Insurance	3%
Space, occupancy, and utilities	4%
Equipment (storage and moving)	3%
Scrap and obsolescence	5%
	30%
(less visible) costs	
Personnel (planners, warehousers, analysts)	15%
Transactions: counting, sorting, moving, retrieving, issuing, reconciling	10%
Inspection, reinspection, return of defective material	10%
Rework, handling damage, loss	10%
	75%

FIG 17-1. *Inventory costs.*

Increased costs due to the labor involved in processing rejected material include those for increased inspection and testing, sorting or reworking the material, the cost of the transaction loop to return rejected material, and the costs of expediting and adjusting the purchase-order records. The "return material authorization" transaction process should be costed in the same way a purchase order is costed. It is often even more laborious and time-consuming.

Additional hidden costs include the effects of the problem materials in your production process and in your finished produce. Warranty repair and lost customer business can be very expensive indeed. One electronics firm calculated the cost of a component failure at stages along the manufacturing process and arrived at the following data:

- Purchase price of the component (each) $ 0.03
- Administration process for rejected material   350.00
- Cost of finding the problem after the part is in production   500.00
- Cost of a warranty repair call to a customer   2500.00

Quantification of these costs and application of a factor to the purchase price which reflects the costs of the rejects that have been experienced will allow for more informed business decisions when choosing suppliers.

THE COST OF TIME

Time has a direct effect on costs, and money has value over time. Anyone who has purchased a home has experienced the time value of money. If a home sells for $100,000 list and the buyer obtains 10.25 percent interest on a 30-year mortgage, the buyer actually pays $322,596 to the holder of the mortgage. The interest on the loan is more than twice the actual cost of the house. The banking industry thrives by taking advantage of the cost of money over time.

Purchasers who understand the effect of time on money are in a better position to minimize the value of purchases. A big consideration is the payment structure that is negotiated with suppliers. Payment within 30 days is a common practice. But if invoices are paid in 60 days rather than 30 days, an additional 30 days of usage of your money has been gained. The exact value of that time depends on the interest rate at which your money is borrowed or invested.

Another issue is consolidated billing. If a supplier delivers many times per month (such as in a just-in-time delivery arrangement), the paperwork to process individual invoices for the deliveries may be more than the accounts payable department can accommodate. Consolidated billing, whereby the supplier keeps track of individual deliveries and submits one invoice at the end of the payment period [month] for all of the deliveries made within that period, can generate significant savings in both labor costs and the time value of money. The value of the use of your money averages to an additional 15 days. If the payment term is net 30 days after receipt of invoice, then the average time from delivery to payment is 45 days.

In the purchase of items of high value and high technology, such as capital equipment, suppliers may ask for progress payments. When negotiating the inclusion of progress payments into a purchase contract, a buyer should balance the cost of the money over time against the value to be gained by agreeing to the payment. If the supplier is assuming a technological risk or major investment that is unaffordable, a progress payment should be considered an investment decision. If there is no such risk, it may not be in the buyer's interest to agree to progress payments. If the operation of the equipment is critical, and acceptance is based on meeting a performance specification, the buyer may wish to make final payment contingent upon successful performance, not upon delivery. There is sometimes a significant time difference between delivery and acceptable performance.

CASH DISCOUNTS

Additional savings can be obtained by negotiating a cash discount for early payment. Suppliers who need to improve their cash flow may readily agree to such a discount. A discount of 2 percent – 10 days, net 30 days means that, for a difference of 20 days, the supplier will give a 2 percent discount. This is equivalent to an annual interest rate of 36.5%, calculated as follows:

$$\frac{X\%}{2\%} = \frac{365 \text{ days}}{20 \text{ days}}$$

Here are some cash discounts and their interest rate equivalents:

TABLE 17-1 Annual Interest Rates Equivalent to Cash Discounts

CASH DISCOUNT	ANNUAL INTEREST RATE
1% 10 net 30	18.25%
2% 10 net 30	36.5 %
3% 10 net 30	54.75%
4% 10 net 30	73.0 %
5% 10 net 30	91.25%

Discounts for volume and for other special arrangements should be carefully weighed against the costs of those arrangements. For example, a discount for volume is designed to encourage the purchase of larger quantities. However, the purchase of a quantity larger than immediately required means storage of inventory. Inventory is also expensive. Is the cost of carrying the inventory less than the savings to be gained from the discount? In order to make the best business decision, it is important to know both costs.

THE COST OF LEAD TIME

Lead time creates expense in two ways—inventory and uncertainty. A buyer may choose to carry safety stock inventory to protect the business against sudden demand within lead time. A lead time of 16 weeks will require a safety stock level much higher than that for a lead time of eight weeks. This inventory carries its expenses.

Uncertainty also affects costs. If the design is changed and the material no longer needed, it will be scrapped. If the sales pattern changes and less is required, inventory levels may go well above even the planned safety stock level. As forecasts go further into the future, they become less stable. A long-lead-time item is purchased based on an unstable forecast. This can generate a significant risk to the business of incurring unplanned expenses. A short lead time fosters stability and lower risk. This translates to lower costs.

QUOTATIONS

A primary purchasing skill is the ability to analyze quotation information and make the most cost-effective decision. Simple price comparison is easy. Frequently, however, there is more to the comparison than price. Creative buyers structure the request for quotation (RFQ) to get additional information that might be of value.

A buyer should structure the RFQ so that it provides a specific and detailed format for basic information, such as price in quantity multiples that are appropriate, delivery charges, and other charges appropriate to the quotation. The RFQ should also provide an opening to suppliers to include anything that may affect the price or the value of the goods or services being purchased. A supplier may come back with benefits of which the buyer was unaware.

Providing a detailed format can also encourage the supplier to quote services separately. Quoting the base price with all other factors spelled out as additional costs or benefits is called option bidding. It allows the buyer better data for determining which services are cost effective and which are not. Additional costs, such as those for transportation, packaging, supplier stocking, and additional benefits, such as extended commitment options, cash discounts, fixed term of price, and reduced lead times, can be evaluated on their own merits. The buyer can then choose which options to take and which to leave. Analysis is much more difficult when the services are buried in the list price. (For additional discussion of option bidding, see Chapter 9.)

Once the quotations have been returned, they must be compared so that proper selection can be made. A convenient way to do this is to use a spreadsheet format. A spreadsheet allows for direct comparison of the base data (such as price) and the inclusion of additional information. The spreadsheet and the quotations should be retained together as reference information during the life of the agreement, as an audit trail, and as a base point for requotation.

A case study of the analysis of quotation information follows:

Mike was asked to establish a contract for one year for the use of meeting facilities at a local hotel. Information was provided by the using departments regarding the frequency of anticipated use and the size of the rooms required. Since the length of the meetings would vary from half a day to five days, Mike specified that the hotels quote their room rates on a half-day and a per-day basis. He also asked them to specify any additional service charges separately. Mike called local facilities to determine the feasibility of asking them to quote and narrowed the field of potential candidates to four. All four returned their quotations promptly, and Mike prepared to do his analysis.

Since the usage would vary, Mike's first task was to establish a standard unit of usage for comparison purposes. He chose to use a one-day meeting with all accessories required as the standard unit for comparison. He first listed those items that he knew would be vital (such as room rate), and left the remainder for inclusion of the extra items that each potential supplier had mentioned.

All data from the quotations was included on the spreadsheet. Where there were questions about information that had not been included or was not clear from the quote, a clarifying telephone call provided the information.

The spreadsheet from Mike's quotation effort is shown in Figure 17-2. Once all information was clear, Mike could total the expense costs for the standard unit of use and make decisions regarding with which hotel to contract, which services to include, and which services to obtain through other means.

A different approach to quotations is possible when a supplier partnership exists. When there is a reciprocal relationship that permits the disclosure of confidential information, the negotiation of price stems from a disclosure of the buyer's market forecasts and quantity projections for the life of the product, and the supplier's disclosure of the costs to manufacture. Both negotiate from open data and look for the best mutually satisfactory arrangement. The analysis becomes one of examining

	Supplier A	Supplier B	Supplier C	Supplier D
Meeting Room:				
Full day	100.00	100.00	75-175	50-250
Half day	50.00	75.00	N/A	25-125
Support Services:				
TV	N/C	N/C	55.00	45.00
VCR	N/C	N/C	with TV	with TV
Flip charts	N/C	N/C	10.00	7.50/day
Overhead projector	N/C	N/C	20.00	25.00
Food Service				
Coffee	$6/pot	N/C	$6/pot	3.50/pers.
Lunch availability	yes	yes	no	no
Other Services				
Parking	free	free	free	free
Cancellation				
- days notice	1 day	1 day	1 day	7 days
- penalty charge	none	none	50.00	25.00
Consolidate invoice	yes	yes	yes	yes
Quarterly statement	yes	yes	no	no
TOTAL charges for 1 day meeting with all equip. and coffee for 20 people (standard unit of use).	$118.00	$100.00	$172.14	$230.00
Supplier suggestions	use of 1 pool	lodging discount		
Buyer comments		closer location		

Analysis:

Suppliers A & B are viable candidates. Supplier B is slightly less expensive. Suppliers C & D are significantly more expensive primarily because of the "extra" charges.

FIG. 17-2 *Evaluation of Mike's Hotel Quotations*

the cost drivers and how they might be reduced. Cost reductions through joint efforts are both feasible and profitable.

FINANCIAL STRENGTH OF SUPPLIERS

Determining the financial strength of suppliers can be both interesting and tricky. It is an important factor if you are considering a long-term supplier partnership that may involve a significant investment on the part of the supplier, or if you are committing to a new technology that the supplier is about to bring to market. The fundamental question to be answered is whether or not the supplier has the financial staying power to remain in the market for the long term and to make the major investments that are of concern to you. The overall picture is composed of several separate pieces of information, plus information that is gathered from the history of your dealings with the supplier.

Perhaps the first step is simply to ask the supplier. Express your concern regarding the future and allow the supplier to respond. If you are entering or already involved in a partnership with that supplier, then the likelihood of receiving a reply with which you can work increases.

In addition to direct conversations with the supplier about its financial staying power, you will want to understand its investment strategy—both current and future. How much is the supplier investing in new product research and development—both in absolute dollars and as a percentage of revenue? Is the supplier making investments in the company's growth and development? Investments in equipment and especially in people may be a key indicator of how the business will be performing in the future.

Look for investment in training. Are there facilities and a stable budget for training? Is there a commitment to training, especially in quality and technology areas? Commitment and financial support for training carry two messages: The first is that there is an understanding of the importance of a skilled work force and a commitment to the long-term development of the work force, and the company is putting its money behind that belief. The second message is that there is sufficient net working capital to fund the investment.

Investment in a skilled work force can also be determined by staffing practices. Does this supplier recruit the best and the brightest for new positions? Does the supplier encourage, promote, and pay for professional certifications? Do they retain their work force, or is there high turnover? Turnover is often an indicator of both investment in wages and morale within the organization. Is this supplier committed to the best work force and willing to invest to retain them, or is it a minimum wage/ high turnover operation? This issue has serious implications for the supplier's future growth and stability.

If you are investigating a potential new supplier and no relationship has been established, you may want to resort to additional sources of information. Two that will be considered here are the annual report and independent verification.

An annual report of the supplier company can reveal some key information. Read the chairman's letter to the stockholders and look for the general tone, indications of the direction the company will take in the future, and an explanation of how the company peformed in the past year. Armed with that general explanation, turn to the figures. The balance sheet will provide several key pieces of information. Look at the difference between current assets and current liabilities; this is the supplier's net working capital, which is the cash it has available to fund current efforts. How much cash is available? And even more important, is it growing or shrinking over prior periods?

Another important piece of information is the size of long-term debt. If the company is growing rapidly, significant long-term debt may not be unhealthy; look for information (either in the footnotes of the annual report or through other sources) to explain why long-term debt exists and what are the plans for retiring it. Divide the long-term debt by the stockholder's equity. This is the "debt to equity ratio," which shows the amount of total debt obligation versus the total assets of the corporation. A high ratio (heavy debt vs. assets) may be acceptable in a young growth company, but it is a risk if growth or sales slow or if net working capital is drained to make the payments on the debt.

The income statement in the annual report shows how much money the supplier made or lost over the year and where. An important line to look for is net sales. Are net sales increasing or decreasing? It is especially instructive if more than one annual report can be compared. Trend information is more valuable than static numbers, especially in net sales and working capital.

When reading an annual report, pay special attention to the footnotes. They often contain exceptions or explanations for the figures and can reveal areas that need further exploration.

Information about payment history can be obtained from financial reporting services such as Dun & Bradstreet (D & B).

The D & B report shows general financial data on the company, gives information about the officers, and gives a credit history indicating how current the supplier is regarding payment of immediate obligations. However, this information is voluntary on the part of the supplier. Those suppliers whose information is not flattering may refuse to give it or may give only partial data.

Independent sources can provide additional data. Look at the trade press and/or market research firms for information about the supplier's market share, whether new products reached the marketplace on time, and the supplier's reputation for quality. While these are not directly financial measurements, when they are combined with the data derived from the annual reports and from payment history, they help to provide a whole picture. Purely financial data is historical in nature. In order to draw sound conclusions about future actions, finance data should be combined with market and business data so that a supplier's potential can be more accurately determined.

CHAPTER PERSPECTIVE

Financial analytical skills are among the most important skills a buyer possesses. A buyer must understand the cost implications involved in all aspects of the business so that he or she can manage the purchasing function in a cost-effective manner. A buyer must also understand the business implications of cost factors. The ability to translate costs into business advantages is required—not merely manipulation of numbers. In addition, a buyer should undertand the implications of quality, time, administration, and inventory for the cost of doing business. In short, sound financial analysis skills allow a buyer to function as a true business partner—both with suppliers and within his or her own organization.

Measuring Purchasing Performance

INTRODUCTION AND MAIN POINTS

Establishing proper measurements of the purchasing function helps to determine the results one gets from the function.

Historically, the purchasing department has been responsible for the price, delivery, and quality of purchased goods. The finance department monitored price performance, production control monitored delivery performance, and quality control monitored the suppliers' goods at incoming inspection. Delivery has been the primary performance measure, followed by price and quality.

After studying the material in this chapter:
- You will know how to identify and evaluate the behavior.
- You will understand which contributions are critical to the success of the purchasing function.
- You will be able to construct a measurement system that encourages people to excel.

ALIGNING GOALS

The first step in the process of constructing a measurement system is to understand current corporate goals and management's expectations of purchasing. Most manufacturing businesses are measured by:

1. Return On Investment (ROI)
2. Profit after tax
3. Predictability
4. Sales dollars per employee
5. Cost of goods sold
6. Gross margin

All of these are financial measures, and accounting is the scorekeeper. Many critical nonfinancial measures are not visible to top management and have only passing significance at lower management levels. These include quality, the cost of product nonconformance, market share, the state of technology, investment in new-product research, customer service levels, and customer satisfaction.

Financial measurements lose their relevance deeper in the organization. For example, purchasing has been measured on 1) supplier delivery performance, 2) variance from standard costs, and 3) percent of rejected lots at incoming inspection. These measures are only loosely connected to the financial measures used by management. For them to have relevance and to support management's financial objectives, there must be a visible and direct alignment between corporate goals and those of each company department.

The problem with financial measures is that they are historically oriented; they account for what has happened and not what should have happened. Measures should encourage the right behavior and support corporate goals.

PURCHASING MEASURES

Measures of the purchasing function include the following:

1. Volume of Activity—Defined as the number of requisitions received and the time between receipt and purchase-order placement, this measure indicates how busy a purchasing department is. It has nothing to do with progress toward better buying or improved corporate profits. The time required to place an order after receipt of a requisition may have nothing to do with purchasing's effectiveness. It may be attributable to requisition backlog in the department, or to the absence or unclarity of specifications, lack of engineering standardization, unavailability of sources of supply, or other factors outside of purchasing. This measure should be avoided, because it rewards business and does not reward smarter purchasing practices. Through use of techniques such as systems contracts and just-in-time release systems, requisition activity in the purchasing department should go down. As the volume of requisitions declines, buyers have more time to devote to profit-producing activities.

2. Cost Variance—This measure is defined by the actual price paid versus standard cost. Standard costs are usually established between purchasing and accounting once a year. Accounting uses these costs to value inventory and to establish product cost. Purchasing sets and uses standard costs as target prices. But since purchasing has a vested interest in achieving a minimum variance, the standard costs become self-fulfilling prophecies. This is a classic example of a measurement that encourages the wrong behavior. If the objective is a minimum variance, what happens when a buyer has the opportunity to reduce prices below standard? If the goal is meeting the standard cost, the buyer will turn down the opportunity—to the detriment of the buyer's company. Standard costs should be used only to value inventory and not as a measure for purchasing.

The real issue is this: What prices are affordable? Past prices (or those that are known to be obtainable) may not match affordable costs. In 1926, Henry Ford said, "It is one of the oddities of business that a man will cite what he has done in the past as proof of what he can do in the future. The past is only something to learn from."[1] What if purchasing were to receive a bill of material with a total affordable price? If the required total material cost cannot be achieved, the company will have no product. Perhaps this might establish realistic cost objectives and force purchasing, design engineering, marketing, and suppliers to work closely together to produce an affordable finished product.

The real cost measures are based on market needs, not on past experience. Therefore, more appropriate measures of purchasing are a) achieving affordable costs and b) achieving lower than those previously paid.

Cost-reduction efforts should be reported to management with uncontrollable influences removed. For example, prices should not reflect the possibility of increased quantities or market fluctuations (e.g., the price of gold). Chart the results in an easy-to-read manner, as demonstrated in Figures 18-1 and 18-2. All measures should be posted conspicuously where management will see and read them.

3. Delivery. Delivery presents a problem in that there is usually little consensus as to the target delivery date. Is one to measure the receipt date against the supplier's lead time, promised shipment date, the requisitioner's request date, or the date on the purchase order? Should purchasing measure the supplier's shipment date or the receipt date?

Only the requisitioner's required date has any meaning, and requisitioners often fail to allow time for purchasing to obtain material. There may be transport delays, suppliers may quote their ship dates and you measure receipt dates, and there may be delays in receiving and inspecting the material. Still, users need the material when they need the material. Therefore, the only delivery measure of any significance is the date on which the user has access to the material.

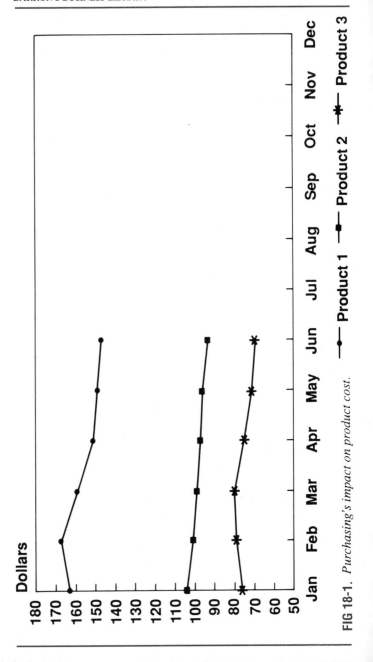

FIG 18-1. *Purchasing's impact on product cost.*

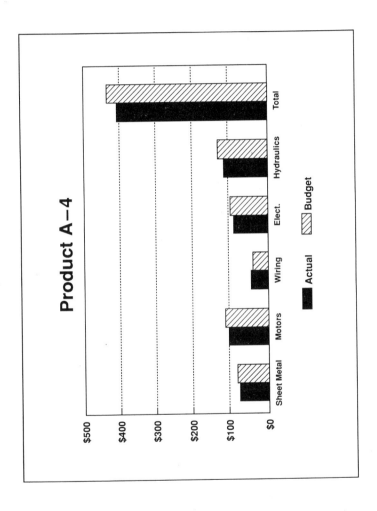

FIG 18-2. *Purchase prices–budget vs. actual.*

The longer the lead time from the supplier, the higher the likelihood of delivery problems. In addition, the goods may be required sooner than was originally estimated. Therefore, it is in purchasing's interest to work on reducing suppliers' lead times, transport time, and the time required to receive and inspect the goods.

THE USE OF CHARTS

Charts should be created and displayed for delivery measures, and other charts should be created that demonstrate purchasing's efforts in reducing suppliers' lead times (see Figures 18-3 and 18-4). Other charts should be created that demonstrate purchasing's efforts to improve supplier performance and, subsequently, production yields and finished-goods quality. The cluster of charts included in Figure 18-5 illustrate some other measures that lend themselves to chart presentation. Use of charts not only distributes information, it promotes action on the information presented.

There is a tendency in some companies to focus on numbers and not on underlying trends. But the trend is what is important, not necessarily the discrete numbers. The objective is to promote and report continuous improvement. Figure 18-6 is a log-log chart for trends of supplier quality. Whether the number for May for incoming quality should have been 1,000 instead of 1,400 is immaterial. The chart shows continued progress, with no stated assumption as to where the lines should have been or where they should conclude. When all three lines drop off the chart (below one part per million), a new chart is drawn reflecting "parts per billion" performance.

Other data that proves valuable are the following:
■ The number of hours or days of buyer training.
■ The number of quality-training seminars conducted for suppliers.
■ Improvements in negotiated terms and conditions (the first offer compared to the negotiated settlement).
■ Improvements in cost reduction.

Trends and results should be expressed in terms of the team or department effort. This develops a team spirit within the purchasing department and prevents a focus on individuals who may be star performers for only a limited time. Similarly, information on supplier performance should be grouped when reporting data publicly. Individual supplier performance is a matter for purchasing and related functions.

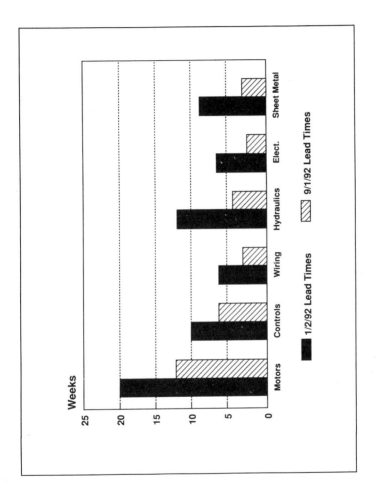

FIG 18-3. *Commodity lead time reduction.*

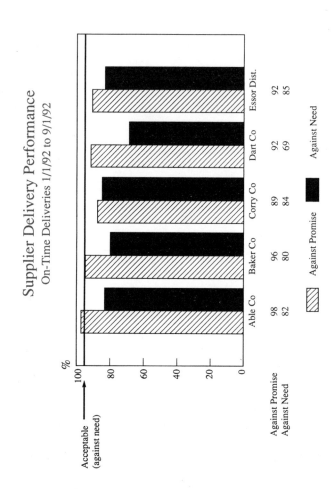

FIG 18-4. *Supplier delivery performance.*

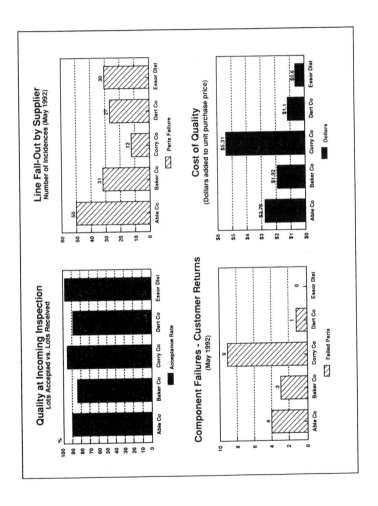

FIG 18-5.

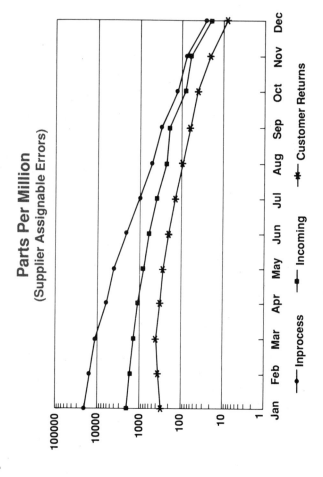

FIG 18-6. *Log-log chart: trends of supplier quality.*

NONPRODUCT MEASURES

A purchasing department manager may wish to set professional-development goals for buyers. These goals may encompass training, such as progress toward professional certification, and the acquisition of specialized skills in such areas as statistical quality control, finance, blueprint reading, negotiation, and traffic management. A chart showing individual buyers' progress toward NAPM certification is in Figure 18-7. The modules represent sets of examinations that must be passed before certification is awarded.

RECOGNITION

Everyone needs recognition for progress toward goals. In a purchasing department such recognition may be simple or elaborate, depending on the circumstances. Either way, it should be sincerely delivered and meaningful to the recipient.

Top management should be invited to participate in the recognition process. Management's involvement has two primary effects: 1) recognition comes from the seat of power and is hence more meaningful to recipients, and 2) top management better understands what is happening in the organization and among employees.

REPORTING

Purchasing should report monthly to top management on progress toward company goals. These reports should be presented in terms of trends and consolidated on simple-to-read charts. Figure 18-8 is an example of such reporting. When submitting reports to top management, a buyer should be certain to acknowledge any assistance received from other departments within the organization. For example, if engineering, quality, finance, or any other function assists purchasing in attaining its goals, lavish those departments with sincere praise and make sure their contributions are known to upper management. This will ensure continued cooperation and may allow for attainment of even higher goals.

CHAPTER PERSPECTIVE

A purchasing department's goals should agree with those of top management. Progress toward those goals should be measured—both for individuals and for the department overall. Key indicators of performance and progress should be reported to top management on a regular basis. These reports should be in terms

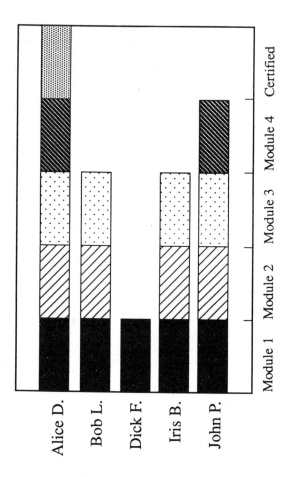

FIG 18-7.

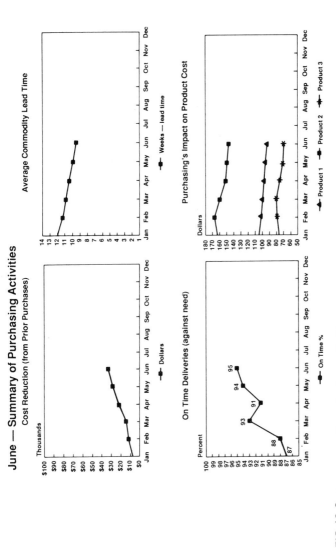

FIG 18-8. *Summary of purchasing activities.*

of trends, not discrete data. Be clear about those items that are to be measured, reported, and rewarded. Be certain that outstanding performance and progress toward goals is acknowledged and rewarded.

REFERENCES

[1]Henry Ford. *Today and Tomorrow,* (New York: Doubleday, Page & Co., 1926), p. 42.

Data Processing Systems for Purchasing

INTRODUCTION AND MAIN POINTS

Purchasing departments process a great deal of information. They must track the performance of suppliers and know the status of purchase orders. Summary information must also be available with which purchasing can gauge supplier delivery performance, supplier quality, and price movements. This information can assist buyers and purchasing managers to make decisions regarding source selection, cost and quality trends, and buyer performance. These needs can be served well by the use of data-processing equipment and appropriate software.

There are many software programs on the market. However, most of these programs are part of a larger system and the purchasing portion is added as an afterthought. An example of this is the purchasing "package" or portion of MRP and MRPII systems. Basically, these packages require that the purchasing department or user change the way they do business to conform to the system requirements. This should not be the function of software programs; programs should support and enhance existing purchasing practices. Even "standalone" purchasing software packages tend to mold existing purchasing practices into a form that may not be in the purchasing department's best interest.

After studying the material in this chapter:

■ You will be able to construct an outline of your own purchasing software program.

■ You will understand what information and formats are important to your operation.

■ You will know how to customize a system to your own needs.

WHY CREATE YOUR OWN SYSTEM?

There is much talk about the advantages of buying "user friendly" software and systems. But the problem with buying someone else's software package is that *it is someone else's software.*

It may be in the purchasing department's interest to create its own software package. Since purchasing designs it, installs it, administers it, and maintains it, it can be nothing but "friendly."

In this chapter, we will concentrate on the logic and format of software programs of use to purchasing departments, and not on specific program language (e.g., Basic, Fortran, RPG, COBOL).

SOFTWARE FEATURES TO CONSIDER

1. Maximum use of English. You will find it easier to use supplier names instead of supplier numbers in the printout and Julian dates instead of week numbers.

2. You may wish, once a month, to break down the run or output by supplier—that is, run one supplier's open orders per page so that you can send each supplier a copy of the run on a regular basis. "Last receipt" information allows suppliers to reconcile your balances and open orders with theirs. This also affords them the advantage of organizing orders the way you have organized them, resulting in a common communication device.

3. You may wish to flag or highlight certain information (e.g., highlight overdue orders or deliveries, short cycled requisitions, early receipts, variances from standard costs). This can be accomplished through exception reports or through special notes on the open purchase order report.

4. You may want a means of tracking rejected material—in a manufacturing environment especially. This is where the four extra digits on the purchase-order number field come in handy. Instead of returning the rejected material to the supplier against the original purchase order (the parts thereby lose their identity), you can close out the old order (assuming there is no balance due) and reissue the old purchase order number, adding the suffix -R1 (identifying the order as a replacement order). This approach can be used to track quality performance and a supplier's sensitivity to replacement schedules.

5. You can make an ally of your accounting department by offering them a cash-flow analysis system that is an easy by-product of your open purchase order system. This gives you dollar commitments by time frame—due dates of orders that have dollars associated with them (e.g., "100 pieces $\times$ \$27.50

each, due June 12, 1992"). If this were done for all orders, you would have an outgoing cash-flow analysis.

6. Are you looking for another ally? Suppose each requisition you receive had a code that identified the end use of the component or the using department, and suppose this information was to be placed on the purchase order and open order run. Now all you need do is to sort the information on the run by this code. Production control or the user would have a listing of materials bought, with due dates, by project or job.

SYSTEM OBJECTIVES

1. A regular, usually weekly, order status report that will monitor delivery status and become a tool for controlling supplier delivery performance.
2. A mechanism for measuring supplier quality (at least the incoming portion).
3. A standard cost-variance report.
4. An outgoing cash-flow or cash-requirements report.
5. A production-control tool.
6. A supplier-usable order-status report.

CONSIDERATIONS

1. Existing systems in place, if any.
2. Method of order entry into the system.
3. Space requirements (e.g., length of part and purchase order numbers).
4. Does current system (if any) support an MRP system?
5. Will your new system run on the company's mainframe or will it run on personal computers (PCs)?
6. Are account numbers, product codes, or other end-item or end-user codes in existence?
7. Approaches and priorities will vary depending upon the type of business in which the system will be used (e.g., manufacturing, distribution, health care, banking, insurance, education).
8. Report-size restrictions—most printers will accommodate a 132-column report.

OTHER DEPARTMENTS TO BE CONSIDERED

1. Management Information Services (MIS), or the resident computer department personnel.
2. Receiving.
3. Production and inventory control (or other planning or

using functions if this is not a manufacturing environment).

4. Finance and cost accounting.
5. The office to which purchasing reports.

CLOSED LOOP

A closed-loop purchasing-status system is one in which all required data comes from purchasing and receiving. Initial data comes from the purchase orders. Similarly, the information is *relieved* by receiving and purchasing input (e.g., amendments and closeouts). Purchasing will also want the responsibility to maintain the integrity of the information.

DETAILED QUESTIONS OF FORM

Once you have decided to construct a system, the following form questions should be answered:

1. What is the maximum number of digits in the part number?
2. What is the maximum number of digits in the purchase-order numbering system. Allow for four more digits than are currently in use.
3. Do you need alphanumeric capability in the part and/ or purchase-order numbers? Alphanumeric capability in the purchase-order numbering system can be quite ueful.
4. Do you have account number, product codes, end-product numbers, user codes, etc.? This will be helpful in relating to production control, end-users, and job-cost accounting.
5. Do you have a unit of measure code?
6. What number of digits do you require for quantity?
7. Will you use other than Julian dates? Is Julian preferred?
8. Does your company have an MRP system that requires single or multiple acknowledgment date(s) column(s)?
9. Do you need the year in your dates, or is the day and month sufficient?
10. Do you use multiple-line-item purchase orders (more than one item per purchase order)?
11. How will you close an order/item? You can have an automatic closeout when an item is received in exact quantity or a closeout within a given percentage of the

ordered quantity (+/− 5 percent or 10 percent). You can also manually close each order/item.

One of the major questions is whether the system will be run on the company's mainframe computer or on PCs. With today's networking capabilities and low cost of PCs, you may want to consider the advantages of a PC hardware system. If, however, your existing production system relies on purchasing input, you may wish to or be required to use the company's mainframe and program your new system into existing software.

THE HEART OF THE SYSTEM

To be usable, a system should "think" the way the user thinks. It should present the information the way the user needs it and in a form that can be shared with others. With this in mind, you may want to sort purchase orders by 1) buyer, 2) supplier, 3) part number, and 4) purchase-order number. Each buyer wants each supplier's orders grouped together for consolidating order administration. Descending or ascending part numbers facilitate part-number location.

The next step is to obtain a pad of 132-column layout paper and start to divide up the real estate. You are ready to create your open purchase-order report.

1. *Part Number*—Allow for the longest part number you can identify in your bills of material and add two digits. *Space two columns between each field or group of information.*

2. *Purchase Order Number*—Allow for the current maximum number and *add four more.* The added four digits will allow you to track rejects/replacement orders—quite a useful feature. Let's say that you have received ten parts on purchase order number 12345. Three of the parts are rejected and the supplier is to replace them. You will make out a debit memo for the three pieces and enter a new purchase order on the supplier for three pieces. The new purchase-order number will be 12345-R1. When you see this purchase order number on your open purchase order status report, you will know that this is a replacement order and will require special delivery attention. If you see an order number like 12345-R6, you will know that you have a real problem with either the supplier or the part. An added feature of this suffix is that, at the end of each month, a subroutine will count up all of the rejected orders and compare the number against the total number of orders received from each supplier, giving you an initial quality rating on each supplier. (This scenario assumes that you have an incoming in-

spection department. Chapter 12 offers alternatives to an incoming inspection department.) Be sure to tell your programmer that you want this field to be alphanumeric.

3. *Print Revision Levels*—You may want to include the revision level on the open order report. This information normally comes from the purchase order. Allow two columns or more if necessary.

4. *Entry Date*—Put in the Julian date on which the order was entered or conveyed to the supplier. This comes from the purchase order. Many systems require use of a work-week code (e.g., wk 33 equals September 22) or a computer such as 0922 or 092292. This becomes difficult to communicate to others who are unfamiliar with the dating codes. We strongly recommend that you provide for the use of 9/22 or 9/22/92, allowing five or eight spaces, respectively.

5. *Quantity Ordered*—It is a good idea to make this a fixed figure—the quantity on the original purchase order—affected only by amendments for quantity processed against the order. Allow for sufficient spaces (digits), and add one to be safe.

6. *Unit of Measure*—Use an existing two-digit code or make up codes of your own if none exist. For example:

EA = each	TO = ton	SH = sheets
DZ = dozen	IN = inch	PD = pad
GR = gross	FT = feet	RM = ream
LT = lot	GA = gallon	PL = pail
OZ = ounce	DR = drum	TB = tube
LB = pound	BX = box	BF = board feet

7. *Price*—Enter the price per unit of measure as it appears on the purchase order. You may wish to have an additional digit to the right of the decimal point if fractions of a cent are important (e.g., $10.725 each).

8. *Quantity and Date of Last Receipt*—Allow for the same number of spaces as in #5, Quantity, and #4, Entry date. This is the one piece of information that depends upon input from a department outside of purchasing—namely, the receiving department. Take each day's receipts and have them posted to the system. This may be done on-line from the receiving department or in batch mode in purchasing or MIS. The most recent receiving information will appear when you run the open purchase order report. When you send a copy of the report to suppliers, they can reconcile shipments and balances by your last receipt information. Allow two spaces between the quantity and date. Tell your programmer that, in the case of multiple partial re-

ceipts, only the most recent receipts are to appear in these columns.

9. *Schedule Quantities and Dates*—The quantities and dates are those from the purchase order and are relieved by receipts. Example:

    a. An order for 100 pieces is scheduled for 50 pieces due March 1 and 50 due June 1, or

          50   3/1
          50   6/1

    b. A receipt is made on March 1, of 60 pieces. The report should show a balance under the schedule section:

          40   3/1

    c. The receipt would also show in the last receipt column:

          60   3/1

Therefore, the schedule quantity columns will reflect a declining balance. These columns can also be altered by order amendments. If you change the order quantity, due dates, or number of releases, you will want these reflected in the schedule columns.

Example: Using the example above, you increase your order by 50 pieces for June 1 delivery. The schedule column would read

          50   3/1
         100   6/1

Your quantity ordered (#5 above) would change from 100 to 150.

Another feature you may want is the ability to not release or schedule all of the quantity on order.

Example: Using the same example, 100 pieces ordered with 50 for delivery on 3/1, the balance of the 50 unreleased might be represented by

          50   3/1
          50   HOLD

Therefore, the date column needs to be alphanumeric. An order amendment would change the HOLD to a specific delivery date.

10. *Overdue Indicator*—It is a good idea to have a single column to provide a flag for overdue orders. An asterisk will appear beside a schedule date that goes back past the date of the report. This facilitates the identification of overdue orders.

11. *Other Column Headings*—This is where you can get creative. You can add, for example:
■ Supplier acknowledgment dates.
■ Standard or supplier quoted lead times.
■ Short-cycled requisition indicator. (Compare the order entry

date and the first required delivery date to the lead time and determine where you are being allowed insufficient lead time by the requisitioner.)

■■ The product or project identifier code. You can identify the purchased item as relating to a product, commodity, customer, production planner, user, etc. You will be able to sort the information on your report so you can give other departments a report sorted by the criteria that is important to and identifiable by them (e.g., a list of all open orders used to fabricate a particular end item).

■■ Early receipt indicator. Any item received earlier than a time acceptable to you (e.g., two weeks, five days) can be flagged on the report for possible return to the supplier or delay in invoice payment.

On the above report format, all information remains unchanged from original input except 1) order quantity, 2) price, 3) schedule quantity and schedule date changed by order amendment, and 4) quantity and date of last receipt, which comes from receiving.

All order information, except the receiving data, should come from the purchase order and requisition. The data can be entered through a keyboard and a hard copy of the purchase order can be printed out.

12. *Summary Data*—At the end of each report or segment, you may wish to have the computer do some "number crunching" for you. For example:

■■ Total number of open orders.

■■ Number of short-cycled requisitions divided by the number of open orders equals percent of short-cycled requisitions.

■■ Number of overdue orders divided by the number of open orders equals percent overdue—by buyer, supplier, or both.

■■ Number of replacement orders divided by the number of receipts for the month equals supplier quality percentage for first orders.

■■ Price on the purchase order versus standard cost or last price paid equals cost variance by buyer, supplier, product code, etc. You may wish to have your report run at the end of each month, with one supplier per page, so you can mail a copy to all or a select number of suppliers. This will serve as a communication device with your suppliers that may encourage them to provide prompt and proper delivery. Since your report shows the last receipt quantity and date, your suppliers can reconcile their records with your report.

Your suppliers, like many American businesses, sometimes

add insult to injury. Not only do they not deliver on time, they force you as the customer to inform them of that fact. This creates an added overhead burden for you, called "expediting." Monthly mailing of your open purchase order report to suppliers will start to address this costly problem.

RECEIVING REPORT

You may wish to have a daily receiving report. A sample is provided in Figure 19-5. A receiving report contains the date of the last receipt, buyer, supplier, quantity, and purchase-order number. Depending on the hardware configuration you have, this information may be entered on-line at receiving or may be batch-loaded at the end of each day.

OTHER REPORTS

Cash Flow Analysis—In your open purchase order report, you have all the elements for a concise cash-requirements report: number of units, price, and expected delivery date. It is a simple matter to gather delivery dates and drop them into monthly time buckets: Calculate the number of parts times unit price, then dump the total into the projected receipt month. Then arrange the items by declining dollars. Either the purchasing or accounts payable department can add the 30 days.

Supplier-Quality Report—You should be careful with this information. Incoming-inspection personnel can detect only gross errors in product quality. The real quality fallout comes in the production process or when the product is in the hands of the user. However, initial quality information can be gathered and reported back to suppliers. The system can search out the "R"-suffixed orders and compare them to the total number of receipts for the month by supplier—lots accepted versus lots rejected at incoming inspection. If you have a line-fallout or production-fallout information-gathering system in place on the manufacturing floor, the rejection and replacement process will be more complete.

Price Variance Report—If you have a standard cost system or base variance on "prior price paid" system, the information in the open order report, when matched with accounting's standard cost or the prior price paid, gives you a variance report.

Since buyer codes are also included in the system, delivery, quality, and price reports can be run by a buyer and used as a measure of buyer effectiveness, with trends plotted. In reality, the performance of the buyer and suppliers is inseparable.

OPEN PURCHASE ORDER FORM

Run Date: 6/1/92
Buyer: Bob Smith
Supplier: Able Electronics Corp.

Part Number	PO no.	Rev	Entry date	Order qty.	U/M	Price
12345-7	84756	B	3/1/92	10,000	EA	1.35
24948-2	82917-R1	4	2/15/92	500	EA	2.25
49846-0	92735	1	5/17/92	100	EA	4.00
51836-1	93726	L	5/22/92	2,000	LB	.875
52701-3	62938	2	2/10/92	15,000	EA	.99

Supplier: Baker Distribution Co.

09273-1	67382-R4	1	5/15/92	50	EA	7.40
39461-4	93428	2	5/20/92	200	EA	10.92

Buyer Summary: Total Orders = 172 Total Shipments = 51
Orders Received On Time = 82% Orders Received Late = 12%
Orders Received Early = 6% Short Cycled Orders = 21%
Incoming Rejects = 2% Cost Variance = −2.1%

Last Receipt Qty.	Date	Schedule Qty.	Date	OD	LD TM	SC	EL	OP Date	LP Date
1000	5/15	1000	6/15		8			6/15	6/15
		1000	7/15					7/15	7/15
		1000	8/15					8/15	8/15
		6000	HOLD					HOLD	HOLD
		500	5/15	*	6			6/15	6/15
		100	6/15		10	*		7/1	7/1
		2000	7/15		6			7/15	7/30
5000	5/1	5000	6/15		12		*	6/15	6/15
		5000	7/15		12			7/15	7/15
100	5/5	50	5/15	*	5			6/10	6/10
		200	7/1		5			7/1	7/1

FIG. 19-1_Open Purchase Order Report_

Figure 19-1 is an excerpt from the Open Purchase Order Report for buyer Bob Smith. In this example, there are two suppliers: Able Electronics and Baker Distribution. The abbreviated headings have the following meanings:

U/M	= unit of measure
OD	= the order or release is overdue
LD/TM	= supplier-quoted lead time
SC	= the requisition was short-cycled

EL   = the shipment was received early or late
OP Date = the supplier's original promise
LP Date = the supplier's latest or last promise

The first item is the part number, 12345-7, and the original order quantity, 10,000 pieces. The last receipt was on May 5 for 1,000 pieces. The supplier's quoted lead time is 8 weeks. The next scheduled delivery is for June 15, and the latest information from the supplier indicates that shipment is on time, as are the scheduled deliveries for July 15 and August 15. The balance of the order, or 6,000 pieces, is as yet unscheduled for delivery. Since the last receipt quantity and the scheduled and unscheduled releases add up to the order quantity of 10,000 pieces, we know that there were no prior receipts.

The second part number, 24948-2, is a replacement order for 500 pieces. Even though the quoted lead time is 6 weeks, we have scheduled the order with no lead time. The order date and the requested delivery date are the same, May 15. This reflects the actual situation in that the goods are needed immediately and are overdue because of the rejection. The supplier has promised a June 15 delivery date.

The third part number is 49846-0 and the quantity ordered is 100 pieces. Since the order date is May 17, the requested delivery date is June 15, and the lead time is 10 weeks, an asterisk appears in the SC, or short cycle, column. The requisitioner allowed for only four weeks lead time on an item requiring 10 weeks. The supplier has acknowledged a July 1 delivery date. Purchasing has an obligation to improve the supplier's delivery date to one that approaches the requisitioner's request date. The SC indicator provides a means for purchasing to track repeated short-cycled requests to determine if there exists a problem at the planning stage of operations.

The fourth part, 51836-3, presents a different scenario. The supplier's original promise met the requisitioner's need date, but subsequent discussions with the supplier revealed that the supplier will not meet the original date and will ship fifteen days later, on July 30. This "repromise" information conveys the new date to production planning and allows purchasing time to investigate the problem with the supplier and to determine if an alternate solution to the delivery extension need be pursued.

The fifth item is part number 52701-3. An asterisk in the early/late (EL) column indicates that the receipt of 5,000 units on May 1 was received either before or after the required date. In this case, the supplier delivered the goods two weeks prior to the requested date. The buyer may decide to return the shipment or to keep the goods and add fifteen days to the invoice payment terms.

Baker's first item has a problem; there have been four replacement orders on this part. Purchasing should be investigating the problem. Is Baker incapable of producing the part with consistency of quality? Is there an internal specification problem where no supplier can provide an acceptable part with consistency? Is there a difference in inspection methods between Baker and purchasing?

INCOMING REJECT REPORT
The monthly incoming quality report might look as follows:

Buyer: Bob Jones

Supplier	Part Number	Year-To-Date Receipts	Year-To-Date Rejects
Able Elect.	09128-1	10	1
	09235-0	5	2
	10237-1	21	4
	12345-7	6	1
	12367-4	17	1
	12948-5	1	1
	13267-1	4	1
	24948-2	4	2
	49846-0	7	1
	51836-1	5	1
	52701-3	3	1
Total		83	16 = 19%

FIG. 19-2 *Monthly Incoming Reject Report*

June

Part Number	Supplier	Units	Price	Total	
09273-1	Baker Dis	50	7.40	370	
12345-7	Able Elec	1000	1.35	1350	
24948-2	Able Elec	500	2.25	1125	
52701-3	Able Elec	5000	.99	4950	
Total June Cash Requirement					$7795

FIG. 19-3 *Cash Requirements Report*

The report would continue through all of the months for which there are scheduled deliveries. The example above lists the cash obligations by part number, but it can also be run by descending dollar values or by supplier. Don't forget to add the supplier terms of payment. This would add 30 days to the payment date.

Supplier	YTD delivery performance	YTD incoming quality	YTD price variance
Able Elect.	83% on time	94% acceptance	1.9% unfavorable
Baker Dist.	96% on time	86% acceptance	2.3% favorable
Carter Mfg.	97% on time	98% acceptance	3.1% unfavorable
Deeker Co.	81% on time	92% acceptance	4.4% favorable

FIG. 19-4 *Buyer Performance—Bob Smith*

		June 15, 1992		
Buyer	Supplier	P.O. number	Part no.	Quantity
Bob Smith	Able Elect.	84756	12345-7	1000
		82917-R1	24948-2	500
		62938	52701-3	5000

FIG. 19-5 *Daily Receiving Report*

ODDS AND EVENS

Figures 19-1 and 19-5 show that the proper quantities are received against the quantities released. In real life that does not happen. Often an odd quantity is shipped against a nicely rounded release quantity. If, for instance, 992 pieces had been received against P.O. 84756 from Able, the "Schedule Qty.—Date" would read 8 pieces due 6/15 and would be overdue on Bob's next open order status report. If 1,005 pieces had been received, the 7/15 requirement would be 995 pieces.

Look again at Figure 19-1 and at the Baker Distribution order number 93428 for 200 pieces of part number 39461-4. Assume that the goods on that order were delivered on time but the quantity received was 198. Baker considers the order complete. The remaining two pieces can be dealt with in one of several ways: 1) the two pieces will reappear as overdue items on Bob's next open order status report and Bob must manually close the order, or 2) there can be a signal built into the software that will automatically close orders when a certain percent of the original order quantity is received (e.g., 2 percent, 5 percent, etc.)

When an order is received complete, or "closed," it will disappear from Bob's report, but the order and all transactions will be stored by the computer for future access by purchasing and for summary reports generated in the weeks and months to come.

CHAPTER PERSPECTIVE

Every industry and every firm has unique needs for information. Purchasing departments have a vested interest in obtaining support systems that assist them in managing the business of procurement. Since many available software packages are generic in nature, they require that the user conform to the format of the software. But software should act as people act, not the other way around.

Developing a purchasing software system with the assistance of a programmer is relatively simple, inexpensive (the system we have described can be installed for less than $10,000), and, since the users construct it, "friendly."

The Future

INTRODUCTION AND MAIN POINTS

Once the purchasing function is working as you would like to see it—material coming in as needed, quality improving, and purchasing strategies in place—consider the future. Where will the company (and purchasing) be in three to five years? How can the process be continually improved? Is there more to life in purchasing than negotiating, placing orders, and receiving goods?

This chapter will consider these questions and assist in creating a vision—one that can change the purchasing function dramatically and permanently.

After studying the material in this chapter:

■ You will understand the changes that underlie long-term improvements in purchasing and its methods of supply.

■ You will be able to create a vision and plan for significant business improvements for your company and your suppliers.

■ You will understand how to put together all of the concepts in this book, along with some new ideas, to create a supply chain that will support your needs now and in the future.

PERSPECTIVE

The functions of purchasing, production control, and inventory control are charged with providing manufacturing (or the using organization) with the proper material at the proper time. This has never been an easy task. In fact, the increasing complexity of products and processes in the past thirty years has increased the difficulty of accomplishing the task. The introduction of tools such as materials requirements planning (MRP), manufacturing resource planning (MRP II), distribution requirements planning (DRP), bar-code readers, electronic data interchange (EDI), cycle counting, material handling equipment, on-line access to information, supplier partnerships and certification, and value analysis have had only minor impacts on the ease of performing the materials functions and on business results.

While there have been additions of more sophisticated tools, the job of supplying materials to users has become more difficult. The result is a draw—little net gain. The problem, in our own processes and at the suppliers', is that there has been no fundamental change in the way we produce products.

An appropriate definition for the word "insanity" is: "Continuing to do the same thing and expecting a different outcome." If all is not well in purchasing, it may be time to consider a different approach to the function. A short while ago, I spoke with an old friend who recently had left purchasing after ten years for another line of work. When I asked why he left, he said: "I finally figured out that it was not all my fault."

In Chapter 8 on Sourcing, the formula for manufacturing velocity is defined as:

$$\text{Manufacturing velocity} = \frac{\text{Cycle Time}}{\text{Work content}}$$

This is a powerful tool. Any effort—manufacturing, administration, or service—can be measured and improved by applying the principle of velocity. For example, a supplier quotes a lead time of twelve weeks to supply a transformer. The actual work content of the transformer is four hours. The difference between four hours and twelve weeks is the supplier's order entry time, the backlog of other orders, the delay caused by working on large lot sizes (only one part at a time can be worked on, while the remaining parts in the lot wait), and the belief that as long as they honor their lead-time commitment, their performance is acceptable to the buyer.

In many companies, the formula produces a ratio as high as 1:80. Companies commonly report a ratio of 1:100 or 1:200. That means for every hour of value-added work, there is 80, 100, or even 200 hours of non–value-added work—queue or wait time. Another way to look at this phenomenon is by defining velocity in terms of physics:

$$\text{Velocity} = \frac{\text{Linear Motion}}{\text{Inertia}}$$

Both formulas illustrate that velocity or positive action is slowed by inertia—in nature as well as on the manufacturing floor. Imagine the impact on purchasing if a manufacturing velocity of 1:10 were achieved! Goods that require 4 hours of processing time would be shipped in 40 hours, or 5 work days.

Time is critical to buyers for several reasons:

1. Demand for an item can change during the lead time. If the lead time is 12 weeks when a buyer enters an order, there are 12 weeks during which demand can change. The buyer's customer may change quantities or delivery requirements.

2. Buyers pay for non–value-added time in the purchase price.

3. The longer the lead-time cycle, the more orders and releases a buyer must manage, which increases administrative labor.

4. Administrative labor also increases in the event of engineering changes issued during the purchase cycle time, and if the change is substantive, material may be scrapped.

IMPACT ON THE SUPPLIER

In order for a supplier to reduce cycle time to approach 1:10, it must reduce lot sizes, reduce setup and change-over times, organize the manufacturing process for an even flow of material, have designs and processes under control to yield excellent quality (unpredictable quality slows production and causes rework or scrap, which causes further delays), and tune in to customers and their needs. This is where the elements discussed in previous chapters —close buyer/supplier relations, process controls, costs based on value-added activities, and small lot sizes—have significant impact.

PRICE

The formula for velocity is not applied to the selling price of an item but to its constituent cost elements. Assume that a sample item follows the national average for cost—60 percent material, 30 percent overhead, and 10 percent direct labor. Also assume that the current velocity is 1:100. The supplier's material costs will not be significantly affected until that suppler applies velocity to its purchased-materials suppliers. Marginal savings can be achieved in direct labor. Some other efficiencies may be achieved by applying the velocity formula, but direct labor and material are the only true value adders in the product. (There are those who argue that product engineering adds value, but if that is the case, and it probably is, engineering should be added to direct labor.)

The primary application of velocity is in reduction of overhead. Overhead is commonly calculated at 300 to 400 percent of direct labor. Overhead has been the largest-growing segment of costs during the past thirty years and is likely to continue to grow if left unchecked. The growth of overhead is attributable to a greater number of indirect people in the production process and fewer direct laborers. It has been shown that indirect labor actually slows the process, whereas direct labor has the capability to move the goods more quickly.

Overhead costs most reduced by application of manufacturing-velocity techniques are those that have been added to cope with the flaws in the current process: quality checking, production planning, inventory planning, order administration, order entry, customer service, expediting, supervision, auditing, and many engineering functions. Applying the velocity formulas to overhead not only reduces a growing cost but speeds the production of goods.

Overhead can be reduced at least one-half to two-thirds. In the process, some overhead functions may be converted to direct-labor functions. When direct-labor people are trained and practice process controls, setup and change-over reduction, and equipment maintenance, these previously overhead activities become direct-labor activities. Accounting procedures that include these elements as direct costs more accurately reflect the actual cost to produce the product and tend to distinguish between activities that add value and those that do not. Further, a buyer can more easily distinguish between costs that contribute to his or her products and those that contribute to products of the supplier's other customers.

TIME

Time is one of the elements in both manufacturing and service industries that is not measured by the standard measures of business performance. Time is critical to a buyer. What added costs are associated with a lead time of twelve weeks versus that of five days? The cost of receiving goods two weeks after the need date? Or the cost of totally unreliable delivery? These costs are not reflected in the purchase price, but they result in the need for backup systems and safety stocks. These added costs also show up in unreliable performance to the buyer's customer—and hence lost business.

The purchase price should reflect a supplier's peformance

against time. The shorter the time to perform, the greater the value a buyer receives.

LOT SIZES

Since the beginning of the Industrial Revolution, a common belief in business has been that economy of scale dictates large lot sizes. It is common for buyers to request monthly shipment of materials. Yet customers use products or components one at a time. The goods are received, placed in a stockroom, and issued to the production floor as needed. This disconnects the supplier from the current needs of the buyer, inflates the buyer's inventories, increases materials handling, and artificially inflates shipment quantities. A better approach is a direct link between the production line of the supplier and that of the buyer. The rate of production for the buyer's line becomes the rate for the supplier's production line. The supplier delivers goods to the buyer's floor as the goods are needed. This may mean that the supplier will deliver goods to the point of use on the buyer's production line on a regular schedule of hours or days.

This approach is similar to the one used by the breadman who delivers bakery products to the point of sale at a grocery store. A month's worth of product is not delivered at one time; there is no stockroom or central storage area; quality is controlled at the point of manufacture (the bakery) and incoming inspection is not required; and no individual purchase orders are involved. Grocery stores use bar codes to reduce the volume of transactions. Inventories are turned 100 to 150 times a year. Suppliers do not hold inventories in anticipation of a buyer's needs. There may be only a few suppliers for each item; usually one supplier is sufficient. Industrial buyers can learn much from grocery stores. (For further discussion of the "breadman" concept, see Chapter 6.)

INVENTORIES

Many companies use large in-house inventories to compensate for unpredictable supplier quality, unreliable deliveries, inaccurate sales forecasts, and poor yields. Inventory is expensive regardless of who holds it, but conventional wisdom holds that it's cheaper than running out. It is often seen as a trade-off. It need not be.

The question is not "What is the right amount of inventory?" but "How can we eliminate the need for and expense of inventory?" The answer to the latter question is to attack problems that make high inventory levels a perceived necessity. Short cycle times and improved quality, for example, permit significant decreases in inventory. In fact, inventory *must* be reduced to achieve short cycle times, or manufacturing velocity; they are codependent.

As inventories are reduced, the problems that created the need for them begin to surface. These problems must be addressed and resolved. Communication with suppliers must increase in order to jointly solve these problems. As problems are solved and inventories are reduced, costs will decrease. As inventories are reduced, many non–value-added activities are curtailed. Those activities include handling and storage, issuing and kitting, and counting and tracking.

Large lot sizes are inventories in process: the larger the lot sizes, the larger the work-in-progress (WIP) inventories; the larger the WIP inventories, the longer the cycle or manufacturing process time. It simply takes longer to complete a large lot than it does a small lot or a lot size of one. (For further discussion of these principles, see Chapter 7.)

QUALITY

Chaper 12 proposed that as quality improves, costs decrease. There is also a correlation between the amount of time a product spends in production and the quality when it exits that process. Therefore, there is a link between quality and time: the shorter the process time, the better the quality—and the better the quality, the shorter the process time.

Quality and time also have another relationship. Quality is more than uniform, predictable parts; the definition of quality includes total business and personal integrity. Max DePree, in his book *Leadership Is An Art,* defines quality in its broadest and most appropriate sense:

> When we talk about quality, we are talking about quality of product and service. But we are also talking about the quality of our relationships and the quality of our communications and the quality of our promises to each other. And so, it is reasonable to think about quality in terms of truth and integrity.[1]

Part of quality, too, is the time in which goods are delivered. Late delivery of goods diminishes their quality; it also diminishes the value of the goods to the buyer.

PEOPLE

There has been an excess of specialization in American business in general and in manufacturing in particular. Workers have been paid for manual dexterity (work), and managers and supervisors have been paid to think. The real questions are: "Do we need every mind working on the problems in the products, in the processes, and with customers?" and "Given American inability to compete internationally in manufactured goods, can we afford to have a significant portion of the working population relegated solely to mechanical activities?" In the current competitive environment, every mind and every skill must be brought to bear on the problems.

In traditional forms of organization, bringing all the required talents to bear on a problem is difficult. American industry has segmented people by formal functions, and these functions do not necessarily relate to the products produced. For example, quality-control personnel are often separate and distinct from manufacturing. They are the ones charged with assuring product quality, but are not usually on the scene as the product is being made. They "police" those workers producing inferior products. This creates an adversarial relationship between quality-control personnel and the work force.

Since quality is created at the point of manufacture (or at the point of delivery of service), doesn't it make sense to have the production workers responsible for the assurance of quality? Similarly, doesn't it make sense to train production workers in routine equipment maintenance? Who knows better when equipment requires lubrication and maintenance? Production workers are also in the best position to assure that production schedules are met. Since production workers live in the process eight or more hours a day, they may have valuable ideas concerning plant and equipment layout. Staff specialists in quality, maintenance, scheduling, manufacturing, engineering, and others would do well to become more closely associated with production workers and the process. These staff people should closely support the line workers and train them to apply a wide variety of skills on the production floor. Specialists become "coaches" to those producing the product. The skills needed to assure the quality and timeliness of production are where they are needed—at the point of manufacture.

This approach requires that line workers be trained and trusted, and that they have the authority and responsibility to manage the production environment. The effectiveness of the specialists is multiplied if line workers have the skills and are empowered to act and make decisions in certain situations. But this situation can also be threatening to both specialists and the line workers. The specialists have to surrender the power of their knowledge, and the line workers have to accept responsibilities formerly assumed by supervisors. It is sometimes as difficult to accept responsibility as it is to relinquish it.

ORGANIZE FOR FLOW

Most manufacturing plants—and some offices as well—are laid out by function. In a plant, all milling machines may be in one area, all injection molding machines in another, and auto-insertion machines in another. In an office, all orders may be entered in one area, credit approved in another, and shipping schedules acknowledged in another area. In these environments, material and information must be moved in large lots from one step to the next. This movement, when flow charted, may look like a plate of spaghetti, as illustrated in Figure 20-1.

Layouts can be rearranged for smooth material and information flow. As Figure 20-2 indicates, this flow can proceed in short straight lines. This requires minimum handling and movement of material and information. Quality checks are performed by the workers. There is little room remaining in the production process to accommodate large amounts of work-in-process inventory. Workstations are close to one another, which allows workers in each area to consult with each other to resolve quality or scheduling problems. The physical process and the time to produce goods are shortened considerably.

THE RESULTS

When a supplier's process time is reduced, quality is improved, costs decrease, and delivery schedules are met. In addition, the supplier is more flexible and can respond to customers' needs, and its profitability increases.

Such suppliers are rare. Buyers must develop more suppliers like these. In the future, purchasing managers will be spending an increasing amount of time working with suppliers so that they may achieve this level of excellence.

There is one important caveat, however: in order to establish and maintain credibility, the buyer's own plant must be moving in the same direction. As Albert Schweitzer once stated: "Example is not the main thing in influencing others. It is the only thing."

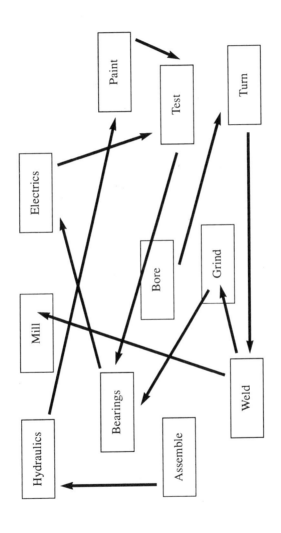

FIG 20-1. *Sub-assembly flow.*

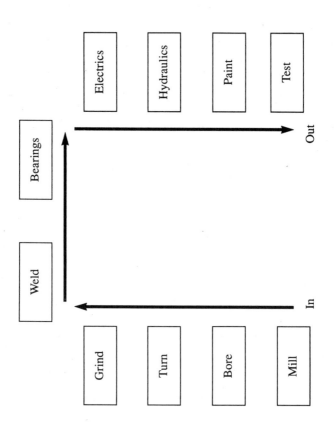

FIG 20-2.

Buyers and suppliers that adopt these powerful tools are in a good position to become leaders in their fields. They do not simply become more competitive; they may be the competition against which all others gauge their success. They can become the benchmarks of excellence.

Ultimately, buyers are the ones who must be satisfied by the performance of suppliers. If buyers settle for mediocre supplier performance, that is precisely what they will get. If, however, they demand world-class performance and can model such performance for suppliers, they will benefit.

COMMUNICATION

Discrete purchase orders, releases, and order amendments are time-consuming efforts that add no value to a product or the buyer-supplier relationship. In place of these written forms of communication, the buyer and supplier can use MRP reports, mechanical signaling devices, and technological advances such as the fax machine.

MRP Communication

A buyer's organization can authorize external production based on a current master schedule and a resulting MRP report. The production planning staff approves the MRP report; that approval authorizes the plant's production for the month and becomes purchasing's authority to acquire material to meet the production schedule. Purchasing has systems or requirements contracts in place for the life of the product. Copies of the MRP report can be faxed directly to suppliers. The MRP report contains current and subsequent monthly requirements. Suppliers use the buyer's MRP reports as schedules for production and delivery.

Mechanical Signaling Devices

Actual weekly schedules may be signaled by empty standardized containers and kanban cards. The container system works like this: Suppliers deliver in reusable containers that circulate between the buyer's production line and the supplier's plant. When a supplier delivers the current requirement to the buyer's production site, the deliverer looks for empty containers. These containers are the supplier's authorization to make deliveries of that quantity on the next routine delivery. The containers have a standard count (e.g., 24 parts per container), and the supplier simply multiplies the number of containers by the standard count to determine the quantity needed. Delivery to the point of use reduces standard transactions such as counting, material movement, and kitting. See Figure 20-3 for a representation of delivery to point of use.

Since the supplier's driver is delivering to the buyer's production line, other product-related issues can be addressed at the same time. If there is a defective part from a previous delivery, the buyer's production worker and the supplier's driver can resolve the issue on the spot with a "one-for-one swap," without the need for paperwork such as a reject notice, return shipping paper, debit memo, or replacement order. The production worker can also act as the receiving department. If the delivery containers are bar coded, the production worker need only read the label or "wand" the bar code. The bar code contains the supplier's name, part number, container quantity; the buyer's software contains the date, time, and delivery location. That information is immediately available to the buyer's accounts payable department.

Some companies carry this process even further. The buyer's finished product is bar coded and the code is "read" at the buyer's shipping dock. The buyer's finished product is the signal that all suppliers have delivered the goods required to build the product. The shipping notice contains the buyer's finished part number; this number is entered into the buyer's MRP and bill of material processor system. All component parts are identified and suppliers are credited with the shipment of components. This reverse accounting for components is called "back-flush." There are a number of MRP software packages that not only include this back-flush capability, but also allow for relieving existing inventories.

Other signaling devices are the kanban and breadman systems. A kanban card contains a bar code that identifies the part, supplier, standard count, delivery location, and other pertinent information. The kanban card is used instead of an empty container as the supplier's authorization to deliver goods. The cards circulate between the buyer's and the supplier's plant.

The breadman signaling system is used by manufacturers to replenish parts based on consumption. These parts are usually inexpensive items, often called "C" items or expendables. The resupply agent circulates through the buyer's plant replenishing parts consumed. This is often merely a matter of refilling a bin or container on the manufacturing floor to a predetermined

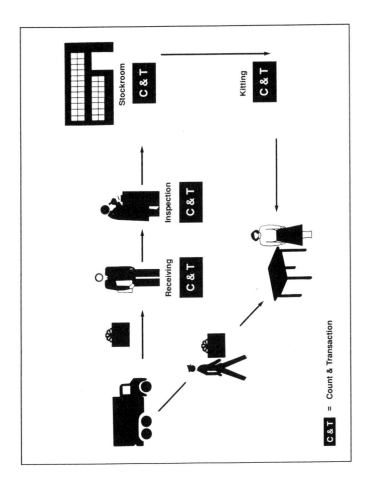

FIG 20-3. *Delivery to point of use*.

level. Some companies place a strip of colored tape on the inside of the container to indicate a fill level.

When buyer and supplier are geographically distant, Kanban cards may be faxed to the supplier. The parts represented by the cards are delivered by contract or common carriers.

CARTAGE

These signaling and delivery methods depend on frequent and reliable delivery of component parts. Local suppliers can deliver in small trucks and use their drivers to deliver goods to the point of use on the buyer's production floor. The driver can also pick up delivery signals such as empty containers and kanban cards, make one-for-one swaps, replace short-count parts and the like.

If the F.O.B. point is the buyer's production line, there is no question about who is responsible for goods damaged in transit, lost parts, and non-conforming parts. The point-of-use production worker will determine the quality of the delivered parts, and corrections, if required, are handled on the spot.

Distant suppliers and local suppliers without delivery trucks can use contract carriers for delivery. These carriers act as agents for the supplier and perform the same duties that a supplier-employed driver might. Distant suppliers may also elect to use common carriers and negotiate customized service with these carriers.

A buyer may elect to use his or her own over-the-road equipment to pick up at suppliers at regular intervals. Routine pickups are known as "sweeps" (see Figure 20-4). The buyer's trucks make sweeps at appointed dates and times. Local suppliers may be on daily sweeps, while distant suppliers may be on a weekly schedule of pickups.

FINANCE

As supplier deliveries increase, a purchasing department should look for ways to simplify the accounts payable process. Aside from implementing back-flushing, purchasing can arrange to receive goods at the point of use, use bar coding or another automated receiving procedure, and pay suppliers on a summary basis. Receipts can be summarized and paid weekly or monthly.

After the receiving process is operating smoothly, individual invoices become unnecessary. The buyer pays based on accumulated monthly receipts. Of course, this is easier if the number of suppliers is low.

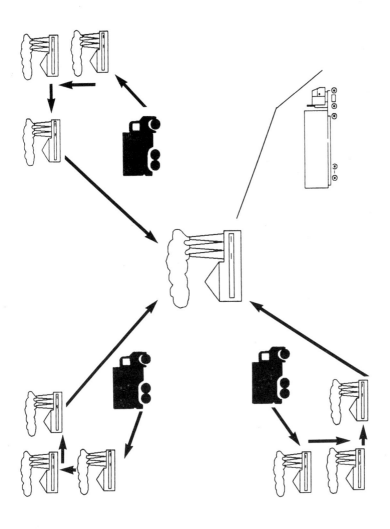

FIG 20-4. *Supplier sweeps.*

PURCHASING'S NEW ROLE

Every purchasing department's role should be evolving from one of placing orders, expediting, finding new suppliers, and replacing rejected material to one of developing and nurturing long-term supplier relations, simplifying processes, and training suppliers in a new way of conducting business.

For that evolution to take place, a purchasing department must create a vision of the way things can be. This vision may be similar to the one described in the past few pages, or it may fit a particular need or environment. It is critical that the purchasing manager create this vision for several reasons:

1. With a clear vision of the future, buyers and suppliers have a direction and can make appropriate decisions to achieve the vision.

2. The purchasing department needs a vision of the future so that its members know that they are working toward change and improvement. Proverbs 29:18 says, "Where there is no vision, the people perish."

3. When a vision is clearly articulated, other company functions, such as quality, finance, engineering, and production, are better able and even eager to assist purchasing to achieve it.

Purchasing will require all the support that it can muster to implement change and work toward its goals. As Nicolo Machiavelli wrote in 1513 in *The Prince:*

It must be remembered that there is nothing more difficult to plan, more doubtful of success, nor more dangerous to manage, than the creation of a new system.

The vision, the journey, and the benefits should be clearly conveyed to all who will come in contact with the new processes. Specific details may be excluded until it is absolutely necessary that they be divulged. They will surface as progress is made.

NEW MEASUREMENTS

What new measurements will be required to support a pursuit of the vision? How will new goals be set? There are two methods of setting goals:

1. Completely analyze the environment, people, products, and current goals. Determine what is reasonable. Have measurements for every activity. Create an organization to create and administer measurements.

2. Any goal created is arbitrary, so why not set perfection as the goal? Keep the system simple. Set only a few measurements, so that people will know what behavior is desired. They

are thus more likely to make the right decisions at the detail level.

The second method has distinct advantages, including simplicity and flexibility. The following are sample techniques for establishing initial goals:

1. Use the square root of current performance. For example:

    a. New Lead Time $= \sqrt{\text{Current Lead Time}}$

    b. New Number of Suppliers $= \sqrt{\text{Current Number of Suppliers}}$

When the square root is achieved, use the square root of the new measure as the new goal. What is desired is continuous improvement, not static and rigid goals. It is important to measure progress, but it may be better not to achieve a goal if doing so harms the ultimate objective. Therefore, goals should be flexible and easily modified.

A goal set quickly may be simpler to implement than one labored over, and it avoids "paralysis of analysis." Elaborate formulas do not work well in business. While graduate schools of business promote the use of such formulas, they simply do not work well in practice. The few formulas that do work are the following:

1. Manufacturing Velocity $= \dfrac{\text{Cycle Time}}{\text{Work Content}} = 20+$

2. Cost of Quality $= \, < 2\%$ of sales

3. Improvement $= \sqrt{\text{Current Practice/Results}}$

4. Profit After Tax $= \, >10\%$

5. Inventory Turns $= \, >20$

6. Customer Retention $= 95+\%$ year to year

7. Indirect to Direct Labor $= \, >1:10$
(coaches to direct labor $= 1:20$)

Nearly all other measurements used in business today work against the interests of good business. These include ROI (return on investment), return on equity, dividends, short-term capital gains, units or dollars shipped in a month or quarter, and price/earnings ratio.

CHAPTER PERSPECTIVE

For a purchasing department to improve itself and achieve its vision of the future, there must be a dramatic change in its beliefs and practices. For example, purchasing must seek out the best suppliers available and assist them to become better—the best in their industry. Also, good suppliers are looking for good customers. Buyers beware!

REFERENCES
[1] Max DePree, *Leadership Is An Art,* (Michigan University Press, East Lansing, MI. 1987), p. 78.

Index